Cultural Studies
and
Critical Theory

For Oskar Edgren and Mathilde Edgren (NM)

Lux mea Kelli, and Morgan (PF)

Cultural Studies
and
Critical Theory

Patrick Fuery
and Nick Mansfield

OXFORD
UNIVERSITY PRESS

OXFORD
UNIVERSITY PRESS

253 Normanby Road, South Melbourne, Victoria, Australia 3205

Oxford University Press is a department of the University of Oxford.
It furthers the University's objective of excellence in research, scholarship,
and education by publishing worldwide in

Oxford New York

Athens Auckland Bangkok Bogotá Buenos Aires Calcutta
Cape Town Chennai Dar es Salaam Delhi Florence Hong Kong Istanbul
Karachi Kuala Lumpur Madrid Melbourne Mexico City Mumbai Nairobi
Paris Port Moresby São Paulo Singapore Taipei Tokyo Toronto Warsaw

with associated companies in Berlin Ibadan

OXFORD is a registered trade mark of Oxford University Press
in the UK and certain other countries

First edition (*Cultural Studies and the New Humanities: Concepts and Controversies*)
published 1997
Reprinted 1997
Second edition published 2000

National Library of Australia
Cataloguing-in-Publication data:

Fuery, Patrick J. (Patrick John), 1957– .
  Cultural studies and critical theory

  2nd ed.
  Bibliography.
  Includes index.
  ISBN 0 19 551294 4.

  1. Critical theory. 2. Humanities. I. Mansfield, Nicholas. II. Title.

001.3

Edited by Jo McMillan and Michele Sabto
Indexed by Russell Brooks
Cover design by Tracey Anne O'Mara
Typeset by Desktop Concepts Pty Ltd, Melbourne
Printed by Kin Keong, Singapore

Contents

Acknowledgments

We would like to thank a number of people who have helped us with this project. Jill Henry at Oxford University Press for her advice, patience, and encouragement, and Jo McMillan for efficient (and considerate) editing. The Royal Netherlands Academy of the Arts and Sciences for a fellowship and a grant for research. Both Macquarie University and the University of London offered financial and practical support. Our colleagues in Critical and Cultural Studies at Macquarie for their help and their belief in another way of doing things. Patrick Fuery would like to thank his family—Kelli and Morgan—who have given so much support, understanding, and love during this project. He also thanks them for taking him to Disneyland Paris, mostly for research purposes. Nick would like to thank Yvonne Edgren, whose research and judgment made his work possible.

Preface

When we set out in 1994 to teach a first-year undergraduate course on theoretical concepts in literary and cultural studies, we assumed it would be easy to find a textbook. We found, however, that many of the candidates, such as Catherine Belsey's *Critical Practice* (1980) or Terry Eagleton's *Literary Theory: An Introduction* (1983), both of which belong to the heady days of the early 1980s, were dated. Others, such as Raman Selden's *A Reader's Guide to Contemporary Literary Theory* (1985), had refined literary theory into a canon— providing potted summaries of the work of 'major' figures or movements. Anthologies of readings, in turn, were always dissatisfying, made up of predictable or unusable choices, and never quite organised into a useful structure. Nor did we want a book that dealt only with the issues of representation and deconstruction that dominated 1970s and 1980s literary theory. We certainly wanted to deal with these issues, but as a starting point to an investigation of the highly charged controversies about power, gender, subjectivity, culture, and sexuality that have defined the humanities in the 1990s, and are its major point of contact with the non-academic world.

This book is organised, therefore, around a set of controversies. We felt that it was not part of our students' education to be made to appreciate the achievements of the theoretical figureheads that had influenced and impressed us. Certainly, the construction of a postmodern canon may sometimes seem pedagogically necessary, but it is more or less a betrayal of what many theorists set out to achieve. Our aim is not to induct students into a particular mode of thinking, but to enliven a set of issues for them, so that they may enter vigorously into the debate from whichever position suits them. Of course, we have conscious and unconscious biases of our own that must be exhibited everywhere in this book. There is also disagreement between the two of us on many of the issues discussed here. But it is our belief that in the new humanities, disagreement is the name of the game. We are aware that we are probably always conforming to present or future orthodoxies of one sort or another, but our hope is that readers will not feel that they are being asked to agree with certain points of view in order to enter the community of the theoretically literate.

Similarly, we have chosen not to pretend that the issues dealt with here can be reduced to simple, unambiguous statements. The area of cultural theory deals with difficult material, and that will sometimes show up in a certain density to our argument. This is partly because the issues dealt with are fundamental to the way we encounter culture, politics, and indeed ourselves. Many theories that have had a major impact on literary and cultural studies have dealt with what earlier generations of intellectuals—at least in, say, English studies—took for granted: subjectivity, sexuality, gender, and so on. There is no easy way in to a lot of these ideas. On the other hand, we have found, often despite warnings from colleagues that we were being naive, that even first-year students have an enthusiasm for a lot of difficult and abstract material when they feel it to be challenging and extending. In fact, we must mark our gratitude to students in the Concept and Controversy strand of ENGL145 and the subsequent CUL 100: Text, Image, Culture (both at Macquarie University) over the last several years, who, through their enthusiasm for much of the material covered here, made us realise that this project was a worthwhile one. Having mentioned our students, it is probably worth noting that we hope this book will also be of value to people working in journalism, the arts and entertainment industries, and those who are interested in general in the issues thrown up by contemporary culture. We hope it will be of interest and service to as many people as possible.

Much has been said about the radical transformation of the humanities in the last thirty years. This has been partly due to the radical expansion of the tertiary education sector in that time, and partly a result of reconsiderations of the social function of intellectual work since the 1960s. It is also due to an expansion in the theorisation of many fundamental issues that touch on all fields in the humanities, whatever their traditional provenance. This book is organised around four key subject areas that we feel summarise the main achievements of this theorisation. First, the issue of *culture*: what is the relationship between the 'new' humanities and the humanism from which they derived? How do the new humanities make us reconsider what 'culture' is, especially the relationship between high, low, and sub culture? Second, the issue of *textuality*: what is a text? How do texts relate to one another, to their authors and audiences? How do they relate to our bodies, and our selves? Third, what is the relationship between texts and their *contexts*: how do postmodern understandings of what texts *do* compare with those of the modern era, and earlier? How does gender, particularly as theorised by poststructuralism, condition our relationship with texts? Finally, what is *subjectivity*, and why has it become so important? In this last section we deal with psychoanalytic and anti-psychoanalytic treatments of the subject, its place in culture, and its relationship to perhaps the most volatile current focus of debate, human sexuality.

The two of us have worked together for a number of years, and have been enriched by the process. However, in the end, we do have different emphases and approaches. This comes out in the topics we have chosen and the way our chapters were written, which on the whole were done separately. Nick has written on post-humanism (Chapter 1); Barthes, Derrrida, and intertextuality (Chapter 4); postmodernism and cultural politics (Chapters 7 and 8); and Foucault and sexuality (Chapters 11 and 12). The discussions of the canon (Chapter 2), phenomenology and semiotic theory (Chapter 3), the gaze and visual culture (Chapters 5 and 6), feminism and film noir (Chapter 8), and psychoanalysis (Lacan and Freud) (Chapter 10) are Patrick's.

We are aware that there are many who will feel that important issues have either been ignored or received the wrong emphasis here. When we set out on this project we had a different impression of what mattered in this field from the one we have now, and our opinions will probably change again. We also know that it is impossible to write a book that perfectly satisfies your own teaching requirements, let alone those of other people, and that the temptation when picking up a book like this in a bookshop is to look for its holes, rather than its strengths. Our aim has always been to be broad and informative in the issues that we feel are definitive for the academic culture of the written word, which was once simply called 'human'.

So contentious has this word become, the most longstanding of definitions of the humanities, that we have never tried to provide the last word on any topic. At no time could anyone pretend that a book like this would not need to be supplemented by other readings. Yet we hope it is as useful as is possible, without being either absurdly general, ideologically dogmatic, or obnoxiously patronising. We hope that it inspires in its readers, not a respect for the big names, or a fixation on specific issues as if only they will ever matter, but an awareness of the volatility of culture, and the absolute centrality of the academic discipline of cultural studies in the long, unending drama of cultural change, from which no one anywhere can ever be insulated.

Introduction

What are 'the new humanities'? To our knowledge the term was first used in the title of a 1991 conference, 'Beyond the Disciplines: The New Humanities', held by the Australian Academy of the Humanities in Canberra. This usage obviously emphasised the potential of recent developments in the humanities to defy conventional divisions between academic subject areas, and produce new formations and processes of exchange between workers in a variety of fields. Many undergraduate students are familiar with the pedagogical consequences of these changes. For example, there may well be an overlap, if not an exact repeat, of subject matter and materials in courses in literature, anthropology, philosophy, and so on. On the other hand, different courses within one of the traditional disciplines may have nothing in common. A course in feminism and sociology may be much closer to a course in gender and literature than the latter may be to a course in Shakespeare. This development raises a number of questions. First, why and how has this happened? And second, where should we go from here?

The answer to the second question is the most fraught. If traditional disciplines like English, history and sociology are being tested at their boundaries, does this mean that they will be replaced by a new set of disciplines: gender studies, cultural studies, and postmodern studies, for example? The course handbooks of some newer campuses encourage you to believe this. Indeed, it seems impossible to imagine a new university, in our country at least, setting up an English department, rather than a department of communication, or of cultural or textual studies. It is one of the most used platitudes of the humanities that divisions between historical epochs are to some extent artificial. As Virginia Woolf's joke goes, modernism did not simply begin at a certain time on the morning of a certain day, and the values and ideas that it supplanted did not—perhaps have still not—simply evaporated. Yet, change happens on the grand as well as on the gradual scale, and it would have to be said that a major change of some sort has been under way in the humanities, one whose origins are in the theoretical debates of the 1960s and 1970s, which still have quite a distance to run. Some thinkers advance the idea that certain new disciplinary formations must be established in order to make academic institutions workable. Students have to be enrolled to study something after all. Other thinkers are more attracted by the idea that any theoretical boundaries are questionable and problematic, and that the broad field of the humanities should be perpetually unsettling and questioning the definitions on which it depends. In many ways, some of the makeshift terms that have been proposed in newer course schedules are an attempt to negotiate some way between these two points of view. If history and English were defined by the object of their study, borrowing this model from what was little more than a caricature of the natural sciences, a field like 'postmodern studies' knows no such simplicity. Its domain is nominally a historical period, yet it must also include certain textual practices, theoretical paradigms, and political and ethical positions. Similarly, not everything that was produced in the nominated period could be called postmodern, and the objects chosen for study could be practices in physics, politics and the arts. There is no doubt that those who formulated this usage were well aware of these problems and would see it as their duty to foreground them as part of—perhaps even the basis of—their teaching. Indeed, it could be the encounter with these problems, rather than any substantive material knowledge about the artifacts of the postmodern era, that is the most important focus of such teaching.

The question of where the new humanities come from does not have a simple answer either. The easiest response would be to say that there has been a radical transformation in the theoretical foundations of the humanities, particularly in the wake of the French movement that has come to be known in the English-speaking world as poststructuralism, and, to a certain extent, the rise of the Birmingham School in Cultural Studies. This book is really as accessible as possible an introduction to the most influential ideas in poststructuralism and though it provides a wide range of material on other subjects, its main focus is in making key poststructuralist ideas accessible to those beginning in the field. We will go into this issue in more detail below as we come to explain the way this book has been laid out. Our focus on poststructuralism is not narrowly ideological nor simply slavish. Indeed in our other work on post-psychoanalytic theory and the politics of sexuality, our aim has been to challenge and subvert many of the staple ideas of poststructuralism. This is not something that can be done from the outset, however, and if students are to understand the new intellectual landscape that confronts them at universities—or indeed if those whose university studies were a number of years ago are to understand the apparently bamboozling rhetoric of contemporary academic debates—they need a thorough, relevant, and up-to-date acquaintance with the theoretical developments that have opened the way for and still to a great extent condition the terms of present discussions.

Yet it is obviously not enough to say there has been a major theoretical reconsideration in the humanities since the 1960s. This reifies a certain historical epoch as more of a watershed in intellectual and social history than it may indeed have been. And it certainly does not explain why *these* changes occurred *at this time*. Another possible explanation is that many of these new fields of study are a direct academic response to changes in society. Gender studies, for example, is a response to the prominence of the women's movement in Western society; postmodern studies is partly a result of the recognition that changes in communication and information technology cannot simply be explained using inherited models of linguistics, economics and textuality; the perceived importance of sexuality as a key to social and cultural dynamics reflects the assertiveness and success of the political activism of the gay and lesbian communities, and so on. There must be a great deal of truth in these conclusions, although the same question arises; by explaining academic change in terms of social change, the problem is merely moved one step further along. Academic change may follow from social change, but why then did the social change happen? There is often a necessary circularity in these arguments. The social change must be the inevitable result of some cultural change; the cultural change was effected by the work of radical academics, and so on, until we return to our starting point. The pragmatic explanation is that social changes cannot be simply explained—there are unique, infinitely complex, and impenetrable social pressures at work that even the most sophisticated theoretical models cannot accommodate, and that it does little good to try and simplify. According to this argument, change happens because it happens, and it is of little advantage to anyone to pretend that our political or humanistic explanations for it are anything more than acts of faith. To those of us educated in the humanistic tradition, which aspired to overcome any such limits in a process of a universal understanding, this sort of theoretical limitation is frustrating, if not unnerving.

The point here is that even when we attempt to answer a simple question about the rise of some current ideas, we can no longer ignore fundamental theoretical problems about the efficacy of traditional common-sense models of, for example, cause and effect, origins and consequences, and so on. Contemporary discussions, such as the ones outlined in this book, can take no such models for granted, and must either be tentative and self-reflexive when dealing with explanations, or let questions about origins stand as provocative, but unanswerable, dynamics.

So far, we have not provided much of a definition of the new humanities. As you will see from some of the chapters that follow, our attitude to many of the contemporary new disciplines in the humanities is that they are not easily defined in the abstract. 'Women's studies' and 'cultural studies', for example, are terms that lend themselves to easy use—in practice, there is little doubt whether or not something belongs to one of these formations. In conventional academic study, only habit has made traditional disciplinary boundaries seem straightforward. Is history the study of anything that has happened in the past, or a specific way of synthesising past events? If the latter, then which way of synthesising those events is the most 'historical'? Much of the most interesting and influential debates in the humanities spring from such controversies, and it would be limiting with the new, as with the older, disciplines to foreclose the discussion too quickly by attempting to delimit subject areas prematurely. The meaning of disciplines is very much in the practice of them, and the controversies, disjunctions, and oppositions varying practices produce.

Although a definition that sets the new humanities up in clear contradistinction to each other and the fields of study they seem to be displacing is impossible, some way of characterising these developments is available. First, it needs to be said that the new humanities are not simply a new set of disciplines that will eventually replace English, history, and so on. This may seem to be the way things are going on some campuses. But on others, practices of the new humanities are at home inside older departments and their engagement with older traditions is something that many of even the most radical researchers would not want to give up easily.

It is from this fact—the engagement of the new humanities with older formations—that we can draw out our way of characterising the new humanities. The new humanities focus on the buried problems and issues that older disciplines took for granted or saw as being outside their domain. The issues of gender, ethnicity, and sexuality, to take some obvious examples, have not been seen as part of the scope of the traditional humanities. Yet, as many writers have argued since the 1960s, the absence of these issues from discussion shows how deeply they have defined and conditioned academic work. If academic researchers, for example, have set to one side the issue of their race, in the name of the elucidation or promotion of universal humanity, then, unconsciously at least, their research has suppressed the effects of racial difference on the work in their field. The consequence of this is that their work diminishes the importance of ethnicity as a condition of the formation of knowledge. This may reflect an appeal to a commonality between individuals that transcends ethnicity, or simply the assumption that academia is dominated by members of a narrow range of social groups, and that an ethnic commonality can be assumed among scholars. This is certainly no longer the case in any simple way, but a generation ago, academics saw little need to consider the sociological differences within their community.

The suppression of the significance of such molar social differences in academia is easily detectable. Other issues, such as the influence of textuality and subjectivity on the conditioning of knowledge, and the reverse, are not. To the new humanities no simple dividing line can be drawn between the ideas conveyed in the text and the way those ideas appear. This will be investigated in more detail below. Suffice it to say here that the textuality of writing can no longer be ignored as a fundamental constituent of the way knowledge is made in societies. This textual self-consciousness may involve an analysis of the way certain writing communities—certain groups of academics, for example—use language in order to structure their various truths. On the one hand, this may mean an analysis of the way information is gathered, explanations are set out, or validation is made. On the other hand, it may investigate certain metaphors and their use in specific branches of human investigation. Why is the search for knowledge understood as a *quest* or an *adventure*, for example? What values and ideals do such metaphors conceal or reveal?

At a deeper level, investigation of the textuality of texts may involve a thorough problematisation of language itself, according to the Derridean model of language now assumed—sometimes uncritically—by many humanities scholars. This modelling of language in terms of an open and unstable field of differences, rather than as a servant of a converging set of meanings, has major consequences for the attempts of researchers and writers to isolate and formulate truth. These issues have produced an endless and still sometimes acrimonious debate in the academy, and it is impossible in a book of this nature to characterise them simply. For our purposes, this issue is reduced to the simple questions: What is the relationship between a text and its author? And what is the relationship between texts and one another?

On the issue of subjectivity, there has been a similarly widespread and contentious range of debates. The traditional rational or expressive model of language assumed by the older humanities holds the text in a complex yet somewhat contradictory relationship with its author and its reader. At certain times, the text 'belongs' to either of these figures—as a product of its author protected by copyright law and academic protocol, or as the material property of its reader. On the whole, however, authors and readers were the two subjects affected by the circulation of the text. According to contemporary theory, this is an inadequate model of the position of the text in relation to the experience of the human community. According to post-Lacanian psychoanalysis, the field of signification is not simply a reflection or tool of individual subjects as they attempt to reach outwards from their enclosed interior life to communicate with one another. Language is the very material of subjectivity, the place in which we have to be produced in order to exist as individuals. Language pre-dates and pre-configures us, according to this theory. Similarly, Foucauldean theory sees the vast and interlocking discourses gathered by institutions and bureaucracies about individuals and their economic, social, and sexual behaviour as the domain in which recognisable and legitimate subjectivity—a subjectivity acceptable to power—is available to us.

Many criticisms have been made of these theories, and we have many reservations about them ourselves. The point of this book, however, is to elucidate them in a way that clearly shows their relationship to specific and unresolved controversies in the humanities. What they produce for us here is an image of the rigorous self-consciousness of knowledge in our time. In fact, to many academic teachers in the new humanities it is the conditions of the production of knowledge that provide a greater insight into the operations of human society and culture than any specific knowledge itself. What is important to understand is that these 'conditions' of knowledge are to be understood in the broadest possible terms—from the institutional structures of knowledge, with its ethnic and gender inequities at one end, to the way knowledge is formulated in language, texts, and subjects at the other.

Some of the practical consequences of the changes that have been taking place here can be seen by a brief look at them in microcosm. Our example is the sort of transformation that has taken place from an introductory course in English to one in cultural studies. As we have mentioned, this book grew out of a first-year course at Macquarie University, Sydney, which aimed to provide an introduction to theoretical controversies that span the traditional and new humanities areas, and our example draws on our experiences with this course. A traditional introductory course in English would usually be structured around a set of canonical texts chosen from a certain period or from a range of genres. The course would deal with these texts in depth, through close reading and textual analysis, in order either to accumulate an understanding of the culture of the specific historical period, or to enumerate the features of a range of genres. Let us take a list of texts from a recent university handbook:

Joseph Conrad's *Heart of Darkness*, Katherine Mansfield's *Bliss and Other Stories*, James Joyce's *A Portrait of the Artist as a Young Man*, and Virginia Woolf's *To the Lighthouse*; the poetry of W.B.Yeats, T.S. Eliot, Wilfred Owen, and the imagists; August Strindberg's *Miss Julie*, George Bernard Shaw's *Heartbreak House*, Luigi Pirandello's *Six Characters in Search of an Author*, and Bertolt Brecht's *Mother Courage and Her Children*. As can be seen, the texts are grouped generically into prose fiction, poetry and drama. Depending on the teacher, lectures would concentrate on a number of different things: the historical background of the texts (usually as it helps us elucidate the text, rather than in itself); clear attributes of the text as a development in the evolution of its genre (experiments by modernist novelists with the stream-of-consciousness technique, for example); and the thematic content of the texts (seen as either a contribution to a transhistorical understanding of the human condition or as an insight into the values and meanings dominant or new in a certain period). There may also be accompanying lectures on research techniques, library skills, essay writing, and perhaps some overview of theoretical material, which may be more or less integrated into the course's textual analyses. Although the historical period exists either as the backdrop to, or goal of, the teaching, the focus of such courses is usually on the texts themselves. Many university calendars include formulations such as 'the focus of study here will be on the close reading of texts'. In fact, the goal and rationale of such teaching usually invests a huge amount of significance in certain texts or types of texts. They are worthy of study *in themselves*. The texts are an access to values and ideas that exist 'before,' 'beside' or 'through' them, but it is the texts themselves that constitute and justify the process of their study. To some teachers, if the students have merely read the texts, then the greater part of the work has been done. Theoretical issues about texts, politics, and culture are subordinate to the reading of texts. They are serviceable only as they aid in the reading of the texts themselves.

In a cultural studies course, on the other hand, these very theoretical issues will usually be the foundation for the teaching. The choice of texts may help to give an insight into the culture of a certain period, but the texts themselves are not necessarily selected because they are thought to be of intrinsic value. For example, a recent course with which we have been involved uses texts from science-fiction film and television (specifically *Blade Runner, The Thing, The X-Files* and *Alien*) in order to investigate issues of alienation and identity (and their relation to the politics of gender and ethnicity as well as their contribution to a model of split subjectivity), textual structure and its relation to social discourses and the construction of national meanings, and the production of various types of audience groups, by industry or subculture. Broader social and historical questions in such a course are its explicit means and goal of study. The texts are chosen as pedagogically useful devices, but a final or total reading of their meaning is not intended. In contrast to an English course, an adequate experience of the texts is not considered sufficient. Indeed, the course could be studied without the texts if students made an adequate investigation of the issues around which the course is framed.

Of course, this sort of characterisation will annoy practitioners both of traditional English studies and cultural studies, but we hope it provides some insight into the contrast between the two areas. As is obvious there is a major overlap between the two fields, and a great deal of shared history. Yet the difference in emphasis is substantial and should not be minimised: one approach selects and promotes certain texts as key material, hoping to give some insight into a historical period, or into the heightened field of cultural values into which it aims to induct its students. The other sees the broad field of cultural practices (which, as we show below, may range from film and book production to dress, food and furniture) as the material for an investigation of the broad construction of meanings and truths with all their social and political interconnections.

This analysis of the contrast between English and cultural studies throws some light on the way the development of the new humanities has contributed to a redefinition of culture. As Raymond Williams reminded us in *Keywords* (1976), there are few more problematic words than 'culture'. In popular usage, the term oscillates between a general summary of the conventions and assumptions of an ethnic or social group (the 'culture of the Australian Aborigine' or 'New South Wales police culture', for example), and a term for the isolation of works of art of particular merit ('it is good to teach the young to appreciate culture'). It is not simple to define the term as it appears in a phrase like 'cultural studies', and to propose a definition would merely invite the impatience and pedantry of those working in the field. Suffice it to say that the new humanities have a major investment in the belief that human behaviour is either determined or mediated by the collective history of human practices. There is thus no simple dividing line between the natural and the cultural, the true and the artificial, the authentic and the inculcated that can be used by human beings to measure their activity. Any such attempt— for example, the Social Darwinism that sought to use the model of 'survival of the fittest' as a basis of social policy—is itself an act of culture, meaningful only in the context of the methods human groups have used to produce and validate the truth.

It is, of course, legitimate to argue that culture is not the mono-lithic and all-encompassing grounds for human behaviour and mean-ing. Common sense, however it may be defined, always seeks to pre-serve some at least hypothetical place for the unsocialised part of human experience. Yet such an assertion cannot itself be expressed without becoming subject in turn to the means and structures of cul-tural mediation: it must be written or spoken in a language saturat-ed with implications, associations, and dynamics that individual lan-guage users can neither recognise nor control. In other words, the outside of culture can only be imagined as the possible space from which we cannot speak. This outside is not easily disputed as a focus of belief, but it is similarly not easily delineated as a basis for analy-sis. If there is indeed an outside to culture in the human world, we can lay claim to it, assert its reality, but only from within the culture it is designed to delimit. The outside of culture can be insisted upon but never mapped or occupied.

In sum, then, the assumption of this book, and of the practices it hopes to clarify, is that the world of culture holds the only intelligi-ble key to the possibilities of human existence. The new humanities do not completely discount extra-cultural influences on human beings, but will always see those influences as inextricably mediated by cultural forms. In this sense, the way to understand the formula-tion of human truth is not by rigorously analysing each truth-claim, but rather by problematising the methods and means by which truth is generated and communicated. The grounds of these practices of truth formation are fundamentally textual. Through an analysis of such textual formulations a new access to the structures and politics of the distribution of materials and meanings in societies can be made available.

How does the layout of this book contribute to introducing students and others to some of the key terms of debate in the new humanities? The first thing that needs to be noted is the scope of the task. When teaching new undergraduate students, what has struck us more than anything else is the growing gap between what is taught in high schools and the ideas long established in universities. It is quite staggering how many of the assumptions that are almost taken for granted in many university humanities courses—such as the post-structuralist model of textuality—are unheard of in schools. Similarly, a continuing a-historical and uncritical approach to canonicity and the humanist tradition leaves many students entering university unable to defend or even to recognise the traditional hermeneutic principles on which their education has been based. This is near scandalous in any intellectual enterprise, where the elucidation and problematisation of first principles should be not only standard practice, but the one concrete goal of pedagogy. Although the aim of this book, and the teaching on which it is based, seems broad, it will have performed its task if it has given readers the most basic awareness of what is at stake in many humanities debates. Since it is unable—for practical reasons—to cope with more than a handful of important ideas and theorists, we hope it will represent a firm starting point for the complex investigations and re-investigations that should constitute the bulk of undergraduate study.

As such, this book performs a balancing act between breadth and depth, the two stalking horses of academic writing, particularly that of an introductory nature. Our tendency has been to give a broad overview of issues, and hopefully to do justice to a range of thinkers, by treating their ideas in depth. These thinkers are, on the whole, the big names of poststructuralism—Jacques Lacan, Julia Kristeva, Michel Foucault, Hélène Cixous, Jacques Derrida, and others. We are well aware that this is already a narrow selection. Yet, when we look around us at the debates taking place in academia, we realise that although discussions range well beyond these thinkers, many of the assumptions—about essentialism and textuality, for example—and many of the asides that plot the course particular intellectuals are taking rely on a basic acquaintance with poststructuralist thinking and its place in the history of thought. This may not seem apparent to many academics whose work has been so conditioned by this movement that they do not recognise that they remain affiliated to it, even or especially when they most attack it. For lack of any other, this statement stands as an apology to those among our colleagues who are unhappy with the emphases of the present volume.

The book is divided into four parts. The first part, 'The Humanities After Humanism', comprises two chapters. The first discusses the vexed and complex history of 'Humanism' and its place in modern debates. Since the 1980s, at least, a critique of humanism has been fundamental to the development of new ideas in the humanities. This chapter surveys how humanism has been presented in these debates. By way of a textual analysis of *Hamlet*, and of the film *Blade Runner*, the key defining values of humanism can be summarised, and their fate in the postmodern era assessed. Although the decline of the humanist consensus among academics is often put down to a kind of heartless scepticism, it is clear that the values that once seemed to motivate cultural work have lost their stable place in Western life in general. The second chapter is a study of the issue of canonicity, which has become one of the most important reference points in debates in the humanities. Why have certain texts been chosen as those most encoding core cultural values and traditions? Why have such texts been seen as the appropriate basis for education? This chapter discusses the key reasons why the claim of a narrow set of texts to define a humanistic education has been disputed in the last twenty years. We present a model of the relationship between 'high', 'popular', and 'sub' cultures in order to outline the fluid and unstable relationship between them, how, in fact, viewed historically, texts move easily, and relatively quickly, from one category to another. The chapter ends with some speculation, using the terminology of psychoanalysis, about the cultural meaning of these different ways of classifying and representing cultural texts.

The second part of the book, 'From Interpretation to Interaction', is divided into four chapters. One deals with the key issues of authorship and textuality as they have developed through twentieth-century theories of language, specifically those of Ferdinand de Saussure, Mikhail Bakhtin, Julia Kristeva, Roland Barthes, and Jacques Derrida. These issues are monumental in scope, and, in order to help focus them, we concentrate on two essays by Barthes on authorship and intertextuality. We do not pretend for a minute that these writings are uncontentious, yet they do provide students with a clear introduction to the gap between the way texts are now talked about in universities, and what they are assumed to be in schools. Put simply, a text can no longer in any sense be seen as the product or property of the body that physically produced it, and that body can no longer be known as its author. Instead, texts are seen as arising in a field of complex interrelationships between one text and another. It is this interrelationship—or intertextuality—that defines their function and fate. We have also included a brief overview of the work that made Jacques Derrida and deconstruction so central to the new humanities. The other chapters in this part deal with various issues to do with the reception of texts. What is 'reading', and how does this process contribute to the making of meaning in texts? Traditionally, reception has been seen as either a passive or an undefinable activity. Recent philosophy and theory, especially that developed in the wake of the Phenomenological movement in philosophy, have tried to analyse and define this process, the various operations performed on a text in the act of reading, and what this can tell us about the relationship between texts and the meaning-making that clusters around them. The related question of the 'gaze' is taken up in another chapter. This issue is one of the landmark debates of the last twenty years of film theory, particularly in the context of the relationship between film and gender. What can theories of watching, as they have developed since the Renaissance, tell us about the way certain audiences and bodies are encrypted in visual texts as the expected audiences for those texts? The final chapter in this part pursues the issues and debates surrounding the gaze as they have been taken up in the emerging field of visual cultures. This is a major development in critical and cultural studies, marking a new direction for some of its key themes. The study of visual culture takes up many ideas from cultural theory (such as meaning, the body, culture, and ethnicity) and examines them in relation to the image, arguing that the image has replaced the word as the dominant mode of discursive practice.

As can be seen from this brief outline, parts one and two of this book concentrate first on the theoretical context in which many new discussions are taking place in terms of the long history of Western academic debates; and second on recent discussions of what texts are, where they operate, and what they have been seen to do. Parts three and four discuss, first, the present social and political function of cultural work, and its place in historical development; and second, the question of the subject, one of the areas of investigation that has received most attention in the postmodern era.

In part three, 'Contextuality', we provide a broad survey of the dominant movements in the cultural theory of the postmodern. The first chapter provides a schematic outline of the key issues in post-modernism and an introduction to work of the most famous theo-rists of the term's meaning and provenance. The third chapter pro-vides a schematic outline of the key issues in postmodern cultural politics, specifically in relation to the confrontation between identity politics and queer theory. Together these two chapters provide a brief introduction to key thinkers in postmodern feminist thinking, espe-cially poststructuralist feminism. Unfortunately, the history and range of a political and cultural movement like feminism is too great for us to provide more than a partial contribution to it. Our decision here was to develop some ideas that relate to many of the other key issues canvassed in this book, rather than attempting an overly reductive account of the whole movement.

Part four, 'Texts and Subjects', introduces some of the key thinkers in the debate about the structure and cultural meaning of the indi-vidual human subject. We begin in the first chapter by outlining some key ideas from the psychoanalytic tradition, and some post-structuralist responses to them, in the work of Lacan and Derrida. In the second chapter, the alternative model of subjectivity in post-structuralism, the one that appears in the work of Foucault, and Deleuze and Guattari, is introduced. The juxtaposition of these chapters provides an insight into the relationship between subjectivity and textuality on the one hand, and subjectivity and power on the other. These have been the cardinal points of discussion here. The final chapter focuses on some key writings about sexuality, which, like the body, has become one of the defining issues of recent discussion. In sexuality, fierce debates about politics, psychology, gender, the body, and social policy mix with and comment on one another. In this debate, more than in any other, it becomes clear what is at stake in the issue of subjectivity—the scale and meaning of culture, and how it defines and administers us.

It is impossible to produce a text that covers all the basic ideas that go to make up the new humanities. As can be seen from the above discussion of the term, the field is so difficult to define that any attempt at theorising it is fraught with uncertainties and unanswerable questions. What are basic starting points to some are irrelevant, marginal, or even unknown to others. Our aim here is not to give a complete introduction to the new humanities, but to cast light on some of the controversies that indicate what has been defining the last twenty years of cultural debate.

PART ONE

The Humanities After Humanism

Introduction

The two chapters in this part examine some of the ways in which the study of the humanities has been radically challenged in recent years. The underlying directives of this part are: to provide a survey of criticisms of humanism; to consider ways of thinking outside some of the dominant paradigms of traditional humanities studies (the example is the canon); and to consider what has happened to the study of texts in the rise of the new humanities.

In one sense, then, this part provides a broad overview, a sort of 'taking stock' of the situation. But in doing so, we want to show how the systems of thought of postmodernism have fundamentally changed the way we look at texts, the way meaning and interpretation have become contested subjects in themselves, and how disciplines have been challenged. For one of the most significant aspects of these theoretical developments has been the self-conscious deliberations on knowledge and its production. And it is in this that we begin to grasp the monumental significance of these developments. For the study of the text is now fundamentally linked to questions of culture, ideology, subjectivity, interpretation, and knowledge, which are in themselves contested areas. So part of the object of the new humanities is to engage in an interdisciplinary investigation, which is also found in philosophy, psychoanalysis, sociology, feminism/women's studies, history, and so on.

The first chapter in this part, 'Post-humanism', examines how English studies in particular have been confronted with a post-humanist sensibility. We pay particular attention to the criticisms of the humanist tradition that have arisen here and become near orthodoxies since the 1980s. This chapter also looks at how we might think about texts in terms of humanism and post-humanism, using *Hamlet* as an example of the first type, and *Blade Runner* as an example of the second. The second chapter begins with an examination of the idea of the canon. However, the real focus is on considering how we can critically position texts within cultural contexts. The chapter proposes a model to illustrate the dynamic and extensive exchange of texts and typologies within cultural and psychoanalytic fields. To this end, the model does not provide a system of analysis, but rather a set of possibilities. It is a model that aims to explore the dynamic relationship between culture, theory, and texts.

1

Post-humanism

One of the things that most clearly defines the break that the new humanities represent is the attitude to humanism. Put simply, many contemporary intellectuals and theorists no longer see themselves fulfilling the cultural project that arose in the Renaissance, which saw the study and fulfillment of human nature as its purpose, and that gave rise to the field of study called the humanities and to the foundation of universities. Originally, the term 'humanist' referred to those scholars in the fourteenth and fifteenth centuries who were dedicated to the study of language and the revival of the literary culture of Ancient Greece and Rome. From the outset, therefore, humanistic culture has had a major investment in the written word, and its perceived civilising, humanising qualities. Many positions staked out in the debates that surround humanism are defined by their attitude to the written word—on the one hand, its charisma and inspiration, on the other, its materiality and unreliability. One of the most important contemporary forms of the debate about humanism centres on the relationship between language and meaning. Those who see themselves working in the humanist tradition still promote the written word as inextricably associated with meaning, even if that meaning is amorphous and subjective. One of the most influential attacks on humanism, the movement called deconstruction, which draws on the work of French philosopher Jacques Derrida, emphasises the instability and volatility of language, and the contingent quality of the meanings ascribed to it.

Humanism, however, is not a simple or even a single thing. In order to define their own positions many theorists have caricatured humanism, ascribing to it any number of unwanted or putatively conservative traits. In order to clarify the contemporary position it may be best to start not with a definition of what humanism is, but with some versions of what it has been seen to be by some critics who reject it. For the purposes of this chapter, we want to draw on two influential introductory works on literary theory from the early 1980s, Catherine Belsey's *Critical Practice* (1980), and Terry Eagleton's *Literary Theory: An Introduction* (1983). Both of these texts come from a British Left critical tradition, and therefore cannot be seen to represent fully the broad range of attacks on humanism that have flourished in the last twenty or thirty years. Throughout this book, we will return to many of the theories that see themselves as post-humanist. For example, we will present in later chapters a detailed description of Lyotard's model of postmodernism as the era of scepticism towards the grand narratives of human history, and Michel Foucault's announcement of the probable end of the human era. At this point, however, our aim is to recap that version of the attack on humanism that surfaced within the context of English studies. This will give students and readers an insight into the changes the humanities have been undergoing in the last twenty years.

Humanism has been attacked for many reasons from many fronts. The simplest way to understand this particular controversy is in the following terms. Humanism, in its broadest definition, sees the identification and fulfillment of a universal human nature as the purpose of cultural work. According to humanism, despite differences across time, place, culture, gender, and ethnicity, we all share certain human qualities that both define us and draw us together. These qualities are always at risk from (among other things) political extremism, intolerance, and cultural degeneracy, and it is the role of the humanities to bolster them and ease their way through history. It is to this project that the humanities have consistently referred to justify themselves, their critique of others, and their interventions in cultural politics.

The general attack on humanism has denied its fundamental premise that there is such a thing as a universal human nature. Indeed, feminists have argued that attempts at defining universal human qualities have been subject to at least a marked gender bias, advancing what are only masculine values and priorities as those of the human race in general. A similar argument has developed in relation to the ethnic bias of humanism, and its concentration on European traditions and priorities as if they were those of all human beings. Indeed, there is ample evidence to show that in the wake of humanism, European culture so idealised the 'human' as an abstract theoretical quality that it became divorced from the simple material reality of membership of the human race. Colonisers encountered ethnic groups they did not necessarily see as human enough by European standards. This licensed at times near genocidal treatment of indigenous populations. In sum, then, in the wake of feminist and anti-Eurocentric criticism, the debate over humanism has polarised around this issue of the assertion and denial of the existence of a common human quality that is separate from the reality of human biology. On the one hand are those who cling to the tradition based on a model of *universal humanity*; on the other, those who see human society as a field of endless and irreducible *difference*.

Let us now turn to the arguments of Belsey and Eagleton. Belsey locates humanism in this way:

> Common sense proposes a *humanism* based on an *empiricist-idealist* interpretation of the world. In other words, common sense urges that 'man' is the origin and source of meaning, of action and of history (*humanism*). Our concepts and our knowledge are held to be the product of experience *(empiricism)*, and this experience is interpreted by the mind, reason or thought, the property of a transcendent human nature whose essence is the attribute of each individual (*idealism*). These propositions ... constitute the basis of a practice of reading which assumes, whether explicitly or implicitly, the theory of expressive realism. This is the theory that literature reflects the *reality* of experience as it is perceived by one (especially gifted) individual, who *expresses* it in a discourse which enables other individuals to recognize it as true (Belsey, 1980:7).

This paragraph summarises a key form of the attack on humanism that has influenced literary and cultural studies in the last twenty years. Belsey identifies the universalising aim of humanism with a specific cultural form, which she names 'expressive realism'. Her aim here is to try to combine an attack on the traditionalism of the literary academy with a subversion of realism, a common strategy among postmodern theorists. Realism was the dominant literary form of the nineteenth century, and its ideology has survived well into the present, even though poststructuralist critics, especially Roland Barthes (in *S/Z*, a booklength study of the French realist Balzac), have mounted a systematic and persuasive attack on its premises. One of the consequences of this is that humanism appears a monolithically conservative formation because of the form in which it has come to dominate English studies. Radical political theorists from Adorno to Chomsky, who have used definitions of human universality as a way of challenging power structures in their societies, may well contest this.

With this reservation in mind, it is worth looking in some detail at what Belsey has to say. What we will do here is illustrate this discussion with examples from William Shakespeare's *Hamlet*. This is done for a number of reasons. First, Shakespeare, and *Hamlet* more than any of his other plays, have always been fundamental to the curriculum and rationale of English studies. Second, the ideas presented in the play, arising as they do at an early point in the history of humanist culture, encapsulate many of the essential ideals of that culture. Finally, *Hamlet* links humanism to a sort of heroic and individual purposefulness that is one of its hallmarks, and one that allows us to see below, in a very different text, Ridley Scott's film *Blade Runner*, the fate of humanism in our time. We are, of course, not claiming that *Hamlet* is a realist text. This would be an incredible anachronism. Our interest here is on the diverse range of individualisms, from the Renaissance to the present, that have carried the torch of humanism into our time.

So far we have spoken about humanism in the most general terms. Belsey helps us to identify some more specific attributes of this world view. She sees humanism as linking idealism and empiricism. Humanism, according to Belsey, takes the human as the origin and measure of all things, particularly the construction of purposeful and progressive action, which we denote as history. Instead of looking to the natural or spiritual world for direction and structure, humanists saw human beings as not only inhabiting the world, but defining and controlling it. If the world was to be known and controlled, it was to be done by human beings themselves according to their own standards and priorities.

The universe therefore, according to humanism, is subject to the analysis and scrutiny of human beings. Human beings *judge* the universe and everything in it. Their attributes and culture are capable of exhaustively measuring and evaluating all things. Hamlet himself is the embodiment of this questioning definition of the human. There is nothing in the universe that cannot be open to Hamlet's judgment. Even the authority of God is subject to human doubt and reconsideration. Not only are the orders of the universe subject to humanist scrutiny, so too are all political and social structures, from the customs of succession that operate in Danish royalty, to the traditional duty of revenge falling on a murder victim's family. Even human perception and sanity itself is subject to doubt. In sum, *Hamlet* locates the human individual as the mediating point between all things and their meaning. No meaning is accepted unquestioningly, and no value is absolute.

It is this last point that leads us to Belsey's comments about idealism and empiricism. One of the problems for humanism is that it must produce a model of the individual that can both embody a continuity and commonality of human nature and identity over and above differences of time and place, as well as engage meaningfully and productively with ever-changing real historical events in the material world. Hamlet must be both philosopher (capable of abstracting from the world the meanings and values that will produce a worthy life) and soldier (capable of violence and resolute action). The humanist individual is defined as the machine that makes these two potentially contradictory attributes compatible. In Belsey's terms, the humanist individual is both *idealist* (a framework of perceptions that refines and accumulates values and meanings as part of an eternal, transhistorical fulfillment of human talent and possibility) and *empiricist* (a concrete respondent and contributor to the material world). Indeed, it can be argued that humanist individualism is a fiction defined in order to make the abstract world of theory and the real world of things and actions connect with one another effectively.

Most readings of *Hamlet* involve the attempt to define exactly which of Hamlet's many and complicated ruminations are the most valuable and conclusive, which, in fact, allow him to act finally to revenge his father's murder. This is to read the play from within the humanist tradition, to take for granted its definition of what a human individual is. This path can only be followed if you have naturalised the humanist individual, if, in other words, you do not see it as possible for human beings to exist in any other way. It may be more useful to see *Hamlet* as merely an attempt to propose this model of human individuality as both necessary, and, in the end, effective. Shakespeare need not produce from Hamlet's thoughts a clear statement of morality or purpose. Indeed, it is not the content of Hamlet's thoughts that count in this context but merely the style of thinking and its eventual linkage to action.

Hamlet also provokes many of the political objections that have been made to the humanist tradition. First, its 'othering' of women. Shakespeare presents women here as disloyal, duplicitous, manipulable, oversexed, or mad. Hamlet's mother, Gertrude, is so blinded by her physical attraction to her dead husband's brother, Claudius, that she is quick to forget her obligations as widow of the late king, and marries too hastily, in Hamlet's opinion. Ophelia is easily overawed by her father and brother, and easily enlisted in the schemes and deceits of Claudius. Indeed, she ends by spying on Hamlet for Claudius. Ultimately, this weakness of character leads to breakdown and madness. Female sexuality is presented either as an object of disgust or a potential distraction. It could not be clearer in this text that the heroic humanist individual is a man, and that the point of view of women is secondary to his epoch-making contribution to his world. Women are *othered* here, and elsewhere in the humanist tradition, many feminists argue. Feminine culture, perception, and experience, the whole of feminine interior life, is presented as unimportant. Humanist culture, because it sees itself as embodying a transcendent human pluralism and generosity, is very sensitive to this sort of criticism. Yet a consistent recent attack has argued that the limited pluralism and tolerance continually proposed by humanist culture is inhibited by the model of universal human commonality. Because it must keep alive the dream of a human experience common to all, humanism is unable to acknowledge fully the broadly divergent experiences and subjectivities that span humanity. Indeed, by arguing that certain qualities are more human than others would seem to lead automatically to the evaluation of some people as more or less central (and others as more or less marginal) to the human project. Humanism inevitably produces hierarchies of the more or less human, despite its most generous intentions. We are all familiar with the term 'human' used by the mass media as a moral evaluation of cultural artifacts, as well as criminal and political behaviour. It is important to notice that these hierarchies have usually conformed to the distribution of power along gender and ethnic lines, which has defined Western politics and society since the Renaissance.

One of humanist culture's clearest betrayals of its historical origins in the Christian tradition is the strong connection made between the revelation of meaning and death. Not only is the quest for meaning in *Hamlet* and other humanist texts triggered by killing; killing is its constant accompaniment and necessary end. Hamlet is not only set on his process of self-criticism and reflection by his father's murder, he must murder in order to continue it (he is directly responsible for the deaths of Polonius, Rosencrantz, Guildenstern, and Claudius in the course of the play, is involved in the deaths of Gertrude and Laertes, and is at least partly morally responsible for Ophelia's death). Similarly, the revelation of an albeit merely rhetorical truth is only possible at the point of his own death. From Renaissance tragedy to hard-boiled detective fiction, there is a strong, sentimental connection between truth and death in Western culture, linked to the humanist project of the elucidation of meaning and value and the pursuit of truth at all costs.

In the postmodern era, the certainty of the humanist definition of individualism has been thoroughly shaken. There are a variety of reasons for this. To Jean-François Lyotard, the twentieth century has been so full of horrors that we no longer can nor should have any faith in the essential unity of the human race. For Michel Foucault, the idea of the 'human' was an accidental mutation in the history of ideas that survived for certain socio-political purposes, and which seems to be passing away. These ideas are dealt with more fully in other chapters. We want now to look briefly at another text from the early 1980s, Ridley Scott's film *Blade Runner* (1982), in order to show how similar questions about the human have been proposed more recently. Although set in the future, *Blade Runner* is in the tradition of detective fiction and *film noir*. The hero Deckard is employed to eliminate androids called replicants, who have rebelled and returned to earth from the off-world colonies (in which they are designed to work) in order to confront their makers. The motto of the Tyrell Corporation, the company responsible for the production of the replicants, is 'more human than human'. The replicants are not only possessed of a skill and strength that is superior to human beings, but they were originally programmed to believe that they *were* human beings, with memories of childhood, family, and so on. In the course of the film, two significant things happen. First, the replicants challenge Deckard with the possibility that despite being artificial, they exhibit a higher, more humane sensibility than the human beings that are hunting them down. The death of the replicant Roy Batty, with his dramatic narration of the suffering he has seen, and the liberation of his soul, challenges the simple dividing line between the human and non-human. Second, Deckard himself becomes more and more threatened by the possibility that he himself may be a replicant. What is to say that his very human subjectivity, his memories and relationships, may not themselves be programmed into him?

Since Mary Shelley's *Frankenstein* (1818), one of science fiction's most important projects has been to use the construction of artificial life as a way of creating an otherness that threatens the human with its sense of consistent and continuous identity and essence, and with its self-image as the highest and most circumspect possible form of subjectivity. The question of what it is to be human has therefore been a focus of much anxiety and uncertainty in Western culture since early in the nineteenth century. The confidence in the human project and the idealist/empirical model of individuality engendered by humanism has been attacked from many fronts, because of the differences among human beings that it ignores, and the perspectives it occludes. But it has also been attacked because of its internal contradictions, the artificiality of its model of subjectivity as the point of engagement between transcendent universality and the material world, and the volatility and uncertainty that inevitably results when human beings study themselves, an uncertainty that humanism originally hoped to suppress.

We have mentioned above how the term 'human' has sometimes been used to evaluate texts—some texts are seen as having more of an authentic human worth than others, of 'speaking' to the truly human quality within us. This idea is one of the hallmarks of the tradition of aesthetic philosophy that began with Immanuel Kant who, in *Critique of Judgment* (1790), wrote of the ability to make aesthetic judgments, that we assess 'the value of other people too on the basis of [their having] a similar maxim in their power of judgment' (Kant, 1987: 228). In other words, to Kant, and the aesthetic tradition he founded, the ability to assess the value of artworks allows us to judge one another. If we are disposed to making aesthetic judgments, we view positively those people with whom we see eye-to-eye, and disparage those who cannot appreciate our perceptions and values. The humanist appreciation of art, therefore, has always involved the selection of specific works that can define membership of a community of sensitivity and sensibility. It is here that we can turn to Terry Eagleton's account of the 'Rise of English' as a subject to be taught at schools and universities. Our focus here will be on the description of the movement that surrounded F.R. and Q.D. Leavis and the journal *Scrutiny*, a movement that has done more to define the meaning and function of English studies (particularly in countries once part of the British Empire) than any other.

What defined the Leavis group was its absolute and rigid adherence to a very specific canon of English texts, its concentration on the 'close reading' of texts, its faith in the 'vitality' of language as an indication of the well-being of a culture, and its resolute antagonism to industrial society and the culture it produced. All these different ideals are interconnected, and we deal with many of them elsewhere, especially the issue of the canon. Put simply, the Leavisite 'myth' of history was that the onset of industrialisation in the eighteenth century had robbed English culture of a vitality and harmony that had been exhibited in its best writing. The aim of English studies was to learn from the texts that most embodied this vitality the habits of moral sensibility and human discrimination that industrial society had flattened out and commercialised. In this sense, the study of literary texts was a highly serious activity, not just a badge of cultural sophistication or taste. As Eagleton puts it:

Scrutiny was not just a journal, but the focus of a moral and cultural crusade: its adherents would go out to the schools and universities to do battle there, nurturing through the study of literature the kind of rich, complex, mature, discriminating, morally serious responses (all key *Scrutiny* terms) which would equip individuals to survive in a mechanized society of trashy romances, alienated labour, banal advertisements and vulgarizing mass media (Eagleton, 1983: 33).

The aim of the Leavis group therefore was to deal directly with the cultural life of its society, to confront and transform it in the hope of at least reviving in an influential minority the sort of values that bespoke the vitality and meaningfulness of pre-industrial society.

Other forms of interventionist political criticism have seen texts as points of access to a historical reality they either represent or embody. Leavisite criticism was not interested in such contextualisation. The historical background of a text was curious, and could perhaps help with references and names, but, on the whole, it was the intense critical engagement with 'the words on the page' that counted for the Leavisites. Most students of literary criticism would find the Leavisite rationale for this kind of literary study surprising, if not bizarre. They would instantly recognise the technique of close reading, however, which continues to dominate high school and university literary studies. In fact, the lack of a clear rationale for this technique, and its dissociation from even the purpose ascribed to it by the Leavises, is one of the most commonly reported frustrations among students and teachers with the sort of English studies still common in high schools.

How could the concentration on words on a page have any relation to outside society? Eagleton paraphrases the Leavis view in this way:

In literature, and perhaps in literature alone, a vital feel for the creative uses of language was still manifest, in contrast to the philistine devaluing of language and traditional culture blatantly apparent in 'mass society'. The quality of a society's language was the most telling index of the quality of its personal and social life: a society which had ceased to value literature was one lethally closed to the impulses which had created and sustained the best of human civilization. In the civilized manners of eighteenth century England, or in the 'natural', 'organic' agrarian society of the seventeenth century, one could discern a form of living sensibility without which modern industrial society would atrophy and die (Eagleton, 1983: 32).

Language was considered the lifeblood of a culture. The debasement of language would reflect and contribute to the degradation of the lives of its citizens. Enclosed in this argument is the still commonly aired view that changes to language almost inevitably involve its debasement, and a subsequent reduction of human sensibility. It also explains the opposition of English studies to studying works in translation. The Leavises are open to criticism that their work identifies unthinkingly an individual's moral education with the language tradition in which he or she is educated. The moral possibilities of texts written in other languages, indeed the fact that an individual's subjective life is always open to influence from a wide variety of ethnic sources, are ignored. Similarly, internal differences between language sub-groups, even when they sound the same, are wiped out in the name of a higher language identity. The particularity of Australian, American, Jamaican or even Yorkshire English, and all the sub-groups within these categories, did not seem to count in the Leavis world view.

Objections can also be raised to the Leavis view of mass culture. The assumption the Leavises worked with, and one still commonly heard, is that the experience of mass or popular culture is a completely passive and mindless activity. Counter to this, recent theoretical work emphasises the ability of individuals to read against texts, and not to be completely subject to their values and prejudices. The American television programme *Friends* seen in Los Angeles, Blackpool, Guatemala City and Wollongong is potentially a very different text according to this view. Indeed, it is common practice for viewers, either individually or in groups, to adopt playfully ironic, sceptical, or even resistant responses to texts as a way of heightening pleasure and making political opportunities. Consequently, texts are produced by writers and directors with this range of possible responses in mind. The superficial qualities of the text are therefore not necessarily an indication of the nature of the response to it. Similarly, the concentration on certain texts rather than others has produced somewhat mindless prejudices against whole genres. The novel of human manners, especially when written by the writers the Leavises admired (most famously, Jane Austen, George Eliot, Henry James, Joseph Conrad and D.H. Lawrence), is taken very seriously. Gothic or science fiction genres, or even film and television *in toto*, are dismissed out of hand as implicitly unserious. In an era such as ours, where much of the innovative and creative work has been produced in such genres and for such media, the Leavis viewpoint has become seriously dated.

Eagleton's main criticism of the Leavisite model of English studies is political, however. Writing in the Marxist tradition, Eagleton sees English studies as having taken up the place left vacant by the decline in the authority of religion. Eagleton says that religion 'at least in its Victoran forms, is a *pacifying* influence, fostering meekness, self-sacrifice and the contemplative inner life. It is no wonder that the Victorian ruling class looked on the threatened dissolution of this ideological discourse with something less than equanimity' (1983: 23). It was to perform this function that the study of English was first tried in Mechanics' Institutes, working men's colleges, and other places (1983: 27). English studies could put day-to-day resentments into a broader context, heading off political discontent by a 'high-minded contemplation of eternal truths and beauties' (1983: 25). Although the Leavises were more interventionist than this, seeing their cultural role as oppositional rather than conservative, their actions never really amounted to a politics, according to Eagleton. He says of them: 'there was never any serious consideration of actually trying to *change* such a society. It was less a matter of seeking to transform the mechanized society which gave birth to this withered culture than of seeking to withstand it' (1983: 33). In other words, despite their oppositional rhetoric and self-image, the Leavises were merely trying to open up a space in which a higher moral sensibility could be lived out, uncontaminated by industrial culture. It is, however, a little easy to make such a criticism. Not much cultural activity would survive the sort of critique that sees molar social change as the only worthwhile aim. Recent theoretical discussions have concentrated on the politics of texts in terms of negotiation rather than revolution. This means that texts or textual reading are not to be seen as possible preliminaries to some major future historical event, but rather as an important component of contemporary life with which we must learn to deal. The ability to understand and resist the political meaning of texts is perhaps the most commonly discussed subject in contemporary literary and cultural studies. In this sense, the Leavisite project may not have been as foreign to much contemporary criticism as it is often seen to be. Its identification of cultural work as oppositional at least paved the way for much that came after. Yet, like the humanism that was its parent, Leavisite criticism undercut its own liberal rhetoric by an unrelieved commitment to hierarchies, to a practice of inclusion and exclusion defined narrowly, and to a refusal to take seriously a variety of under-represented perspectives. Like humanism, Leavis-style criticism was pluralistic, but only on its own terms. It generalised its own priorities till they obscured anyone else's, and sought to establish itself as the arbiter of what variety of tastes and behaviours would be deemed acceptable. Again, like humanism, its acceptance of difference was to be policed, or at least balanced, by a clear and loudly announced insistence on the universality of certain human attributes, and a strict definition of those attributes. It was inevitable that the greater complexity of postmodern life would make such a balance appear simple-minded and impossible.

This survey of the critique of humanism within English studies represents only a fraction of the range of images and ideas that could be seen as post-humanist. In fact, the greater part of this book is an explication of other post-humanist writings: the critical ontology of Michel Foucault, which sees the 'human' as a mere mutation in the history of thought that arose at the beginning of the nineteenth century and is now beginning to pass away; the cyborg politics of Donna Haraway, which sees us as occupying an unstable and shifting zone that overlaps with nature at one end and technology at the other; and the sceptical but thrilling inspirations of Queer theory that refuse to acknowledge any prefixed 'natural' limits for our desire and, consequently, our subjectivity. The study of post-humanism within English studies shows us how a transition has been made from an intellectual cosmos defined by the human to one suspicious of it. The postmodern cultural world that has resulted is infinitely more dramatic, creative, and surprising, however, and it is to these inventions and interventions that our discussion will continually return.

Further Reading

The literature on humanism is voluminous, particularly works treating humanism in the Renaissance. Any library catalogue will provide a starting point. In terms of issues closer to those discussed here, a good place to start is Terry Eagleton's *Literary Theory: An Introduction* (1983) and Catherine Belsey's *Critical Practice* (1980), where you can find the extracts discussed above. A useful recent edition of Kant's work on aesthetics is Immanuel Kant, *Critique of Judgment* (1987). The Leavisite tradition is usually traced back to Matthew Arnold's *Culture and Anarchy* (1869). If you are interested in the Leavises, F.R. Leavis's essays on poetry are collected in *Revaluation: Tradition and Development in English Poetry* (1964), and his influential definition of a canon of the English novel is in *The Great Tradition* (1962). Q.D. Leavis's most important work is *Fiction and the Reading Public* (1932). Those interested in English studies and questions of the moral or social value of culture should see Tony Bennett's *Outside Literature* (1990), and *Culture, A Reformer's Science* (1998), Andrew Milner's *Literature, Culture and Society* (1996), and John Frow's *Cultural Studies and Cultural Value* (1995).

2

The Text, Culture, and the Unconscious: Life Without the Canon

The idea of the canon has been around for a long time, and its powerful presence in the discussion of texts—in particular the literary—makes it a difficult structure to ignore. This chapter will focus on why the idea of the canon has outlived its usefulness as a critical device (if indeed it ever had one), while at the same time acknowledging that certain types of analysis of texts are still dominated by this idea. The ensuing discussion will note some of the problems of using the canon as a form of analysis, and also consider why we need to go beyond it. That said, it is important to recognise that the concept of canonicity cannot be ignored, not simply because it has informed studies in the humanities for such a long time, or that it continues to dominate certain fields of that study, but because the canon is something that any research in the humanities has to come to terms with in order to understand the processes of categorising, analysis, and change. Quite simply, we need to acknowledge the *idea* of canonicity in order to understand what changes have taken place in a postmodern aesthetic. This, in turn, allows the canon to be deconstructed not by discarding it, but rather by using it in the processes of analysis.

To define what canonicity means is as difficult as examining the devices used in determining the canon itself. As a working definition the following is inadequate, but it will get us started: The canon is a body of texts institutionally determined and culturally 'accepted' as constituting 'Literature', or 'Film', or 'Art', and hence the literary/

filmic/aesthetic work of art. This definition introduces further issues, such as the idea that certain forms have been seen as canonical. The most obvious example is the way film studies struggled to be recognised within the academy because it was continually judged against literature. Similarly, television studies 'adopted' the methodologies of literary analysis in order to seem more acceptable. Any definition of the canon—this one included—works on a number of assumptions based on value, cultural acceptance of the criteria for inclusion and exclusion of texts, and the certainty of the elements that constitute it. What is essential to acknowledge, however, is that any work defined as canonical exists as such through a set of value judgments placed on it, which are in themselves entirely arbitrary. This immediately creates a number of difficulties.

If the idea of the canon is based on value it then becomes necessary to decide what is to be done with ideas such as 'good' and 'bad', or 'literary' and 'non-literary', or 'cinematic' and 'non-cinematic', or 'art' and 'non-art'. Adherence to the canonical ideal means that the works themselves must be seen to have an intrinsic quality that makes them 'good' or 'art'. There are three major problems with such an idea: first, this line of argument fails to recognise that any work becomes canonical not for what it is or does, but through external forces that define it as such; second, works drift in and out of the canon, but nothing in the works themselves has changed—in other words, forming the canon is a political, cultural and social act, rather than the aesthetic one it purports to be; and third, the very terms of debate, such as 'good' and 'bad', are impossibilities in themselves. How is it possible, for example, to speak of a 'good film'? What is the criteria for good? What, or who, is it good for? This is part of the reason why studying the canon is useful in itself. Consideration of what a culture has come to determine as canonical reveals some aspects of that culture. For example, negotiations of the 'artistic' and pornographic have depended on a sense of the canon; James Joyce's *Ulysses*, for example, moved from being considered pornography to high literature through a determining system of the canon, and demonstrated a change in ideas about sexuality, aesthetics, and politics; Kubrick's final film *Eyes Wide Shut* (1999) is viewed differently because of the *oeuvre* of the director that precedes it.

Rather than try to establish a canon, what is more useful—and more interesting—is to examine the dynamics of change and diversity. Rather than attempt to detail and sustain an élite criteria for 'Literature' or 'Film', we can consider the heterogeneity of the literary work or cinematic work. Instead of trying to argue what is a good text, it is more useful to consider how texts engage in a wide, diverse, and often contradictory set of processes. It is in this direction that the new humanities have begun to develop. A simple example will illustrate this.

One author to be found in most, if not all, lists of the Western canon is Shakespeare—his inclusion would seem to be automatic. But, critically speaking, such an assertion yields very little. On the other hand, if we place this sense of the canonical in parentheses, and instead consider Shakespeare in different contexts, then much more is revealed. Shakespeare's work positioned not as élite/canonical culture, for example, but in the context of popular culture, immediately produces ideas and reflections on such cultural contexts. We could examine how Shakespeare was a figure of the popular culture in his time, considered much more an entertainer than an artist. Or we could look at Shakespeare's works and our own, more recent popular culture—at how *The Tempest* came to be translated into the science-fiction film *Forbidden Planet* (Fred McLeod Wilcox, 1956) or Peter Greenaway's arthouse film *Prospero's Books* (1992). Or we could consider Franco Zeffirelli's comment on casting Mel Gibson as Hamlet after seeing *Lethal Weapon* (Richard Donner, 1987) (so the film's main character can be seen as a reinterpretation of Hamlet), and in doing so aligning Shakespeare with a form of popular cinema. What this means, in effect, is that in such discussions there is a foregrounding of the *ideas* and *concepts*, and a relinquishing of the privileged site of the artist/creative genius. It is just as possible to use either *Hamlet* or *Lethal Weapon* to illustrate the idea of the loss of the will to live and the incapacity to act. In such a scenario what is important is not the canonicity of the text, but the ideas and theoretical issues at hand. This inflection, this radical transformation, is what has taken place over the last twenty or so years in the postmodern humanities.

Other examples would be the recent development of Queer theory and its examination of Shakespeare in terms of the practice of cross-dressing (boys or young men always played the part of women in Shakespeare's time), or its re-reading of the sonnets as homo-erotic, as opposed to the canonical view of dividing them into sonnets about love addressed to women, and sonnets about friendship addressed to men. Similarly, the political aspects of postcolonialism have been discussed in terms of *Othello* and *The Tempest* to great effect. What is significant is that all of these readings can take place without any reference to the canon, to value, and to notions of good and bad. So it is not the value of Shakespeare that is brought into question, but the ways in which the works are read, the context in which they are positioned, and the processes of analysis traditionally used to study them.

The shift in recent times has been away from élite notions of high art, and towards a wider study of textual practices. A consequence of this has been the need to examine cultural processes themselves. This has been part of the rise of cultural studies, some of which will be taken up later in this chapter. One of the key aspects of this shift has been not simply to negate the idea of the canon, but to evaluate critically its function. By examining relationships between texts and culture, aspects such as the two-way flow between contexts and texts, and the significance of the reader and the problematising of the status of the author have been articulated.

Text, Culture and Psychoanalysis: A Model

The model below contains all of the problems of this type of analysis: it oversimplifies certain aspects; it cannot address certain issues; it raises more questions than it yields answers; and it operates at an abstract level. However, none of these produce impossible difficulties, and some are of a distinct advantage in this type of examination. A model in this sort of discussion should always aim beyond itself— after all it does not purport to be a diagram for a scientific experiment. With this in mind the following diagrams are designed to consider essentially five issues in the interrelations between the text, culture, and different textual forms. Part of this agenda is also to consider the interdisciplinary nature of such analytic tools. The model:

(i) suggests the flow and dynamic between divisions of cultural forms, and how texts move across them;

(ii) locates some of the relational contexts between texts, historical forces and culture;

(iii) positions the divisions of culture (high and low; elite and popular) in terms of one another and other contexts;

(iv) considers the idea of culture and texts, and their operations, in terms of ideology; and

(v) suggests some ideas on culture and texts in terms of a cultural unconscious.

We will also be concerned once more with how recent theoretical developments relate to established issues, such as the canon. The model draws on ideas from semiotics, the anthropological work of Lévi-Strauss, and Freudian/Lacanian psychoanalysis. In doing so it is as much concerned with demonstrating the usefulness of such approaches (and combinations) to cultural studies, as it is with applying them to such a study. It is also important to note that the model operates very much on a comparative basis. This means that all of the elements and all of the processes within the model are defined and understood more by their comparative position to the others than by any qualities inherent to them. Ultimately the model becomes one concerned with issues in the study of culture and so a few words on this are necessary before we proceed.

One thing seems to be certain regarding the issue of cultural studies at this moment of critical investigation: that no one is really certain exactly what cultural studies as a discipline is. In fact, a great deal of the critical energy invested in this branch of study has been devoted to discussion and argument on, and dispute of, a definition. It would be unreasonable to proffer a definition here, but we will offer some broad notes towards a defining of the territory, so that we might consider how the model ties in with some of these issues.

Cultural studies is difficult to define partly because of its history. It originates from a diverse set of disciplines, including sociology, anthropology, history, linguistics, semiotics, Marxism, literary studies, film studies, and philosophy. Depending on the emphasis from these (and other) sources, what appears under the banner of cultural studies can look bewilderingly heterogeneous, and quite often antagonistic. If we were to compare the 'historical' cultural studies of Foucault (for example, *The Order of Things*[1]) with the 'philosophical' cultural studies of Derrida (the essays of *Writing and Difference*[2]) not only would we have the difficulty of making connections along the lines of the study of cultures, but we would also have to contend with the arguments that neither of these appear to be cultural studies to a sociologically based study. The two options that seem to present themselves in such a situation are either to have a definition of cultural studies that is so broad it can comfortably contain all differences (a problematic option because it greatly reduces the effectiveness of the term), or to enter into the debate on exactly what defines cultural studies. A third option, which we will take, is to say that the actual definition of cultural studies should not be of primary concern, but attempts to define it should continue through the processes of analysing texts. This is to suggest a performative definition of cultural studies—that is, cultural studies is the enacting of analysis which necessarily goes beyond any definition from the academy.

While not pretending to be a definition within the current context, cultural studies will be taken to be concerned with the investigation of how we read cultures, how cultures generate and sustain meanings and interpretations, how cultural perspectives are generated, and how cultural differences (both external to a culture and within a specific cultural order) operate. In other words, cultural studies is a set of (performed) analyses on how we might interpret the interpretative gestures of cultures. The other thing that marks cultural studies is that its textual base—that is, the texts examined—is very wide and far reaching. Literature, film, media, fashion, language, the body, gender, architecture and sport form only a part of the textual range that cultural studies has investigated. Indeed, it is this diversity that

---

1 In *The Order of Things* (1970), Foucault examines how cultures produce *epistemes*, that is, models of meaning and interpretation. He considers how across hundreds of years—from the Renaissance to the twentieth century—the same sorts of issues of classification produce different cultural perspectives, but also how systems of classification themselves operate to produce forms of knowledge.

2 Some of the essays in *Writing and Difference* (1978), specifically address issues of culture. 'Cogito and the History of Madness', Derrida's famous reply to Foucault's book *Madness and Civilization* (1967), is very much concerned with the position of meaning within cultural and philosophical contexts. Similarly, 'Structure, Sign, and Play in the Discourse of the Human Sciences' can be seen as a deconstructionist analysis of the cultural production of centres and margins'.

defines cultural studies as a discipline, for it sees itself as an academic field that must consider all facets of a culture. Texts become significant both in themselves and as ways of reading a culture. This is partly why the issue of the canon is completely refigured in a cultural studies context. The focus shifts from a question such as 'what is a canonical text?' to 'why does the idea of a canon exist and what function does it perform in the culture?' Interestingly, once such a question is asked the issue of canonical texts can also be broached. To address questions of this type it is necessary to consider texts from as wide a range as possible.

The Model

We want to sidestep the difficulties of defining 'culture' as it would take us too far from the issues at hand, and most likely not produce any satisfaction. Enough of a definition will seep through the following to make such an act redundant anyway. We can begin with the cultural 'system' (see figure 2.1), which provokes a number of difficulties. The terms 'canonical', 'popular', and 'sub' culture are selected not because they are necessarily viable terms of analysis, but because they exist in our cultural discourse already.

One of the issues that needs to be considered is how relationships operate between textual types and ideological orders of culture. To illustrate this three diagrams representing the relational context of each cultural type to the ideological mainstream appear below. 'Ideological mainstream' is taken to mean that order of ideology which is perceived as the dominant one within the culture. White, late-capitalist patriarchy, which celebrates the ruling class, is an example of such an ideological order. The entwined circles demonstrate how relationships between the ideology (of the dominant, popular or subcultural) and the textual order shift. The ideology of the punk movement, for example, is quite different from that of other subcultural groups, just as it is from the dominant ideology. But, perhaps more useful than this, the diagrams in figure 2.1 also try to show a relationship between ideological paradigms and textual utterances. The two circles represent logical types—that is, they are self-contained, are defined external to each other (in terms of certain aspects), and

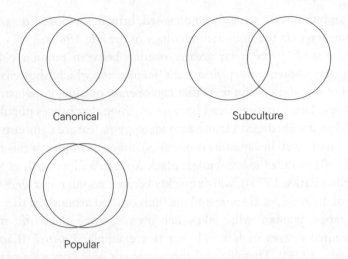

Canonical   Subculture

Popular

Figure 2.1 Textual orders and simple interrelationships

act in a categorising fashion. Yet there is also a set of processes that align the textual order and ideological groups. This is where the idea of canonicity is formulated and sustained.

'Canonical' culture is most often used to defend the idea of the artistic, but part of it is also aligned to the ruling class, or a particular ideological order that defines itself as such. Texts that become part of the canonical order may or may not be aligned with the current dominant ideology. When Joyce published *Ulysses* it quickly became part of the literary canon, yet it was denied the status of literature by the ideological processes of the canon. In the latter half of the twentieth century it is much closer to the common mid-ground, largely because of its positioning in academic work and as a common requirement in university courses on modernism. A text that has shifted in the opposite way is Shakespeare's *Macbeth*. It was written specifically for James I, the first Scottish king of England, and included aspects such as witchcraft because of the king's interest in the supernatural. The play was both canonical and a part of the ideology of the ruling class. Today *Macbeth* retains its status as part of the canon, but is much less noted for its ideological alignment with the ruling class of late capitalism. Interestingly, when Roman Polanski made a film version of the play the metaphors of power, violence, and ambition were strongly emphasised, bringing it closer to a social commentary on the dominant ideology of the late 1960s.

There tends to be a far greater overlap between popular culture texts and contemporary dominant ideologies, which shortens the band of popular culture texts that can operate outside of mainstream ideology. This situation arises because anything that proves popular is quickly subsumed into mainstream ideology (a feature demonstrated particularly well in capitalist economies). Some examples of this from the 1970s include the low-budget Black American films (such as *Shaft* (Gordon Parks, 1971)), which quickly became popular and were then part of mainstream cinema; and the films centred around the theme of the raped woman who takes her own revenge once the male-dominated system of law fails her (for example, *Lipstick* (Lamont Johnson, 1976)). These films demonstrate not only how a set of texts is recouped into the ideological system, but also how different political agendas are diffused. The rising power (political, economic, and social) of Blacks and women at this time in the United States, coupled with a burgeoning film industry, caused Hollywood to hegemonically subsume these divergent ideologies of non-White and non-male. The raped-woman films seem to suggest the misogynistic elements of patriarchy, and the inability (and perhaps unwillingness) of its laws to protect women. But ultimately these become pseudo-feminist texts because the moral structure always returns them to the very patriarchy that they initially resist or rebel against. The women who employ violence against violence are never allowed the autonomy and lawlessness of Harry Callahan in the 'Dirty Harry' films, made around the same time. The whole genre of revenge films also illustrates the phallocentric politics through the point of revenge itself. Women usually have to seek revenge because of a wrong committed against them personally (usually rape), whereas the revenge sought by men is generally the result of a wrong committed against their 'possessions' (women, land, objects of power). This inflection of revenge reveals how a signifier (revenge and motives for it) can be determined through gender and cultural politics.

The movement from a thin band of popular culture that operates outside the dominant ideologies—in effect, hegemonic control—illustrates the structure of relational contexts between subcultures and these ideologies. Unlike the large overlap with popular culture, subcultures tend to operate outside of the dominant ideologies, often offering sites of resistance to such ideological contexts. Part of the reason for this is that they often define themselves precisely as the 'other'. Subcultures often survive because of a radical and subversive identity, and their demise, somewhat ironically, is often due to a growth in popularity. When punk culture first appeared in the mid-1970s it was a social manifestation of an extreme reaction to Thatcherite politics. Its political and social force depended on it being *outside* the mainstream ideology of capitalism. However, once it gained popularity, its dress became fashion, its music was played on mainstream radio, and it left its context of mid-1970s England to appear in countries like the United States and Australia, it lost its political venom. The same phenomenon has occurred in the mid-1990s with rap music and fashion. Initially a cultural form directing its anger at Reaganism (and its after effects), it sought to operate outside the harmonics of White radio and reflect the social angst of poor, Black America. Its demise as a subculture with a political message is reflected in the sanitised versions being recorded by White, middle-class 'boys', and its entry into the world of advertising. In terms of our diagram (figure 2.1) this is represented as a shift from the subcultural position, which exists outside of the dominant ideologies, to one that becomes part of them. Of course once this takes place, the subcultural has become part of the popular culture.

The triangle of 'canonical', 'popular' and 'sub' cultural suggests that there is a relationship between these cultural forms, and each one is in fact attached to the others. The way that these groups 'communicate' is through texts shifting positions, and the act of reading. It is the reading process that formulates such connections, and a more accurate diagram would include a fourth point of 'reading/spectatorship' at an apex. Such a pyramid would have a base of cultural orders. Now we will turn to this aspect of the flow between these cultural orders.

There are three common movements for texts or groups of texts in this triangle: first, the movement from a subculture to popular culture (for example, punk or rap music); second, from a subculture to canonical via popular culture (for example, cult films such as *Blue*

Velvet (David Lynch, 1986) or *Casablanca* (Michael Curtiz, 1943));
and third, from a subculture directly to the canonical (for example,
the artistic movements of Dadaism and Surrealism, Van Gogh's
paintings—these examples also demonstrate a further movement,
that of the canonical to the popular). There are, of course, movements 'against' such flows—the example of Van Gogh's paintings
becoming part of popular culture from the site of canonicity is one.
Popularity through adaptation is a common process (Victor Hugo's
Les Misérables moved from the literary canon to popular culture
when it became a musical; Conrad's *Heart of Darkness* became the
film *Apocalypse Now* (1979)). What is perhaps more interesting is
what happens to the defining principles of the cultural forms when
this happens. The texts of pop art (through people such as Andy
Warhol, Roy Lichtenstein, and Jasper Johns) were based very much
on this deconstruction of divisions, and film-makers such as the
Coen Brothers (*Blood Simple* (1984), *Miller's Crossing* (1990), and
Barton Fink (1992) are all good examples) and Quentin Tarantino
(*Pulp Fiction* (1994) in particular) defy classification because their
works can be located in any of the three categories. Such texts are
analytically useful because they illustrate the problems of trying to
locate any cultural form in such a manner. They also demonstrate
how it is more the act of reading (with the attendant issues of cultural and historical processes) that determines a defining point,
rather than anything that might be in the text itself.

The next part of the discussion shifts the emphasis from the sociocultural to the psychoanalytic. We can overlay on the existing triangle a second one made up of the conscious, preconscious, and
unconscious (see figure 2.2). These Freudian terms have passed into
current language, but a brief and highly simplified summary will help
locate them within the current discussion. The conscious part of the
mind involves the everyday dealings of the subject as he or she moves
through the social world. It is a repressed, contained, and managed
system of thinking, dominated by what Freud termed the 'super-ego'.
The super-ego is responsible for the subject behaving in a socially
acceptable manner—it controls the mechanisms of repression that
deny manifestation of the extremities of the id. The id is dominated
by the sex drive and the death drive. It is deeply anti-social, with no

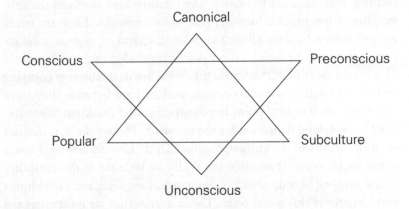

Figure 2.2 Textual orders and the unconscious

sense of morality or ethics. The third part of what Freud termed the 'topographical divisions' of the mind is the ego. This is a force that is concerned entirely with the self, including the immediate gratification of demands for the self. Both the id and the ego constantly strive for expression and for this immediacy, while the super-ego represses and demands postponement. Freud argues that it is through things such as dreams that the repressed and censored material of the id and ego is allowed to be manifested in the conscious mind.

Freud's other two topographical divisions are the preconscious and the unconscious. The preconscious exists just under the conscious mind and, according to Freud, can be reached with some effort. In other words, thoughts and memories in the preconscious are absent from the conscious mind, but can appear with some prompting. The unconscious, on the other hand, is always denied direct expression in the conscious mind. Thoughts that come from it always undergo strict and complex repression and censorship, hence its manifestation is based on disguise. This notion of repression is highly significant in Freud's work, forming a cornerstone for a great deal of psychoanalytic theory, and will be returned to in a later chapter.

Before discussing in more detail some of the implications of these Freudian terms for our model we would like to introduce a further three. Lacan developed the idea of the 'imaginary', the 'symbolic', and the 'real' in order to explore the relationships between the subject, his or her psychic identity, and social contexts. They are terms we will return to throughout the ensuing chapters, and so a definition will be accumulated, rather than expounded at a single point.[3] This is necessary in part because the terms are in themselves complex and require significant elaboration, and in part because they have come to form a central point in poststructuralist thinking. What follows is a working definition for the moment. The symbolic is derived from the works of the anthropologist Claude Lévi-Strauss and refers to the social order. It is called the symbolic because of the centrality of the symbol (word, object of exchange, language, etc.) that binds and formulates this social order. Lacan argues that we must enter the symbolic in order to engage in the social, to become socialised, and to acquire language. The imaginary is linked to Lacan's idea of the 'mirror stage'—a moment in the subject's development when he or she moves from a domination of an egocentric status into the symbolic order. The imaginary is defined by, and orientated around, a sense of the self. The real is perhaps the most difficult of the three to define. At this stage we can simplify things by saying that the real, on one level, is most closely linked to the unconscious and the drives that constantly seek manifestation. The real must not be confused with notions of 'reality', for it is much more a part of psychic processes than any structures of the external world.

By locating these psychoanalytic issues in terms of the cultural paradigm of 'canonical', 'popular' and 'sub' cultural we are attempting to develop a model that shows how different interpretative systems can be used in the analysis of texts. There is also a sense of the subject's position in various cultural orders—and this is where we witness more forcefully the actions of the reader. The combination here will allow us to consider a particular inflection of the cultural in terms of the psychoanalytic, and the psychoanalytic in terms of the cultural.

---

3 For further definition of these terms see Jacques Lacan, *The Four Fundamental Concepts of Psychoanalysis* (1977) and *Ecrits: A Selection* (1985). In terms of the definition given here a more extended commentary is to be found in Patrick Fuery, *Theories of Desire* (1995). Further discussion can be found here in Part 4 'Texts and Subjects'.

Let us now return to figure 2.2 and suggest some possible combinations. The line of connection between the canonical and the popular can be located within the sphere of the conscious. In other words, we can speak of a type of cultural consciousness, dominated by certain textual practices. The variants of the canonical and popular (which also includes those texts that actually combine the two) are aligned with the conscious because, as in the Freudian model of the mind, they are the most apparent, most manifest, most produced (as a social unit), and demonstrate a greater level of homogeneity of all the cultural artefacts. They are also the areas most likely to be contorted through repressive devices (this time generated by ideological processes of a culture, such as censorship, moral codes, and ethical constraints). Even the idea of the canon carries with it both repression and an escape from censorship. Joyce's *Ulysses* or D.H. Lawrence's *Lady Chatterley's Lover* eventually escaped cultural and social (that is, legal) repression when their status changed from the pornographic to the artistic/canonical.

In this sense the canonical/popular/conscious paradigm is part of the symbolic order (see figure 2.3). It is in this area that laws are stated, rules performed, and structures solidified. This is an ideological dimension and function of the symbolic. It is also significant

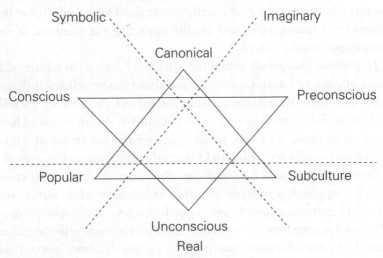

Figure 2.3 Textual Orders and Lacan's Schema

that the symbolic is the area where systems of exchange are organised and articulated, and the text operates openly as a commodity within such systems.

The connection between the canonical and subculture can be seen to operate like the preconscious. In this sense these texts, once more either as a variant from the other textual practices or as a set of texts that combine the two cultural conditions, are there in the social order, but are much less apparent as part of that order. This evokes the idea of a cultural preconscious—that is, a paradigm where texts are situated just outside of the dominant symbolic. As a consequence, issues such as repression are treated differently. When a film festival is held, for example, films normally requiring classification or even censoring by the moral codes are allowed to be screened free of such conditions. The festival creates a space like the preconscious, having restrictions, but restrictions substantially different from those in the symbolic. It is no coincidence that films at such festivals are seen as being both canonical and subcultural. This liminal zone reflects certain aspects of what Bakhtin (1968; 1973) describes as the 'carnivalesque'. This is a time (or space) where the conventions of social order are overturned and usurped and the figures of authority and power are replaced by those usually repressed. Sydney's gay and lesbian mardi gras or the carnivale in Rio are demonstrations of groups whose subjectivity is usually constrained taking control of the streets for a limited time, and usually attracting the attention of the mainstream media as well.

To position this group within the imaginary may seem a little odd. After all, one of Lacan's specifications about the imaginary is that it negotiates the relationships between the subject, its sense of the self, and the social contexts in which it is placed. For this to be useful here we need to think not of the subject's imaginary, but rather of a type of cultural imaginary. This would enact the same sorts of issues—the reflection of the culture to itself, an illumination of the contexts in which it operates, a struggle with the inadequacies of its status, and so on. These two cultural forms are included here and not in the popular not because they are inherently invested in such self-consciousness, but rather because once popular culture becomes part of the imaginary, it also tends to be redefined. The television show *The*

Simpsons, for example, is strongly invested with a self-reflexivity about popular culture itself. In other words, it is a text that draws attention to its own cultural site and lineage. It has moved from the status of subculture to popular to a type of canonicity. In doing so it has also operated as part of the cultural imaginary. Similarly, *The X Files* depends and draws on a cultural and textual knowledge of a range of established texts. It does not introduce new terrors, but feeds on the ones already devised within the cultural imaginary. This is not simply generic shorthand, but is part of the way a cultural sensibility is formed through self-reference. Another example, which has undergone a similar set of developments, is the pop art movement of the 1960s. The self-reflexive nature of these paintings commented on the idea of painting, aesthetics, and the canon, and in doing so drew attention to itself as a set of texts in the cultural order. What this suggests is that, like the symbolic, the imaginary can be 'translated' into a language that a culture uses in a self-reflexive fashion.

The third connection, that of the popular and subcultural, is most like the unconscious because it is subject to the strongest forms of repression and censorship by the dominant ideologies. This positioning relies on the notion that the dominant ideology is often reflected in the formation of the canonical. The Western canon, for example, is dominated by male writers, and represents a humanism that expounds élitism and individuality. A paradigm of the popular and subcultural is potentially dangerous to such dominant ideologies because it carries both the subversive and popular. This is not a scenario of 'better' and 'worse' ideologies, for the range within the subcultural is immense. A political example would be the far left and far right. Both are subcultures with manifestations of different cultural groups (for example, the left-wing Red Brigade and the extreme right-wing skinheads or the militia groups in the United States) which oppose the dominant ideology, but have little else in common.

An example of the popular and subcultural would be the emergence of rock music in the 1950s. Its movement from this status to popular culture relied on a defusing of its otherness. Its origins in Black music made it subcultural until White performers (such as Elvis Presley) made it more acceptable to the economically dominant White population of the United States. A different example is pornography. Whereas rock music shifted status with relative ease, pornography has always been located in popular culture (it is mass consumed and represented in all media forms) and subculture. Like the unconscious, its existence is continually suppressed, yet it infiltrates the social order in many guises. As with the Freudian definition of the unconscious and the 'pleasure principle' (which are discussed in more detail in a later chapter), pornography is a textual order that demands immediate satisfaction, and has little regard for social conventions and sensibilities.

This final grouping is most like Lacan's notion of the real because, like the unconscious, its sense of 'reality' only operates within the context of the group itself. A dream, which originates from the unconscious, can make little sense to the conscious mind, but within itself it has a 'realism' that follows an exact logic. Pornography can only be sexually exciting if it is located within its own textual and cultural conventions. This may be partly why the definition of what is pornographic varies so much from culture to culture and across time. The pornographic is not always simply sexually explicit material; in more recent years the emphasis (especially in terms of a definition) has been placed on violence rather than sexuality. The irony here is that many cultures seem far more comfortable with the graphic depiction of violence than with any form of sexuality.

The cultural real, like aspects of the unconscious, contains elements that much of the social order refuses to acknowledge as being part of its systems. The whole history of sexuality is constructed around such refusals and denials—this is a key point in Foucault's three-volume study on sexuality (1980a; 1985; 1986). It is the pervasive and powerful processes of making something like sexuality into a discourse that controls it. Foucault's point that the Victorian age saw a type of repression of sexuality, but at the same time an explosion of discourses on and about it can be seen as a production of a discourse in the symbolic, and a restriction of the cultural real. Similarly, Foucault in *Discipline and Punish* (1977) speaks about the restraining, controlling and management of the body through social institutions such as hospitals, prisons and schools. These social discourses enforce a symbolic structure on the body to deny or refuse its legacies from the real. The body in pornography is an impossibility within the symbolic because it functions in sexual extremes. All the characters have voracious sexual appetites and no sense of restriction. That it is a male-orientated and dominated textual form reflects the phallocentric bias of the cultures that produce it.

Our model of the three textual forms and the cultural and psychoanalytic concepts is useful for demonstrating the problems of classification, rather than an analytic tool in itself. Ultimately what becomes apparent in such a model is that we are always dealing with heterogeneity and plurality in these texts. The forces that shape how we read them, position them, and make sense of them lie in part within the texts, in part through cultural contexts, in part within our own reading praxis. It is this final aspect of the act of reading that will be of concern in the following chapters.

Further Reading

A curious aspect of the notion of the canon is that it exists almost without direct critical support. This is largely due to the fact that it is historically determined and institutionally derived. Perhaps the best place to begin is a recent book that intentionally sets out to define and defend a canon of literature, Harold Bloom's *The Western Canon: The Books and Schools of Ages* (1994).

Locating texts within different contexts, particularly cultural and psychoanalytic ones (as this chapter attempts to do), will always produce different reading lists. Because Foucault is so self-consciously aware of the mechanisms of determining categories and interpretative systems, he is a good place to start; and one of the best works to consider is *The Order of Things* (1970), especially the introduction, in which Foucault is at his playful best. Three other works that illustrate how Foucault tackles the relationship of culture and knowledge through madness, the body, and the subject are *Madness and Civilization: A History of Insanity in the Age of Reason* (1967); *Discipline and Punish: The Birth of the Prison* (1977); *The History of Sexuality, Vol. 1: An Introduction* (1980a).

To study Freud's ideas on the topographic divisions of the mind— which are vital to so much of his theory—the best place to start is *The Interpretation of Dreams* (1986). Apart from being a lucid and enjoyable read, this book is essential to any further readings in psychoanalysis. His *On Metapsychology: The Theory of Psychoanalysis* (1987a) contains important essays on drives, and the pleasure principle. To come to terms with Lacan's ideas on the Imaginary, Symbolic and Real requires a careful working through of his seminars, as there is no single point at which he spells out exactly what they mean. The essays in his *Écrits: A Selection* (1985) are useful, particularly 'The Subversion of the Subject and the Dialectic of Desire in the Freudian Unconscious' and 'The Mirror Stage as Formative of the Function of the I'. However, to witness the way in which Lacan uses the concepts it is better to look at a text such as *The Ethics of Psychoanalysis* (1992). A further advantage is that this is a complete collection of seminars, rather than a selection.

PART TWO

From Interpretation to Interaction

Introduction

This part is concerned with the ways in which ideas regarding the relationship between author, reader, and texts have come to be examined. It maps out the changes that have taken place in the study of texts, and concentrates on the postmodern move towards the open-endedness of texts and interpretation.

The first chapter offers a summary of two major fields of reception theory: phenomenology, with its roots in philosophy, and semiotics, which has its origins in linguistics, structuralism, and psychoanalysis. One of the issues for discussion is how the reader has come to be seen as a creative and pro-active agent in the function and analysis of the text. Following on from this, the next chapter considers how theories of the author and textuality have changed. The focus here is on the idea of intertextuality—that is, the cultural and textual matrix formed in the act of reading. We are concerned not simply with the relationship of texts to texts, but of how the reader and cultural contexts formulate relational processes between texts.

If the first two chapters are companion pieces, each taking a different approach to the issues of the agencies of reader, text and author, then the next two are more specifically concerned with the ways in which these theories have influenced the study of texts. The third chapter looks at how theories of the gaze operate as models of reading, drawing specifically on theories from Lacan and Derrida. One of the underlying themes of this chapter is how we, as readers, engage in the text, and how texts shape us as subjects. This idea feeds into the fourth chapter, which looks at the rise of one of the key developments in cultural and critical studies in recent years: visual cultures. The chapter considers some of the main concepts and influences in this rapidly growing discipline, including the study of cultures through their visual representational systems (film, television, painting, advertising, fashion, and so on). It also looks at how different theoretical models have become part of this tradition.

3

The Readerly Question: Phenomenology, Semiotics, and the Act of Reading

What exactly is it that we do when we read? Does it make any difference what we are reading? Do we, as readers, make a difference to the text, and does the text make a difference to us? These are difficult questions in themselves, but that they can be asked at all (within a critical context) is a relatively recent phenomenon. The model that has for so long dominated literary, filmic, and art studies—in fact all of the humanities—has been that of the artistic genius who produces the great works, which are in turn to be read and celebrated by the reader. Critical analysis in the humanities concentrated on understanding the 'genius' of the author and its effect on the reader, rather than what the reader did with the text. By reading these works, so the line of thinking went (and still goes in some studies), we discover some fundamental truth about the world, ourselves, and our culture. But, as we have seen in an earlier discussion, all of these notions of genius and greatness, and even truth itself, have come under sustained examination and their basic tenets have been questioned. Furthermore, the whole idea that there might be some universal and profound meaning embedded within the text by the author and waiting for us, the reader, to discover it is highly problematic. Quite simply it relies on a site of authority that authenticates the text, positions it within a register of value ('high' art, 'popular' culture, etc.) and predetermines the reading stance. Yet we know that reading is a highly dynamic process, and the range of possible interpretations is as wide as the reading audience itself.

This chapter will introduce some of the theories that have shifted the emphasis away from the discovery and celebration of the author, and instead have focused on the act of reading. Some of these issues will also be developed further in Chapter 4. It should be noted at the outset that many of these theories, although dealing with a similar conceptual field, have markedly different ideas and approaches regarding these issues. This is largely due to the history of the ideas, and that they owe their development to different disciplines (mostly philosophy, psychoanalysis, cultural studies, and linguistics). To understand some of the dominant models we shall focus on the two major forms of reception theory. These are 'phenomenology', and the closely related area of reader response; and 'semiotics', and the related developments in cultural/audience response. However, the emphasis here is not on a history of these various schools and interpretative gestures, but on the interplay between the reader as an active and creative agent in the formation of the text, the textual processes themselves, and the act of reading as a cultural and historical construct. We are interested in examining some of the ways in which the reader has been theorised. For this reason the chapter will proceed by looking at a few key concepts and illustrating them with examples from texts. The significant thing here is that the text is no longer seen as a single voice (of the author), but as a complex matrix of polylogue—that is, of competing voices, contradictory voices, and, ultimately, creative voices—which is derived as much in the act of reading as from any elements within the texts themselves.

Phenomenological Approaches to the Text

Perhaps one of the earliest developments (in terms of recent studies) in this type of theory originated in phenomenology. Phenomenology is a branch of philosophy developed largely from the writings of the German philosopher Edmund Husserl (1859–1938). Husserl's main concern was with the actual processes of analysis. In other words, he wanted to know what it was we did when we performed any analytic (or even perceptual) procedure. How do we order the world, make sense of it, and then speak with such certainty (or lack of certainty for that matter)? These are questions that haunt all fields of study: in any area there must always be a level of abstraction that allows the practitioners a point from which to view their own subject and its methodologies. Philosophy is especially good at this sort of thing because self-reflection forms part of its own domain, but other fields have similar processes. Perhaps one of the most interesting thinkers in recent times to provoke such questions to the point where they become a method in their own right is Foucault. Foucault consistently challenged systems of thinking, and in doing so recognised that his own works could well fall into the same trap of seeming to be authoritative and impartial. Foucault's way around this dilemma was to develop what he called a genealogical study, which focused on the relationship of power to knowledge. His later writings continually stressed the self-conscious necessity of any form of analysis. For Foucault this was the only way to avoid becoming a part of what he was trying to critique.

For Husserl the focus must be on figuring out the essence of the subject of inquiry. Most discussions on phenomenology seem to start with furniture, so we will follow tradition for the moment! When we look at a table at what point do we know what it is, or even acknowledge its existence? Husserl wanted to know what the essence of the table is—its 'tableness'; but more than this, he wanted to know how we could arrive at tableness. The key to this for Husserl was human consciousness. It is the act of consciousness that enables us to deliberate on the tableness of tables. The difficulty is that we always encounter tables (and everything else) through mediation. Husserl wanted to develop a method that would allow investigation of the essence (the *eidos*) itself, outside of these external processes and in the everyday world—what phenomenology calls the natural attitude and the *lebenswelt* respectively. This is the beginning of the phenomenological method—an attempt to understand the acts of consciousness as they are directed towards something.

Phenomenology points out that there is never simply consciousness, but rather consciousness towards or of something. In other words consciousness is always directed at something. Husserl called this the 'intentionality of consciousness'—when we think, we think of something; when we are happy, we are happy about something; when we dream, we dream about something. It was this intentionality that

Husserl wanted to investigate. Part of this process involved splitting the processes of consciousness into two: the *noesis*, which is the act of consciousness; and the *noema*, which is the 'object' to which the conscious act is directed. The other key part to this phenomenological method is phenomenological suspension or *epoché*. Husserl believed it was necessary to suspend (that is, bracket off) the *lebenswelt* and natural attitude in order to perform eidetic reduction and so move towards an understanding of the essences of things.

One of the main theorists to adapt Husserl's ideas to literary work was Polish philosopher Roman Ingarden. Ingarden wanted to see how Husserl's phenomenological method could be applied to investigate the literary: to see, for example, the act of reading in terms of the intentionality of consciousness; to examine what makes literature literature—what is its *literariness*. There is insufficient space here to investigate and summarise Ingarden's ideas, so a few key terms and an example will have to suffice.

Ingarden argued that reading the literary text is an intensely creative and dynamic act of consciousness. Once more we must be aware that even though Ingarden concentrates specifically on the literary, much of what he argues can also be seen in terms of other textual forms and practices. We will mention just three of the ways that Ingarden, and this branch of reception theory in general, sees this creativity in operation. The first is called *Unbestimmtheitsstellen* or *lacunae*—or spots of indeterminacy. The argument here is that no matter how complete and full a description is given in a literary work, there will always be elements that the reader supplies. This is part of what Ingarden describes as *concretisation*, or the determination of elements of the text. For Ingarden part of the definition of the literary work is this aspect of incompletion, but of equal significance is that it can never be completed: 'We can say that, with regard to the determination of the objectivities represented within it, every literary work is in principle incomplete and always in need of further supplementation; in terms of the text, however, this supplementation can never be completed' (Ingarden, 1973a: 251). Rather than seeing this as a negative attribute, Ingarden, and other phenomenological-based critics, argue that it is in fact part of the appeal of reading. In one way this is part of the critical approach that allowed Barthes to formulate ideas about texts of pleasure and texts of *jouissance*.

'Filling in' the *lacunae*—that is, performing acts of concretisation—is something we do more or less automatically. However, sometimes the text will draw the reader's attention to this very act and so produce a type of self-reflexivity; or the actual *lacunae* themselves are so enigmatic that they resist all attempts to concretise them. A few examples will illustrate these processes in action. In Krysztof Kieslowski's film *The Double Life of Veronique* (1991) the final image has Veronique running her hand over the bark of a tree, while the *leitmotif* of Weronika wafts in the air. This follows the scene in which a puppeteer tells of a story he is writing, which actually mirrors the film we have just watched. Veronique stops her car to feel the bark of the tree, but we are never told why. The *lacunae* here resists any specific, single meaning, but we, as readers, continue to supply them. The connections of wood, for example, flow through the music of Weronika's singing, Veronique's father's wood making, and the wood of the puppets. But we could equally read this action as a *lacunae* based on contrasts (the soft hand against the hard bark, the country scene juxtaposed against the city scenes), which would follow from the film's theme of similarities and distinctions. Whatever reading we attempt, what we are left with is an open-ended image that invites concretisation and interpretation, but does little to confirm any. Compare this to Kieslowski's later film *Red*, the ending of which offers a curious synthesis of the characters from the trilogy of *Blue* (1993), *White* (1994) and *Red* (1994). In a sense the final images of *Red* close down the operation of *lacunae* as much as the final image of *The Double Life of Veronique* opens it up. Another example from film, and once more a closing shot, is Paul Verhoeven's *Basic Instinct* (1992). Throughout the film the tension pivots around the threat of Catherine Tramell to men in general, and specifically to the detective who becomes obsessed with her. The final scene, which gives a number of false endings, fails to deliver the likely ending of an ice-pick murder of the detective. However, the slow panning shot to an ice-pick under the bed re-ignites the possibility of such a killing, or suggests that she had considered such a murder but felt that it was too risky, or even that the pick had simply fallen under there.

Another example in which the *lacunae* is much less overt, yet still operates in a highly complex and significant manner, will help illustrate this point. The final lines of Cody Jarrett in Raoul Walsh's *White Heat* (1949) have a number of indetermined spots. Cody, the psychotic, oedipal-driven, megalomaniac gangster stands astride the burning gas tower and shouts to his (dead) mother: 'Made it Ma! Top of the world' before being incinerated in the explosion. Cody's obsessive behaviour towards his mother and his drive to achieve power drive the narrative, and his mental instability is so constantly shown throughout the film that this final act is consistent and not that surprising. However, it does create an interpretative gap that needs to be 'filled'. Why does Cody feel that he has 'made it' when clearly everything in his life has ended tragically? All of his paranoid fears have been fulfilled (a girlfriend who cheats on him, a best friend who turns out to be an undercover policeman), his gangster power has gone, he is wounded and trapped—yet he calls out in triumph. The simple way of filling in this indetermined spot is to argue that this is just the final demonstration of Cody's mental derangement— he has mistaken the situation of powerlessness and defeat for one of triumph. But how different an inflection we get if we read these signifiers as escape! The immoral gangster defies the law; the psychotic, mother-obsessed killer determines a fate for himself outside of the moral strictures of society. Such a reading subverts the usual moral directive that criminals must not triumph.

Basic Instinct illustrates one of the key ways in which *lacunae* are developed in texts—through genre. Certain generic forms openly use the reader's concretising to create emotional effects and illicit responses. The horror and thriller genres are the most obvious examples. Horror works best when it is formulated through *lacunae*—witness how this operates in a film such as *Seven*, or in Henry James's *Turn of the Screw*, which is built almost entirely on textual and interpretative gaps. Compare also the ways in which different types of horror are created; films such as *Scream* (Wes Craven, 1996) use the parodic to create a perverse humour that acknowledges the *lacunae*, while *The Blair Witch Project* (D. Myrick/E. Sanchez, 1999) bases its entire horrific effect on the unseen. Similarly, the genres of suspense and detective/crime rely almost entirely on the promulgation of such indetermined spots. Once this aspect of emotive response is introduced things become even more complicated. Does a reader from a different cultural background (or gender) fill in the *lacunae* differently? Or do such differences in readers actually produce different *lacunae*? How do we engage with and resolve moral *lacunae*?

Ingarden's examples of *lacunae* seldom, if ever, venture into this domain, instead focusing on what he himself admits are relatively trite examples. In *Cognition of the Literary Work of Art* he uses a simple example:

> If a story talks about the fate of a very old man but does not say what colour hair he has, then, theoretically, he can be given any colour hair in the concretization; but it is more probable that he has grey hair. If he had very black hair despite his age, that would be something worth mentioning, something important about the old man who has aged so little (Ingarden, 1973a: 392).

What is perhaps more useful about Ingarden's example is that it indicates that readers tend to concretise/visualise along certain lines, which are usually culturally formed. If we read about a character called Ingrid who lives in Norway, we will tend to visualise her as blonde-haired, blue-eyed, and fair-skinned. If Ingrid turns out to be dark-skinned, with a lilting West Indian accent, we would expect the narrative to explain why this is so. In other words, the way in which we concretise is embedded in a number of cultural practices. We usually concretise a character's sexuality as heterosexual, and if it turns out that the character is lesbian or gay this often becomes an issue in the narrative. Heterosexuality becomes established as the norm for the concretising of sexual identity. Neil Jordan's film *The Crying Game* (1992) exploited this tendency by challenging the way in which the reader not only concretises sexuality, but also gender itself. In a different, but related way, the final shot in Billy Wilder's film *Some Like it Hot* (1959) relies on the enigma of the look of the male character (still in drag); but it is an enigma that draws on a certain codification of gender and sexual identity.

The other point to be made here is that the reader tends to note those elements that are mentioned, which in turn affects other acts of concretisation. Within the first few lines of Emily Brontë's *Wuthering*

Heights (1989) Heathcliff is described as having 'black eyes', which immediately enforces a certain type of concretisation about his characteristics and mental state; it is the same sort of reading we gain in the description of Kurtz's eyes in Conrad's *Heart of Darkness*: 'the eyes of that apparition shining darkly far in its bony head' (Conrad, 1989: 99). The difference is that we have had a long build up to this meeting with Kurtz, so the concretisation of dark eyes confirms much of the material already given, whereas Heathcliff's 'black eyes' are the first mention of his character in Brontë's narrative. Because of the literary and cultural practices of concretising such signifiers, the reader immediately begins to position Heathcliff in a certain way. This act of projection raises a further issue in the act of reading.

Phenomenology also describes the act of reading as one that is not so much linear, as one that continually moves through what it terms 'protension' and 'retention'. The idea here is that the reader accumulates information through the text, while at the same time projecting a number of possibilities. As these projections become confirmed or denied they are either retained or abandoned. Similarly, established readings of the text are either adapted to accommodate the new information, or abandoned. The significant aspect about this is that it once more reveals the dynamic activity that reading actually is. A filmic example will illustrate this. In Ridley Scott's film *Alien* (1979) there is a debate as to whether or not the crew member who has had an alien attach itself to his face should be allowed back on board the ship to receive medical attention. The heated discussion is between Ripley and Ash, with the former demanding they observe quarantine procedure and not allow the stricken member inside the spaceship. Ash overrides her authority and allows entry. During the debate we are presented with the moral dilemma of the sacrifice of one crew member in order not to risk the others, or a show of compassion for a comrade. The fact that the seemingly cold, harsh, and logical case is argued by a woman (who is later shown as maternal and nurturing) and the compassionate and illogical by a man (who, again ironically, is later shown to be an android, and not human at all), reverses the cultural stereotypes of gender.

As we watch this scene the acts of protension and retention become invested in a number of narrative elements. The moral choice of whether or not to open the door, and the possible consequences of this are foremost. There is also the generic information that we use in such processes—before the film even begins we know it is a horror/science-fiction film, so we concretise and project possibilities within the context of constant threat and danger. When Ash opens the door we may congratulate his compassion, and retain this throughout the narrative, until it is revealed that his real motivation was to bring an alien back for the Company. Once we gain this information we go back to the scene of the door opening and reread it, not as a debate on the one versus the group, but (perhaps) as a struggle between the social group and the immoral ethics of the Company. Perhaps more than this though, the reader who 'sided' with the seemingly compassionate option presented by Ash must re-assess all subsequent interpretations.

Apart from these sorts of investigations of the act of reading performed by phenomenological approaches, another area of interest is the defining of the literary work itself. This is a complex issue, and would take us too far if we attempted to cover everything here. We have observed a number of key points already—*lacunae*, and protension and retention are reading activities that partly define certain textual forms (narrative in the literary and filmic). Another example is the idea of quasi-judgments. Ingarden argues that, unlike scientific discourse, the literary is made up of a unique type of utterance. These are statements and descriptions that operate as if they were factual (within the created world order), but are noted by the reader as true only within the text. Quasi-judgments mark the literary because they are only found within that form. In doing so, Ingarden argues, they distinguish it from other discourses, thus becoming part of the literariness.

Semiotics and Cultural Studies

The other major area that has been concerned with theories of reading is semiotics, which has a strong basis in certain areas of cultural studies. If phenomenology, and the related field of reception theory, has focused on the interaction between the act of reading and textuality, semiotics, it can be argued, has concentrated on the social and cultural constructions that take place in reading. Another field that has been left out here is that of audience-response studies. These are heavily indebted to sociological methodology and so are less concerned with acts of reading and textuality, and more with the wider implications of the reader and the text as a social phenomenon. To cover this aspect would take more space than is available here. Just as we concentrated above on some specific ideas from a key figure (Ingarden), below we will draw mainly on the work of Umberto Eco and Barthes.

In different ways Eco and Barthes represent a particular facet of semiotics, often more influenced by philosophical issues than the linguistic ones of other semiotic studies. Eco's *Semiotics and the Philosophy of Language* (1984) is more concerned with some of the philosophical implications and contexts of semiotic studies, than with elements of language. However, it is important to acknowledge that one of the central aspects of semiotics is the interplay between systems of communication, social contexts, and how we make sense and meaning from signs. Semiotic studies are directed towards this interrelationship between the social constructions of meaning and communication. A short review of the two fundamentals of semiotics—the nature of the 'sign' and the operation of 'codes'—will allow us to consider the idea of the semiotics of reading.

It may seem too broad and sweeping a statement, but it is essentially the case that in semiotics anything has the potential to be a sign. Composed of a materiality (signifier) and an abstract potential (signified), the sign is at once concrete and shadow. The materiality of the sign—that which we grasp, see, hear, and so on—cannot be separated from the abstract—that which we understand or interpret. Furthermore, the material base of the sign is social conventions, which we understand because we know the conventions themselves. The letters we use to construct the word 'cat' make sense, and can communicate such a sense, only within a social context. This is what semiotics argues is the arbitrary nature of signs—they mean what they mean (or, rather, we read them in a certain way in order to establish a meaning that may or may not be shared) through social understanding.

Semiotics defines certain types of signs according to the degree of this arbitrary link between the material aspect of the sign and what it stands for. The division of icon (signs that most resemble their object, such as a photograph), index (where the link is less obvious or seems more tenuous), and symbol (where there is no link except that established by a culture, such as words) is always susceptible to collapse, however. Even the most iconic of signs will also rely on a leap of faith by the reader to make the link between the sign and the object of reference; and the connection between the signifier and its signified is also derived from a cultural process of sense making.

From this impossible division between materiality and the abstract ideas represented by signs, semiotics divides the sign into its 'denotative' and 'connotative' elements. The denotation of the sign is the material aspect, as well as the first level of meaning. When we use the word 'tree' and look out of the window and see one, we are using the sign at a denotative level. However, additional meanings are in constant operation within all signs (none ever operate purely at the denotative), and these are the connotative. 'Tree' refers to the tall, green and brown object outside the window, but its connotations can include the environment, nature, the ozone layer, wood chipping, Robin Hood, Tarzan, and so on. The tree we look at now has a different set of connotations from the one Veronique stops to touch at the end of *The Double Life of Veronique*—we have already seen how some of those connotations operate. Semiotics argues that all signs have a never-ending set of connotations—Barthes calls this the cultural operation of myth (1973) and Eco calls it unlimited semiosis (1984), that is, the continual roll of possible connotations. One of the implications of this is that we can never attach a single, fixed meaning to a sign. This raises the question of how it is that we can begin to understand and have a shared reading of signs.

One of the ways we do this, semiotics argues, is through codes. Essentially codes do four things in the construction of meaning: they limit the range of possible readings of the signs; they provide a framework for the construction of possible readings; they exclude and include signs; and they provide the rules of combination. Grammar, for example, is a type of code for it allows us to construct words and sentences out of a given range of signs, which will be (reasonably) understood by others in the culture. Similarly, composition of perspective in Western painting, the editing of shots in film, the positioning of notes and harmonies in music, are all types of codes that operate through a culturally shared understanding of combination and exclusion.

Both the creators of such signs and the readers can break or exploit the codes. This is something that takes place quite regularly for varying reasons and effects. There is a sequence of shots in Jonathan Demme's *Silence of the Lambs* (1991) in which the serial killer hears a knock on his door, which is followed by a second shot of FBI agents knocking on a door. There is a series of cuts, the knocks getting louder as the killer walks to the door, the FBI agents seen hammering on the door, and so on. Only when we see the killer open the door to a single figure, followed by a shot of the FBI bursting into a deserted room, do we realise that the intercutting has been a trick that relied on our understanding of the way to read the code of montage. Because this code is so well established, the reader has every right to expect the knocking on the door of the killer to be the same knocking being done by the FBI. Such rapid intercutting also relies on the cinematic device of creating tension. This is another established code—the more rapid the cuts the more the reader 'reads' tension. Alfred Hitchcock pushes the code to its extreme with the shower scene in *Psycho* (1960); the cuts here are so rapid that they almost foreground the actual process itself.

Part of the coding process is to interpret signs, both the known and the new. Eco argues that when we are confronted with a sign that is so different or new that we do not know how to read it, we perform a different sort of encoding process. We either attempt to locate it within a pre-existing code, or we invent a new code to read the sign. During this process we may well introduce a sense of meaning to the sign, but there is also the likelihood that the codes themselves will come under scrutiny. The form of realism, developed in the nineteenth century as a reaction to romanticism, was a radical theorising of the notion of verisimilitude. As a code, realism produced and organised its sign with a very distinct relationship to the world it represented. But no matter how much the code insisted on the realism of its signs, ultimately it relied on the reader to adopt this coding practice. If the code is challenged in the reading act, the underlying assumptions about the codes themselves come under scrutiny. When

Picasso painted figures with two faces the challenge was not simply at the level of the code of portraiture, but also of realism. The code of nineteenth-century realism is based on the exact reproduction of life, a mirroring in effect. But Picasso's paintings represented the 'reality' of the multiplicity of our subjectivity. Read in this way can we say that Picasso uses a more 'realistic' coding practice than, say, Constable? Similarly, is Joyce's stream-of-consciousness technique more realistic than Balzac's attempt to be the secretary of his culture? In other words, what renders realism in signs is not their closeness to what they denotatively stand for, but the codes we use to read and understand them. Foucault and Derrida argue that the whole system of representing is tied to the construction of knowledge—that is, the schemas we use to represent are a vital part in how a culture makes sense of itself and others.

Apart from such textual codes, there are also cultural codes that are used to determine social systems and interpretations such as morality or sexuality. These codes inflect the signs with an ideological bias, which often operates invisibly within the text. Indeed Barthes argues that ideology is the process of turning the cultural into appearing natural and therefore is rendered invisible, except through analysis (Barthes, 1973). It would seem that part of the function of texts is specifically to challenge these types of codes. Arthur Penn's film *Bonnie and Clyde* (1967) was seen as immoral because it represented gangsters in a sympathetic and psychologically complex way. It broke the socially and cinematically acceptable practices that had developed in Hollywood. Similarly, in Francis Ford Coppola's film *The Godfather* (1972) Don Corleone dies not in a morally determined way (that is, at the hands of the police), but playing with his grandchild in the garden. The social and moral code that once demanded that those who broke the law must pay through the legal system is broken by this death.

What happens, however, if a reader (either deliberately or through a lack of knowledge) reads against the code? Or if there is considerable ambiguity in the coding process? Because semiotics is so grounded in explaining cultural contexts and their effects these sorts of textual questions usually lead to issues of the social. It must be remembered that semiotics, perhaps even more than phenomenology, actually attributes to the reader a strong creative process. This is the philosophy behind Barthes' ideas of the readerly and writerly texts, and the texts of pleasure and *jouissance*.

Barthes argues for a typology of texts that are defined by the emphasis placed on the creative acts of reading. The writerly text is open, plural, and dynamic, while the readerly is contained, restricted, and narrow. What is perhaps most significant about Barthes's division is that it is impossible to define a text as being either readerly or writerly within itself, but the act of reading shapes such a sense of the text. The fact that some texts *seem* more writerly (or readerly) than others is a result of the contexts in which they are read, rather than of qualities within the texts themselves. Similarly, the text of pleasure is defined by its adherence to cultural sensibilities precisely through the act of reading, and the text of *jouissance* is a rupture of such a relationship. Barthes defines them as follows: 'Text of pleasure: the text that contents, fills, grants euphoria; the text that comes from culture and does not break with it, is linked to a *comfortable* practice of reading. Text of *jouissance*: the text that imposes a state of loss, the text that discomforts ... unsettles the reader's historical, cultural, psychological assumptions, brings to a crisis his relation with language' (Barthes, 1975: 14). Where it is possible to have texts that operate in this manner through cultural, historical and aesthetic contexts so that they have the appearance of being inherently readerly or writerly, or as a part of pleasure or *jouissance*, it is the act of reading that determines such perspectives, and they are always prone to change. The textual and conceptual innovations of Orson Welles's film *Citizen Kane* (1941) or Samuel Beckett's play *Waiting for Godot* (1956) make them seem to be texts of *jouissance* and to demand a writerly approach by the reader, but the factors that contribute to such a status are dependent on other contexts and texts. In this way it can be said that the act of reading creates the text/sign. One of the ways in which this is done is through the manipulation of signs and codes.

Different readings and interpretations are produced through an aberrant reading of the codes and signs. If, for example, we take the concept of 'Literature' as a code (it designates certain signs as literary, it excludes others, it prescribes signs, it proposes and confirms combinations, etc.), when we read in *Wuthering Heights* the line 'The front door stood open, but the jealous gate was fastened, as at my last visit' (Brontë, 1989: 249), we have no real difficulty making sense of the idea of a jealous gate. We recognise metaphor as an essential part of the literary sign. Who or what the gate is jealous of allows the reader to continue the effect of the metaphor throughout the narrative of the story, and in particular the relationship of the narrator to the narrated. The code of 'Literature' allows sense to be made of a jealous gate, makes it not seem like nonsense or clumsy writing. But this code also allows the concept of jealousy to be read in a certain way. Freud's use of the term in the essay 'Some Neurotic Mechanisms in Jealousy, Paranoia and Homosexuality', or his case study of Dora, is *intended* to be read as scientific. What happens to it if it is read as literary transforms the whole nature of the sign. A curious aspect about certain analytic processes is that they themselves challenge such categories: Freud can be read as literature (the Dora case study is superb as a narrative), and *Wuthering Heights* can be read as a treatise on, say, jealousy. If we follow this line further we could use *Wuthering Heights* as an illustration of Freud's idea of jealousy as a manifestation of bisexuality. In doing so we produce a different sort of reading of Brontë's novel. Consider the following lines from Freud as a description of what happens in the novel: ' … a man will not only feel pain about the woman he loves and hatred of the man who is his rival, but also grief about the man, whom he loves unconsciously, and hatred of the woman as his rival; and this latter set of feelings will add to the intensity of his jealousy' (Freud, 1987b: 197–8). We produce a quite different reading of the classic romantic novel if we see either Heathcliff or the narrator in this light.

This process of reading against the intended or the accepted, the historically determined or culturally sanctioned, or even the textual evidence itself is an important part of recent developments in theories of spectatorship and sites of reading. It also demonstrates the complicity of the nature of the act of reading, and the creativity involved. The politics of a prescribed site of reading, and the resistance to it, has become an area of increasing interest. Feminism, Queer theory, and postcolonial studies have provided rich ideas in this area, mainly because these theories are concerned with sites of power and control, of challenging the given perspective and readings, of allowing a pluralism of reading and interpretation of the signs themselves. A very important agenda in these critical models is to propose an act of reading that often consciously reads against or outside the established coding practices. Similarly, many of the texts created within these sorts of domains attempt to develop new or different sites of spectatorship. A major reason why this is so significant is that theories of reading are linked to ideas on power and knowledge.

Further Reading

To come to terms with phenomenological approaches to the act of reading it is not necessary to 'return' to Husserl himself, but if you are so inclined the best place to start is his *Cartesian Meditations* (1960), in which he attempts to offer an introduction to his works and ideas. Similarly, Husserl's *The Paris Lectures* (1975) provides some good background points. Those wishing to dip more than a toe in this Husserlian water can try *Ideas: General Introduction to Pure Phenomenology* (1969) and *Ideas Pertaining to a Pure Phenomenology and to a Phenomenological Philosophy* (3 vols, 1980)— both are foundational works in the development of phenomenology as a philosophy.

For works more specifically directed to the phenomenological study of texts and reading, the influential works of Ingarden are *The Literary Work of Art* (1973b) and *Cognition of the Literary Work of Art* (1973a). It is possible to engage in this area without going back to these sources, but for serious research these are key works. Two theorists who have used the works of Husserl and Ingarden are Wolfgang Iser, see especially *The Act of Reading* (1978) and Horst Ruthrof, see *The Reader's Construction of Narrative* (1981) and *Semantics and the Body* (1997). Ruthrof's more recent work *Pandora and Occam: On the Limits of Language and Literature* (1992) provides an excellent example of just how far phenomenology can be pushed in the study of literatures and discourse. Finally, it is also important to recognise that much of Derrida's work (especially the early work) engages in the issues of phenomenology and Husserl's work. Any time spent coming to grips with this should help in reading some of Derrida.

For a study of the semiotics of reading the two major figures to consider are Barthes and Eco. In this area, the best place to start with Barthes is his *The Pleasure of the Text* (1975) and *A Lover's Discourse: Fragments* (1990). Both of these are subtle and pleasurable works on the act of reading. Barthes's *Mythologies* (1973), although an early (and perhaps dated) work, contains the essay 'Myth Today', which is useful in considering some fundamentals of semiotics. *S/Z* (1974) is Barthes's complex and detailed reading of a short story, but more than demonstrating how semiotic analysis can work, it provides a number of significant points on the theory of codes. For a different perspective on semiotics Eco's *A Theory of Semiotics* (1976) is important. His *The Role of the Reader* (1979) addresses the issue of reading much further, while *Semiotics and the Philosophy of Language* (1984) sees Eco returning to his concerns with language, meaning, and culture.

4

Deconstruction, The Death of the Author, and Intertextuality

'What is a Text?'

In the last thirty years, the word 'text' has come to be applied to any cultural object, from writing to dress, food, and even the human body. What are the assumptions that lie behind this development, and what does it say about our changing relationship to the world, to each other, and to the things we make and do? What *is* a text, and how does it connect to the people who produce and consume it? And how has this redefinition changed our understanding of what writing is?

What we will do in this chapter is look at two influential articles by Barthes, 'The Death of the Author' and 'From Work to Text' in the light of Jacques Derrida's early work on deconstruction. Our aim will be to explain how in contemporary cultural theory we no longer see the author as the main source and measure of a text's meaning. Nor are texts to be seen as isolated from one another, to be read as separate entities. Instead, texts connect with and reflect one another in a vast network of what is called 'intertextuality'. In this intertextual network, the constituent parts of a text refer back to, quote, and react with all the other texts, indeed all the other signifiers, that exist around them, and that have existed before them. A text, therefore, only operates as a part of all the different practices of textuality that create its context.

This conception of texts as part of a network not only changes our understanding of literary and cultural studies, but also our relationship to the world. If one text can refer to another, then all the different networks to which that text connects itself—the nations, cities, and social groups it describes, the historical events and economic systems it analyses, even the physical and emotional episodes it dramatises—all come to be seen as part of the same vast interconnecting collection of images, representations, meanings, part-meanings, ideas, impressions, and memories. In this way, the textual network comes to define a relationship with the world, where the world is to be considered on the model of the text, a text that may be read and interpreted in the same way as a written text. This 'textualisation' of the world has been an important development in twentieth-century cultural theory in the West, and has produced semiotic readings of things as disparate as dress habits, menus, landscape design, and sporting ritual, as well as theories, such as those of the psychoanalytic philosopher Jacques Lacan, which see the individual human psyche—or 'subject'—as being structured like a language.

The rise of a movement called structuralism as a dominant school of thought, first in linguistics and anthropology, and then in the 1950s and 1960s in literary and cultural studies, represents one of the most important developments here. Barthes was a major figure in the structuralist movement, particularly in the founding of the discipline or practice of semiotics, and it is therefore worth opening this chapter with a short history of these earlier developments in order to show the broader context of the intertextual model. The basic premise of structural linguistics is that any sign—such as what we would commonly call a word, but not only words—is divided into two constituent parts: a 'signified', a concept or meaning that motivates the sign and that the sign communicates, and a 'signifier', the material vehicle of the signified. There are other important principles of structuralism. For example, the relationship between the signified and signifier is arbitrary—there is no logical necessity why the concept of a 'cat' should be expressed using the particular formation of symbols 'cat'. Another important principle is that signs communicate by their difference from one another. 'Cat' becomes a meaningful term because of its difference from similar signifiers, like 'rat' and 'bat'.

This is a very brief and sketchy introduction to the principles of structuralist linguistics. Much more would need to be said to give a complete picture of this movement. What is important for our purposes is that the structuralist distinction between the constituent parts of the sign—signified and signifier—soon became a model for the analysis of human behaviour in general, first in the work of the Belgian anthropologist Claude Lévi-Strauss, and later in Barthes's analyses of contemporary French life and popular culture *Mythologies* (1957). Barthes's aim in this book was to look behind simple social practices to find their historical and cultural meaning. The things he looked at were some of the dominant social images and practices of the 1950s, ranging from the theatrics of wrestling to the iconic portrayal of Greta Garbo's face. Barthes looks beyond the common or literal meaning of a social practice to discover how it exhibits or betrays social values. He writes: 'the universe is infinitely fertile in suggestions. Every object in the world can pass from a closed, silent existence to an oral state, open to appropriation by society' (Barthes, 1973: 109).

In *Mythologies*, Barthes was interested in analysing individual cultural artifacts more or less in isolation. By the time he wrote 'The Death of the Author' and 'From Work to Text', which were published in 1968 and 1971 respectively, he had become interested in how all signs were conditioned by their interaction with one another, more than by what they meant in isolation. Things no longer seemed to be the simple signifier of a single signified. Instead, they were now criss-crossed with many different impulses and associations. They could no longer be seen as stable, and the expression of one meaning alone. Structuralism had been radically questioned, particularly in the work of Derrida, the leading philosopher of deconstruction and arguably the most influential figure in the theory of language in cultural studies.

Deconstruction had a huge impact on literary studies in North America in the 1980s and even became a movement—deconstructionism, whose most prominent members were Paul de Man, J. Hillis Miller, Geoffrey Hartman, Barbara Johnson and others. This movement has faded as a coherent event in the academy, but more as a result of the spread of Derrida's ideas rather than their exhaustion. The understanding of language he developed has become so dominant in most branches of the new humanities that it is often taken for granted by contemporary academics. This is despite the fact that

Derrida's work is difficult and challenging—to its critics, meaningless and self-indulgent—upsetting the whole of the Western philosophical tradition and the assumptions it has bequeathed to our everyday common sense.

What are Derrida's key ideas about language and textuality? I will give a brief account of Derrida's early work *Of Grammatology* (1967), because this has been the text most known to researchers in the humanities, and was the first to fully map out his main attitudes towards language and philosophy. *Of Grammatology* is fundamentally a study of the attitude of the Western intellectual tradition towards—and the value it places on—writing. Traditionally, writing, despite its apparent modern legal authority, has been seen as having lesser status than speech as a means of linguistic communication. Speech has been held to be the closest form of language to the intention of the speaker, who is inevitably physically *present* at the point of articulation. Writing, on the other hand, is seen merely as the transcription of speech. The speaker, who ostensibly gave rise to the language, is *absent* from the written form. Translated into the structuralist model of linguistics that was introduced early in this chapter, the spoken signifier is the envelope and medium of the living signified, a dramatisation of the speaker's living intention. The written signifier, on the other hand, harks back only to the spoken signifier. It is one stage further removed from the signified, which is identified with the speaker's intention. The signifier of speech is the signifier of a signified; the written signifier, in contrast, is a signifier of a signifier.

Derrida challenges this assumption about the difference between speech and writing, by returning to two key principles from Ferdinand de Saussure's work. First, as we mentioned above, according to Saussure the relationship between signifier and signified is arbitrary. There is no necessary reason why one particular combination of sounds or marks on a page is used to denote a specific concept. There is no necessary connection between the marks on a page 'WALL', and the part of a building that it denotes. It is centuries of collective linguistic enterprise that have delivered this particular usage to us. Derrida argues that if there is no logical connection between signified and signifier, then it is impossible to see one as subordinate to another. If the signified does not determine the signifier, then it is impossible to establish a hierarchy between signified and signifier, and indeed between one kind of signifier and another. They may be connected with one another, but they cannot be seen to cause or determine one another. The signified does not determine the spoken signifier in any way that can be seen as superior to its relationship with the written signifier. He writes: 'from the moment that one considers the totality of determined signs, spoken and . . . written, as unmotivated institutions, one must exclude any relationship of natural subordination, any natural hierarchy among signifiers or orders of signifiers' (Derrida, 1976: 44). In fact, since the connection back from the signifier to the signified can only be arbitrary, there will always be a gap, a disjunction, an incommensurability between any signifier and the signified itself. No signifier, spoken or written, can claim to be in direct correspondance with the signified, or have the signified present to it. All signs are built around arbitrariness and absence. All signs, therefore, conform more to the traditional understanding of writing, the signifier of signifiers. Derrida writes: 'language is a possibility founded on the general possibility of writing' (Derrida, 1976: 52).

This is where the second structuralist principle of language becomes important: the idea that language is a system of differences. Saussure had argued that language could only function because its users recognized the slight but significant differences between one sign and another that allowed subtle variations in meaning to become possible. The undeniable separation in meaning between, for example, the signs *vast, cast, mast, fast, last, past* bears witness to the dependence of language, in practice, on marked differences. It is only the difference between signs that makes meaning possible. To Derrida, this difference does not only exist between signifiers but also within each signifier itself. The arbitrary relation between signifier and signified institutes a gap within the signifier that can never be reduced or simply wished away. The spoken signifier can never be perfectly attuned with the signified, thus abolishing the difference between the spoken and the written signifier. The latter seems now to be no more removed from the signified than the former. Thus, there is always an absence in every sign. The signified is never present to the signifier. Indeed, the signified can now be seen to be purely hypo-thetical, the dream of an imaginary speaker's clear and accessible intention. But this moment of absolutely clear intentionality—even if it exists—can never anchor language. The signified will always be irrecoverable.

The consequences of looking at language in this way are boundless. To Derrida, the idea that speech is more authentic than writing rests on the belief that we can rise above the flux of the material world and enter a pure domain of eternal truths and universal meanings: in the same way that we can supposedly move from the signifier (built around an absence) to a signified (in contact with a presence), we are able to trace our origins back from our culture to our nature, from body to spirit, world to god. The opposition between speech and writing valued one of these two terms more than another. All the binary oppositions that structure our thought and values prefer one term to another: man to woman, heterosexual to homosexual, us to them, coloniser to native, the living to the dead, the immigrant to the local, and so on. Yet Derrida's analysis of the breakdown of the opposition between speech and writing, in which the two are seen to have the same structure (which he comes to call *différance*) becomes a model of the way in which all these oppositions can be broken down, or to use Derrida's term, derived from Martin Heidegger, *deconstructed*.

Deconstruction works according to the logic of supplementarity. Let us return to the example of speech and writing. Traditionally, speech has been seen as self-contained and the original system of human language-use. The assumption is that speech predated writ-ing, and that some cultures never needed to develop writing. Writing, therefore, comes to speech from the outside and later. It is added to a complete and self-contained order of communication. Yet, Derrida's analysis has already proposed that speech and writing share a struc-ture, that the absence that has been seen to define writing is part of the logic of speech as well. Writing is said to come from the outside, to supplement speech, yet it is shown to already be part of the struc-ture of speech. It is both after speech and its contemporary, both out-side and inside it. It is alien to it, yet part of it. It is impossible to keep the opposition between the two stable. In Derrida's usage, all binary oppositions function in this way. The twin terms of a binarism are normally seen as a hierarchy in which one term is superior to another. The lesser term comes from the outside to supplement the superior term. Yet its function as a supplement can only be made possible if the lesser term is *always already* part of the identity and structure of the superior term. We are used to seeing our present oppositions between speech and writing, or nature and culture, as inevitable. We believe that there was a speech that pre-existed writing, and a nature that pre-existed culture. Yet, if there was no writing, there would equally be no need for the term 'speech': such a distinct category would not need to exist. Similarly, if there were no culture, we would not have to identify things as natural. There would be no distinction to be made between the natural and non-natural. The term 'nature' would be redundant. All our identities are like this, according to the logic of supplementarity. The completeness and self-sufficiency of the superior term is an illusion. Speech needs writing, nature needs culture, the local needs the immigrant, the heterosexual the homosexual, and so on. Each identity requires an inferior other that can be measured against it. The other is not something outside and alien. It is a necessary part of the identity that thinks it is using the other as something to define itself against. The outside is truly inside. The different is truly part of the same. In this way, all binary oppositions can be deconstructed.

Yet, our systems of knowledge all depend on such binary oppositions: between truth and falsehood, form and content, meaning and chaos, subject and object. If all these oppositions can be broken down, then what can be known and what can we be certain about? A common response to Derrida's ideas is to reject them as nihilistic, as a threat to all human values and to truth itself. Poststructuralism is suspicious of truth and meaning, which it sees as a construct that often serves specific cultural or political ends. Yet Derrida's work does not inevitably lead to an abyss of meaninglessness and relativity. What it insists on is that all knowledge has to take into consideration the cultural logic in which it is situated, the binarisms that it assumes, and the language, or systems of representation, on which it depends for its formulation. If the signified is not recoverable from the signifiers that are supposed to transmit it, any attempt at formulating truth will remain entangled in the textuality in which we first encounter it, whether that text is verbal, visual, corporeal, or electronic. Hence one of Derrida's most (in)famous phrases, 'there is nothing outside of the text' (Derrida, 1976: 158). This does not mean that there is no reality outside of books, which is what some of Derrida's critic have argued it means, in their attempt to present his work as completely unreal and abstract. The meaning of the original French ('il n'y a pas de hors-texte') is closer to 'there is nothing that is extra-textual'. It conveys the idea that there is nothing in inter-human practices, or in the relation between humans and the world, that is not conditioned by the structure and practice of language and textuality. Textuality must therefore always be taken into account. In a sense, we find here the ultimate expression of the textualisation of the world that has become so dominant in the new humanities. Every human practice, according to poststructuralism is conditioned by, indeed is part of, textual practice, and the logic of textuality must always be considered when we attempt an analysis.

Barthes's most famous contribution to this reconsideration of the text is his discussion of authorship, and it is to this issue that we now turn. In 'The Death of the Author', Barthes reminds us that words never simply transmit a single indisputable meaning. Every communication is open to a variety of interpretations. Anyone who has studied literary texts is aware that they always cause disagreement between readers. Usually this is explained in terms of the different perspectives different readers bring to the texts. Barthes argues, however, that differences of interpretation are not simply the result of individual differences between different readers. Words themselves have an unstable relationship with meaning. Writing is a volatile field, producing within itself many complex, sometimes even contradictory, meanings and implications. Barthes asserts that 'writing is the destruction of every voice, of every point of origin. Writing is that neutral composite oblique space where our subject slips away, the negative where all identity is lost, starting with the very identity of the body writing' (1977: 142). Writing is such an unstable space that we seek some way of controlling it, of stabilising it and freeing it of the burden of uncertainty and ambiguity. One of the traditional ways of doing this is to refer to the author of the text. The author's life provides us with a set of simple, reductive truths that we can use to explain or conceal every complexity within the text. In this way, we can control the text's rich energy, its expansive and unstable sense of possibility.

For example, we say that Van Gogh's paintings have bright colours because he was mad, or because he lived in a hot and sunny climate. The distinctiveness of that rich and vibrant colour—its startling, even confronting, quality is neutralised by this simple reference to the impersonal, unambiguous fact. The weakness of this practice is obvious. It draws attention away from the art work towards something external to it, which may or may not be an explanation for why the work is the way it is. This example may well be a caricature of author-centred styles of reading. Yet, even reference to complex theories of historical causation, or elaborate models of the relationship between social factors and individual psychology involve some attempt to reduce or simplify the text, to find some way of controlling its uncertainties.

This reference to the real conditions of the author's life is not the only form of author-centred criticism. When we construct the author as some phantom figure behind the text who is sending a single meaning, or even a simple set of meanings, to us, we are seeking to use an idea or image of the author as a way of giving our individual response some authority. Barthes's argument, therefore, is not one for an individual's right to interpret how he or she will. To use Susan Sontag's phrase, Barthes is 'against interpretation' altogether. He writes: 'to give a text an Author is to impose a limit on the text ... to close the writing' (1977: 147).

What is the alternative to author-centred reading? According to Barthes,

> the space of writing is to be ranged over; writing ceaselessly posits meaning ceaselessly to evaporate it, carrying out a systematic exemption of meaning. In precisely this way literature (it would be better from now on to say *writing*), by refusing to assign a 'secret', an ultimate meaning, to the text (and to the world as text), liberates what may be called an anti-theological activity, an activity that is truly revolutionary since to refuse to fix meaning is, in the end, to refuse God and his hypostases—reason, science, law (1977: 147).

Assigning an author to a text is part of a consistent cultural pattern, in Barthes's view. The search for meaning reflects a cult of authority that ranges from the religious belief that the universe is inhabited and explained by an ultimate, and absolute meaning—God—to equally authoritative and authoritarian systems of civil and scientific law that, ironically, often see themselves as opposed to religion. Meaning, then, is a tyranny, and our search for it encourages all these systems that narrow or distort the possibilities of human existence. By resisting the temptation to pin the text down, by reading not for meaning, but for a plural meaninglessness in the text, we can free ourselves from God-like authority figures, and anyone who tries to impose on us a single way of thinking. In this way, what Barthes now wants to call 'writing' opposes all the systems of thought that dominate society. Political ideologies, religions, academic disciplines, economic orthodoxies—all rely on some sort of unity or convergence of meaning, which Barthes considers oppressive and authoritarian. He claims that reading against meaning is therefore an act of political—to use a word fashionable in the era in which he was writing, revolutionary—subversion.

What does it mean to 'range' over a text? This leads us to the question of each text's location in a broader, ever-expanding, and mobile field, where it is defined by its interdependence on and correspondence to other texts, in the broadest possible sense. This field is called 'intertextual'. Barthes did not coin the term 'intertextuality', nor was he the first to theorise it. The term itself comes from the early work of Julia Kristeva, for example, the essay 'The Bounded Text' (Kristeva, 1984a: 36–63). Before Kristeva, key versions of the intertextual model of the text can be found in the writings of Bakhtin, and other work that developed in conjunction with the Russian Formalist movement of the 1920s. Bakhtin's terms for the plurality and fragmentation of language were 'dialogism' and 'heteroglossia'. For Bakhtin, language is a field of contending voices thrown up by the dynamism and struggle of the social world. Official, or dominant, culture attempts to impose unitary models of language on this dynamic social field, educating users in 'correct' or preferred models of language use. The tension between this authoritarian imposition of such a unitary language, and the entropic

author that gave rise to it, rather than the open and general field of language in which it is located.

The tracing of influence requires some foreknowledge on the part of specialists. You can only claim that Patrick White was influenced by Jung if you have read both authors, and you can identify a writing style and a set of ideas common to them. Yet, for Barthes, this is not the fundamental thing about the intertextual relations of each text. His way of describing this is to say that 'the citations which go to make up a text are anonymous, untraceable, and yet *already read*'. Every reader is affected by the many levels of association between one text and another, whether simply by recognising a predictable plot device or reliving the emotional response to one art work in the middle of another. And as we have said, this experience goes beyond art works. Words and phrases dominate all social exchanges. Narrative structures influence our understanding and representations of politics and history. Our way of presenting ourselves and analysing the behaviour of others also involves complex processes of reading and reference, comparison and interpretation. In this way, we live in a world of signs as much as a world of things, the intertextual network reaches out to incorporate all our experiences and desires.

Thus there are two ways of understanding the significance of the intertextual model, although they are not completely separable. First, intertextuality is a model of culture itself, and the relationship of the human subject to it. In this way, we live in a dynamic and often obscure field of multiplying cultural meanings out of which our values, truths and experiences are generated. When we position ourselves in society—by taking a moral or political stand, for example—we construct ourselves in relation to the whole range of discourses, part-discourses and casual remarks that have produced the context in which we live and speak. The second way of using intertextuality returns it to the more literally textual domain. J.D. Salinger opens his novel *The Catcher in the Rye* with the apparent refusal of his narrator to speak in detail about his family background, repudiating what he calls 'all that David Copperfield kind of crap' (Salinger, 1958: 5). Kathy Acker opens her novel *Great Expectations* with more or less the same words as the opening of Dickens's novel of the same name, before she launches into a monologue about her narrator's suicidal thoughts and sadomasochistic relationships. These authors are not positioning their work in relation to Dickens's texts in order to pay tribute to an influence they want to acknowledge. They are positioning their own, sometimes mildly ironic (in the case of Salinger), or wildly hostile (in the case of Acker), judgment of the Dickens text, and the sort of literary culture it has fostered. The intertextual relationship here is a highly conscious one, aware of the literary precedents that it may seek to distinguish itself from or attack. Out of the disjunctions produced by the relationship between the earlier and later texts, whole new meanings become possible— meanings to do with the changes in family and social life that have taken place in the intervening period, and, in the case of Acker, the inhibiting gender and sexual stereotypes in Dickens that her text aims to subvert. In the intertextual relationship, therefore, texts call on one another to problematise and challenge the cultural meanings with which they have become connected. In the uncertainty and volatility made available by these clashes, new sites of controversy and debate are produced.

Further Reading

Ideas about intertextuality are among the most influential and commonly discussed in recent literary and cultural studies. Roland Barthes's work can be approached from a number of different angles. The essays discussed in detail here are found in the collection *Image-Music-Text* (1977), and although difficult at times, they are short and rewarding. A good place to start on Barthes's semiotics is his *Mythologies* (1973). Barthes's final major statement on textuality is *The Pleasure of the Text* (1975), which he describes as an attempt at formulating an 'erotics' of reading. A good place to start investigating Mikhail Bakhtin's work is the collection *The Dialogic Imagination* (1981). Those particularly interested in Bakhtin should look at his most discussed books *The Problem of Dostoyevsky's Poetics* (1973), and *Rabelais and his World* (1968). Julia Kristeva has become one of the most important figures in contemporary cultural theory. Most of her work, however, is in the field of psychoanalysis. Her work more specifically devoted to textuality appears in the early volumes

Revolution in Poetic Language (1984b) and *Desire in Language* (1984a), which contains the article discussed in this chapter. Derrida's output has been immense. The most common place to start is with the early work, such as *Of Grammatology* (1976), or the essays in *Writing and Difference* (1978) or *Margins of Philosophy* (1986b). Useful and recent introductory overviews of Derrida's works include Niall Lucy's *Debating Derrida* (1995), Julian Wolfreys' *Applying to Derrida* (1996), and Marion Hobson's *Jacques Derrida: Opening Lines* (1998).

5

Seduced by the Text: Theories of the Gaze

Why the Gaze?

The analysis of 'the gaze' has become a well-sustained topic of discussion for some time now. What we might generously call the postmodern theories of the gaze (say from the 1950s to the present) represent a theoretical order that has been dealing with a set of issues dating back at least to the Renaissance. This is not to argue that what has been developed in the second half of the twentieth century is simply a continuation of a historical model. In fact what we find in these recent developments is a mix of acceptance (through derivation and reference) and rejection of many of the earlier theories of the gaze. Before we go on to consider some of the critical developments of these issues it is important to understand why the gaze became, and has continued to be, a site of critical debate and significance.

One of the key reasons why the gaze has figured so prominently in critical writings of poststructuralism and postmodernism is what has also shaped its theoretical history. This is the idea that the gaze is bound up with formations and operations of subjectivity. This means that the gaze is not simply the mechanism of perception, but rather a fundamental structure in the ways in which the subject relates to the cultural order, and, perhaps even more significantly, the way in which subjectivity itself is formed through the mechanisms of the gaze. What is being argued here is that the gaze, rather than being a hermeneutic structure that flows 'out' of the body/subject, is also something that impacts on, shapes, and contorts the body/subject. This is a complex line of argument and one that we must take slowly and carefully.

As this chapter develops, this idea of the formation and insertion of the subject through the gaze will be examined. Before we begin, however, it is important to consider why the gaze, and not other physical modes of perception, has come to feature in such a manner. At one level it is true to argue that the gaze has become a dominant concern, but it is also significant that it is not the only one. With the challenge to the Cartesian *cogito* by poststructuralism came a much more problematic definition of subjectivity, one based on uncertainty and fragmentation. Part of this rupture stems from the challenge to a set of theories developed during the Enlightenment. In terms of the present discussion what is marked in poststructuralism is the acknowledgment that the body is a fundamental part in the construction of subjectivity, as well as the formation of relational contexts between that subject and his or her social world order. So rather than the model proposed by Descartes, with its focus on the certainty of the mind and the deceit of the body, certain theoretical paradigms in the twentieth century have reinserted corporeality into issues such as subjectivity and the formation of interpretations. A few examples will demonstrate this, after which we can consider in more detail the gaze itself. These examples are how the voice and the ear have featured in similar ways to the construction and deconstruction of the subject.

The voice—language and speech—became a fundamental part of the formation and analysis of the subject with the development of psychoanalysis. When one of Freud's patients coined the term 'the talking cure' to describe his psychoanalytic method, she underlined the significance of the voice and language. For Freud, and his followers, the voice—the retelling of dreams, the parapraxis of slips of the tongue or forgetting names, the recounting of pasts, and so on— came to represent one of the most important techniques to engage with, and map, the unconscious. With such strong emphasis it is little wonder that psychoanalysis came to be of great interest to the humanities, and to literary studies in particular. The emphasis on language as an analytic device is clearly something that the study of literature has always marked as central to its enterprise. Much more than, say, trite investigations into the author's psychology, it is this quintessential aspect of language and the voice that made the connection between the two disciplines both viable and productive. It is no surprise that Lacan, one of the key poststructuralists and great rereaders of Freud, based so much of his work on a combination of psychoanalysis and semiotics.

As with the gaze, the various examinations of the voice in poststructuralism concentrate on its relationship to the formation and declaration (to others) of the subject. In Chapter 8, for example, we will witness how feminist theories developed around the idea of the need for a different voice to articulate a language 'outside' patriarchy. The idea is that language and the voice construct and deconstruct subject positions within the social order—we come to exist or vanish according to the ways in which we are spoken by the discourses of the social order[1]. The implications of this are far-reaching, not the least being what happens to the definition of the subject when it operates outside of the mainstream language. Two examples will serve to illustrate this.

If we can speak of a literary voice—that is, a language in which the idea of the literary is carried—then for a great deal of the time in the development of literary studies this voice has been understood as the 'canon'. Part of this definition has been based on the 'elevation' of language, so that the canonical text's relationship to language (and the voice in which it is articulated) is seen to be more creative and reflexive. We have already noted how problematic such vague concepts are, and the notion of the literary voice illustrates this. Part of the defence of the canon has always rested on the study of a certain type of voice or language. Texts were included in the canon, or even came to define it, because of their voice. At the same time other texts were excluded because their language was seen as somehow less significant or innovative or timeless or complex—all terms that were developed from an élitist perspective. So the language of Shakespeare carried greater presence in literary studies than lyrics from the

---

1 The idea that subjectivity is based on absence and that language and the voice is a strategy to feign presence is discussed in Patrick Fuery, *The Theory of Absence* (1995b).

Rolling Stones. Yet the Rolling Stones also became canonical—just as the Sex Pistols did, no matter how much 1970s punk tried to resist such hegemonic control. Even though this is a canon of a different type, the same principles apply—a certain type of voice includes or excludes the particular text. And the reader or listener becomes a part of or a part from the text according to their (cultural) positionality to that voice.

The second example lies more in the political domain. In this sense, to have a voice is to be heard, and to be silenced is a far more repressive act. Any so-called minority group is often defined as such not through some numerical weighting, but rather through the possession or dispossession of a voice. Women in a patriarchal order, non-Whites in an apartheid system, gays and lesbians in a sexually repressive society, are not minorities because of their number in the society, but because of their lack of access to the ruling voice. Such groups are silenced and rendered absent because the voice of their subjectivity (the feminine, the negritude, the different erotics) is denied. Such groups have recognised the power of having their own voice, how their social existence depends on the ability to articulate their differences, and have developed strategies to maintain or create a voice outside of the restrictions of the dominant language. When gay communities began to refer to themselves as 'queer' they reclaimed a derogatory and politically violent term and allowed it to represent a different voice, one that they themselves possessed and controlled; a similar political manoeuvring took place when Australian Aborigines realigned the formerly racist term 'blackfella' to be part of their own discourse. Other examples of this inventing a voice have been the open rejection of the dominant, disempowering language. Many Black African writers refused to write in the colonial languages of French or English and 'returned' to their original language, thus confronting the very mode of the literary (the oral against the written).

The voice and articulation of languages have become powerful issues in recent studies because they have been so closely tied to the social and cultural formations of subjectivity. From the psychoanalytic emphasis on the analysis of the voice to gain access to the unconscious, to attempts to formulate a voice that will allow for a fuller expression of difference (in sexuality, race, ethnicity, gender, etc.), what is common is the link between the physical and political, between the subject and his or her negotiations of the order of things. Another related example, but perhaps one less developed, is the ear. If the voice is a symbol of giving presence to the subject and his or her values and beliefs, then the ear must represent the capacity to receive differences. The example we want to use here illustrates such differences at the level of translation. Here the term 'translation' has both its literal sense of translating one language to another, and a more metaphoric one of the relationship between subjects who try to understand each other as they negotiate the alienating process of language.

One of the most apparent examples of the ear in poststructuralist theory and practice has been the play on words and sounds. Because a great deal of the material is French there is the double inflection of the play on words in the original as well as the differences in the translation. We, as readers, need to train our ears to the sorts of sounds these writers (such as Derrida, Lacan, Luce Irigaray and Kristeva) are making. They continually draw attention to the differences that the sounds and spellings make. Perhaps one of the most famous examples is Derrida's *différance*—a term that sounds the same to our ear, but looks different to our eyes, and draws attention to the impossibility of translation. A legacy of this type of word play has been that these theorists have drawn on something that the artist has long relied on—the imprecision of the language (be it written, spoken, visual). Poststructuralism celebrates the polysemic nature of communication, along with the multiplicity of language, to illustrate the difficulties of constructing meaning.

A different, less developed, and perhaps more complex example of the ear and subjectivity can be drawn from Derrida. He ties the issue of the ear—that is, of being heard and therefore having confirmation of one's subjectivity—to translation and autobiography. In an analysis of Nietzsche's autobiographical work *Ecce Homo* (1992), Derrida traces the line between what is said in the text and how it is then read and interpreted. His motif is the ear, rather than the eye, of the reader because, Derrida argues, it is at this level that we engage in understanding itself. To make more sense of this we can refer to a key passage:

The most important thing about the ear's difference, which I have
yet to remark, is that the signature becomes effective—performed
and performing—not at the moment it apparently takes place, but
only later, when ears will have managed to receive the message ... In
other words, to abbreviate my remarks in a very lapidary fashion, it
is the ear of the other that signs. The ear of the other says to me and
constitutes the *autos* of my autobiography (Derrida, 1988:50–1).

Derrida goes on to argue that the ear is the 'organ for perceiving
difference' (1988: 51) and that all texts rely on this. What is at stake
here is the possession of the text, that is, how it is formed and interpreted outside of the author's act of creation. Derrida is arguing that
as readers we must have keen ears, not simply to understand what
was intended by the author, but rather to allow the text to exist at all
and for us to have a relationship to it. It is the capacity to hear that
brings the text about, that makes it different. What is surprising
about Derrida's example is that he argues these concepts in terms of
the autobiography. This strategy of choosing a form that would seem
to be self-contained is an interesting one. One of Derrida's points is
that we seek to be heard by others, by our culture, or future cultures.
In doing so we seek to be heard and understood by the other because
in doing so we seek confirmation of our subjectivity outside our
'self'. Some textual examples will help clarify this.

Both Hamlet and Macbeth continually strive to be heard by the
other. In both cases the other represents state authority (the father
for Hamlet, the ideal king for Macbeth). Both men's actions and
speeches are directed at the ear of this patriarchal other because both
are uncertain of their position as potential kings. The woman's ear,
or counsel, is not sought because in these patriarchal world orders
only a masculine confirmation will do. Hamlet slips into one of his
strongest acts of madness (probably feigned in this scene) when
Ophelia enters at the end of the 'To be or not to be' soliloquy. This
autobiographical statement is aimed at the ear of authority (his
father, himself, God, and perhaps the reader) and so he openly denies
Ophelia his speech through word play. Similarly, Macbeth directs
less and less speech towards Lady Macbeth as the tragedy unfolds
and he becomes embroiled in his own form of madness.

A different example can be found in Tarantino's *Pulp Fiction*. When Jules first delivers his speech from the Bible it is directed at four different sets of ears: to those of the other characters about to be shot; to those of Vincent, his partner; to those of the film's audience; and to his own. Each time it is heard it operates in terms of difference. For the other characters it establishes the difference between killer and victim; to Vincent it signals impending violence—a signification it takes on for the audience once the code is understood; and for Jules himself it shifts from a symbol of violence to a more 'literal' interpretation made by someone for whom violence is no longer acceptable. In this last example we witness how the ear of the other shifts the same words into a different meaning altogether. The interpretation of the biblical quotation is heard differently and Jules's subjectivity is radically transformed, but only because of the ear of the other. In the final scene Jules even works through the range of interpretations possible, demonstrating how the same words can be heard differently, with different people taking the point of reference.

The Gaze

Theorising the gaze can be traced back at least as far as the early stages of the Renaissance. The whole concept of perspective can be seen as part of the desire to understand and even manipulate the gaze of the reader. Early examples of paintings that were important steps in the development of perspective in Western art include Duccio (1278–1319), *Maestá Altarpiece*, with its division of spaces in terms of perspective, and Uccello (1397–1475), *Battle of San Romano* (*c*.1455), in which the fallen figures are attempts at foreshortening in order to give a sense of depth. However the construction of perspective in these examples is incomplete. By the time of the late 1400s artists, such as Mantegna, who produced the *Camera Degli Sopsi* fresco, demonstrated both a command of perspective and a willingness to play with it. So in a relatively short time the rules of perspective became fixed in Western painting, relying as much on the reader's propensity to accept it as 'realistic' as on the artist's skill to create it. This mode of painting came to be the dominant form of Western art for the next 500 years, being challenged only by artists such as Van Gogh (see, for example, his *Night Café*) and Picasso (see his famous *Demoiselle D'Avignon*). Integral to the heavily codified practices of perspective is a mechanical/formal aspect. At a purely denotative level, perspective is an enabling process (albeit a culturally learnt one) that allows us to view the painting. But what perspective really does is create a position of preferred reading. That is, it locates the position from which the text is supposed to be viewed and so aims to control the gaze.

This idea is not restricted to painting—in fact all textual forms have variations on, and manifestations of, this device. Point of view in narrative forms such as film, the novel, and drama operates like perspective by creating a site from which the reader perceives and interprets the created world order. It is a relationship between what is represented, how it is represented, and the way the reader reads it. However, this site is neither mechanical nor innocent. There are cultural/ideological and psychological agendas attached to such sites. By this we mean that the position from which the reader enters and subsequently reads the text has cultural, political, and historical frames of reference. Part of the analysis of such sites is to ask what position is being offered when we read the text? What, for example, is the site offered by the filmic texts from Hollywood in the 1950s science-fiction films and the 1980s Vietnam-revenge films? The politics of the Cold War inflects many of these films with a certain cultural paranoia: *The Invasion of the Body Snatchers* (Don Siegel, 1956) and *Rambo* (George P. Cosmatos, 1985) depend on readers occupying a specific viewing site in order to align themselves with the morality of the narrative. This issue of a prescribed viewing position was taken up in the 1970s and 1980s by feminist film theorists (such as Laura Mulvey, Mary Ann Doane and Annette Kuhn). Their concern, however, was with the relationship of the representation of gender and sexuality to the spectator. Many of these writers argued that the viewing site offered was male-orientated, and therefore denied women access to the pleasures of the text. There are some difficulties with this idea and we will return to it in a moment.

The devices that prescribe the viewing site are usually constructed and have passed into the conventions of textual form in such a way that they are largely invisible. Some texts, however, actually draw our attention to these processes, and in turn they may become part of the conventions of that form. Historically, documentary film-making used the hand-held camera because it often required on-the-spot filming and a short time in post-production. However, this quickly became a convention of the form, and a shaky camera shot came to connote veracity. Then in the 1980s television police dramas in the United States (such as *Hill Street Blues* and *NYPD Blue*) and England (such as *The Sweeney* and *The Bill*) began to employ the hand-held camera convention to replicate a sense of realism and immediacy. The line between fiction and documentary blurred even more because the viewing perspective was based on a technique linked to real-life recording. Even in the 1990s police shows tend to avoid the smooth, seamless camera shots in order to draw on this device, which has become a convention of the genre. Given the themes of this type of programme (police work and crime) it is easy to see why the replication of a documentary style was attractive.

Another example is the French New Wave cinema. Directors such as Jean-Luc Godard, Jacques Rivette, François Truffaut, and Claude Chabrol exploited filmic techniques such as the jump-cut, structures of montage and *mise-en-scène*, and even character development, as much to comment on film structure and the act of viewing as to make a film. In these examples the actual narrative would take second place to the explorations of the devices of narrative. What these textual forms share is a foregrounding of the elements of the text and the acts of reading, with a key effect being a challenge to the positioning of the reader's gaze. By drawing attention to itself the text openly acknowledges the artificiality of itself.

These examples illustrate another aspect of the site of the gaze, which is connected to genre. It is by accepting the generic viewing site that the conventions of the form are understood. Horror, comedy, tragedy, eroticism, and so on, all rely on the reader adopting a certain point of view. We are free to reject this perspective, of course, but to do so is also to read against the generic codes and so develop a totally different text. If, for example, a reader refuses to see Jonathan Swift's *Gulliver's Travels* as a political satire, as is the accepted generic site, it becomes a quite different book for that reader. This is similar to, yet different from, not being frightened in Stanley Kubrick's film *The*

Shining (1980) (or seeing, or not seeing, irony in his *Eyes Wide Shut*, 1999). This emotional response during the film viewing does not necessarily mean that the reader has not acknowledged that this is part of the horror genre. What the two aberrant readings of *Gulliver's Travels* and *The Shining* share, however, is that the established point of the gaze is not being taken up and so a different set of meanings are being produced. For many years now *Gulliver's Travels* has been reproduced as a children's story, with no real reference to its political background. Significantly, it is difficult, if not impossible, to argue that such readings are less valid. To remain with the horror genre example, if a reader watches Wes Craven's *Nightmare on Elm Street* (1984) and reads it as a film about the social repression of teenage sexuality, or as a moral tale about not transgressing White, middle-class American values, this is not incorrect, even when compared to the reader who engages in the text at the purely emotional level of being frightened. The difference is what meaning is produced and what the reader has done with the text's established viewing position.

It is now time to turn to one of the key theoretical issues of the gaze, which was developed during the 1980s, but has its origins much earlier than that. The combination of semiotics, psychoanalysis, and feminism in film studies in the 1980s led to a sustained examination of the theory of the gaze. One of the points of origin for this discussion came from an article by Freud called 'Triebe und Triebschicksale', which was badly translated as 'Instincts and their Vicissitudes'. (The problem in the translation stems from the use of the term 'instincts', and so to avoid confusion we have preferred the term 'drives' here). In this article Freud discusses the term 'scopophilia', or the pleasure of looking. We do not need to concern ourselves too much with Freud's analysis here, what is important to note is that he argued that the development of the subject's relationship to sexuality and pleasure involves the scopophilic drive. In Freud's schema this drive begins as an auto-erotic, but then changes to a projection onto the body of others (1987a: 127–8). This is an important issue in Freudian psychoanalysis as it connected with theories of narcissism, voyeurism, and masochism.

In terms of certain film theories, it was argued that the gaze is part of the scopophilic drive and the act of watching a film is inevitably tied to acts of pleasure. It is important to note that in such a (Freudian) construction pleasure is a complex process, linked both to the formation and the operation of the unconscious. Pleasure may well include those aspects we might usually relate to such a term, but it also includes the operations of repression and disguise. This is why Freud speaks of the pleasure principle and the reality principle as being determining processes in our psychic make-up and in everyday life. This is discussed in Freud's essay 'Beyond the Pleasure Principle'. In terms of the issues at hand, part of this pleasure is related to the projection of the self (the auto-erotic), through the gaze, into the film. This is not a one-way flow, and a great many of these theories concentrated on not only the reader's gaze towards the film text, but also the ways in which the text controls and shapes that act of viewing. One of the most significant articles of the time was Laura Mulvey's 'Visual Pleasure and Narrative Cinema' (1975). Mulvey argued that the forms of scopophilia developed in mainstream cinema were male-dominated—that men had the power and pleasure of the gaze, while women were the objects of that gaze. Mulvey's thesis was premised on the idea that scopophilia is engendered and formulated through patriarchy. As important and influential as Mulvey's writings have been it is necessary to acknowledge that there are some fundamental flaws in them (not to mention that they now are really historical documents rather than viable theoretical processes), the major one being that her interpretation tends to pacify the whole act of looking, and attributes too much power to the text. More recent theories have instead focused on the idea that there is much more free play in the act of looking, with readers continually adopting positions outside of those proffered by the mainstream gaze. This is not to deny that the dominant position of scopophilia in Hollywood cinema, for example, is engendered towards a masculine perspective; but we do have to look further than the idea of passive acceptance of such a viewing position.

Mulvey, as well as other theorists in this area, has drawn heavily on the works of Lacan, whose writings on the gaze have had far-reaching effects, not only in film studies, but across the range of the humanities. Lacan himself uses Freud's theories of scopophilia, but goes beyond them by arguing that the gaze is a fundamental part of the formation of subjectivity (as well as a significant aspect in the study of psychoanalysis itself). The gaze, for Lacan, is an issue of being and existence. And because of this Lacan connects the whole issue of the gaze to the foundations of psychoanalysis. Indeed the whole issue of the gaze recurs throughout Lacan's writings and seminars. One example will serve to illustrate how Lacan connects the gaze with formations of subjectivity.

Lacan recounts how as a young man he went fishing with a local fisherman, Petit-Jean (Lacan, 1977: 95–6). Lacan begins the story by establishing the social, economic, and personal differences between himself and Petit-Jean. As they are sitting in the boat a sardine can floats past and Petit-Jean asks the young Lacan if he sees it. Lacan acknowledges that he does, to which the fisherman retorts 'Well, it does not see you' and bursts into laughter. Lacan admits he didn't see the humour in the comment. Part of the significance of the story is that Petit-Jean's question and outburst of laughter forces the young Lacan to realise he doesn't actually exist in that harsh world of fishing, economic struggle, and early deaths. That the sardine can does not return his gaze signifies that the objects and people of that situation do not see him, that is, he has little or no relevance to them. Lacan's point is that this story is a metaphor for a larger and more universal psychic struggle we encounter and engage in throughout our lives. We constantly seek the gaze of some other (person, group, institution, ideology, etc.) in order to confirm our sense of presence. Making sense of a text—that is, having a sense of relevance for the text, and from the text—is part of this process. When we read we are seeking confirmation from the gaze of the text; we want the gaze to see us. We must now turn to the issue of how we negotiate this in terms of the politics of the text's gaze.

We have already noted that the theory of the gaze has developed in such a way that it involves not simply the looking at, but also the idea that the viewer is looked at and positioned in a certain way. In other words, there is a two-way flow in the relationship of the gaze. One of the effects of this is that our subjectivity becomes a text for the text. This may sound a little odd, but its essential argument lies in the interplay between the reader as subject and the institutional processes of the text. The implications of this are far-reaching, so an example from film studies will serve as an illustration, and also help narrow the focus somewhat.

The influence of psychoanalytic theory on film studies produced the idea of *suture*. Initially this is a metaphor that draws on the medical usage of stitching up a hole in the body. In these theoretical workings, *suture* came to mean the stitching of the eye to the image/narrative (what the film theorist Christian Metz called *diegesis*, which is the composite processes of filmic narrative) on the screen, and so illustrates this idea of the reader and text caught up in one another through the formation of the gaze. It is also the way in which the reader enters the filmic text. The psychoanalyst Jacques-Alain Miller offered the following comment on this concept: '*Suture* names the relation of the subject to the chain of its discourse ... it figures there as the element which is lacking, in the form of a stand in' (Rosen, 1986: 219). What Miller is getting at here is that the dynamic interaction between the subject and the different forms of language and communication (what Miller calls, after Lacan, the chain of discourse, which in this example is the film text) is negotiated through *suture*. This whole relationship, however, is derived from an absence—that is, a lack. So the scopophilia of the gaze, or the compulsion of the language of the symbolic, operates through absence, which we, as readers, attempt to fill or occupy. An example will help explain this.

The opening scene of Luis Bunuel's film *Belle de Jour* (1967) shows a young woman, Severine/Belle, riding in a horse-drawn carriage. After she resists the sexual advances of her companion, the carriage stops, she is dragged into the nearby woods, tied to a tree, and has her dress stripped from her back. She is then molested and whipped by the two drivers of the carriage. To this point the film demonstrates all the elements of mysogynistic and sadistic fantasy. The camera then cuts from the close-up on Belle's face as she is whipped, to her being woken from a daydream. We are initially sutured into a viewing position that seems to be masculine and sadistic, but are then forced into another that is shown to be feminine and masochistic. Of course the third, perhaps unifying, position is one which allows both: the masochistic feminine is in fact a fantasy of the sadistic masculine. However, the narrative twist in *Belle de Jour* is that the source of scopophilia jumps from the masculine to the feminine. This twist can only take place because we, as readers, have come to occupy, or at least negotiate, a site of absence offered by the text—the site of the gaze—which is then undercut by our expectations. The politics of the pleasure of the gaze then become essential to how we read and make sense of the text. Something like propaganda relies precisely on persuading the reader to take up and accept unconditionally a very exact site, whereas *Belle de Jour* constantly questions the viewing position, which in turn forces the reader to question his or her own perspective. This is the gaze as it turns against itself.

Further Reading

The development of theories of the gaze in poststructuralism and postmodernism can be traced back to Freud's key work '*Triebe und Triebschicksale*' ('Instincts and their Vicissitudes') collected in *On Metapsychology: The Theory of Psychoanalysis* (1987a), which he wrote in 1915. It is well worth starting with this short essay as much that follows takes it as common knowledge. In film studies there were three converging 'schools', all operating around the same time (the 1970s), which shaped much of the theory of the gaze as it currently stands. The first of these are ideas derived from the works of the film theorist Christian Metz, whose early writings were concerned with a semiotics of cinema (see, in particular, *Film Language* (1974)). However, in his *The Imaginary Signifier* (1982) Metz develops a sustained film theory based on ideas from Lacan, thus moving towards psychoanalysis. The second influence came from the British film journal *Screen*, which in the 1970s and 1980s presented many of the ideas from French philosophy and psychoanalysis in translation. The third development was a form of feminist film theory, which engaged in these psychoanalytic models. As mentioned above, one of the most influential pieces was Laura Mulvey's 'Visual Pleasure and Narrative Cinema' (1975). Although dated and flawed this is an important article to read within these historical developments. More of the critical ideas are pursued in Fuery *New Directions in Film Theory* (2000).

Feminist film theory has continued to investigate the politics of the gaze. Some recent examples include Teresa de Lauretis, *Technologies of Gender: Essays on Theory, Film, and Fiction* (1987); E. Ann Kaplin, *Psychoanalysis and Cinema* (1989); Annette Kuhn, *Women's Pictures: Feminism and Cinema* (1982); and Tania Modleski, *The Women Who Knew Too Much: Hitchcock and Feminist Theory* (1988).

In terms of the theory of the gaze and psychoanalysis it is important to witness Jacques Lacan's deliberations. He returned to the issue of the gaze and its relationship to subjectivity often, and it formed an important part of his overall views on the role and function of psychoanalysis. Perhaps the best place to start is his *The Four Fundamental Concepts of Psychoanalysis* (1977), where many of his key ideas are expounded. There are also interesting discussions in *Freud's Papers on Technique* (1988a). For a different, yet connected, reading of the gaze in these terms see J.L. Baudry in Philip Rosen (ed.), *Narrative, Apparatus, Ideology* (1986).

Surprisingly, the development of these ideas in the other visual arts has been less rapid than in film studies. One writer who has used poststructuralist theory for the analysis of painting is Norman Bryson. One of his key works is *Vision and Painting: The Logic of the Gaze* (1985).

6

Visual Cultures

First Scene:

To get to the Freud museum in London you have to make your way along a busy roadway before turning up a steep and narrow footpath. This takes you past a school of red brick and high walls to a beautiful tree-lined street of expensive, well-kept houses. The house where Freud lived for the last few years of his life, after fleeing the Nazi terror in his native Austria, is quite plain from the outside. However, once inside the visitor steps back to Freud's own time: the furniture and books are carefully arranged and preserved to appear as if they are still used. This illusion that the house is still occupied, still exists in the late 1930s, drives the whole experience. Everywhere one finds traces of Freud, but there is one room where his presence is most acutely felt. This is, of course, Freud's study and treatment room. The visitor entering this double room is faced with cases of books that reach from floor to ceiling. Old books with leather covers, in German; books on science and art; Freud's favourite literary texts (Goethe and Shakespeare—quotes from their work recur throughout his writings). And beyond this space of books, in the second half of the room, is Freud's desk, positioned in the centre of the room. Its surface is almost covered with tiny antiques, with a small space for a writing pad. There is an ashtray with a cigar resting on the edge, and Freud's glasses lie on some paper as if their owner has just put them there. The whole image creates the effect that Freud will, at any moment, return to the desk and commence work once more. The walls around this area are lined with shelves holding many more antiques (Freud was a great collector of items from places such as Egypt, Rome, and Greece). There are some famous pictures on the walls, including one of Charcot lecturing and the figure of Gradiva[1]. And then, opposite this desk, against a wall is perhaps the most famous couch in the world. It is covered with rich blankets in sombre colours and at its head is Freud's chair where he would sit, out of view of the patient. If Freud's desk is set up as if he has just stepped out for a moment and will return shortly, this couch and chair seem remarkably empty.

Freud's house, converted into a museum, is like all such houses. There is a sense of phantoms, of time slippage, and of the presence of the original inhabitants. Visitors come to these places for a variety of reasons, but mostly, it would seem, to experience a sense of a mixing of the past and the present. This study and treatment room is arranged to reproduce Freud's presence, not simply to record his working environment. We look for the everyday things of Freud so we can experience a sense of the extraordinary. The driving emotion within all this is to allow the ghosts and traces to be seen.

The Idea of Visual Cultures

One of the most rapidly growing disciplines in critical and cultural studies over the last ten years has been visual cultures. Perhaps two of the clearest indicators of its rapid rise have been the recent introduction of university departments and degree majors in visual cultures, and (in the truest sense of capitalism abhorring a vacuum) bookshops with sections devoted to this area. Like many fields in the new humanities, its history is one of hybridisation, evolution, and innovation. Its subject matter is very diverse, and its critical tools come from a vast range of areas of study. And because it is still becoming established, the potential for new modes of analysis in this field is immense. This chapter can only offer a brief summary of

---

1 Freud studied under Charcot and was strongly influenced by his theories on hypnosis and hysteria. In many ways, the teaching of Charcot directed the young Freud towards psychoanalysis. Freud's essay on a story about the image of a girl walking, and the associated image of Gradiva (the name given to the girl), is one of the key pieces of Freud's work on interpretation and sexuality.

what visual cultures might look like as a field of study. The 'Further Reading' section at the end of this chapter provides additional direction and resources. Ultimately, however, the reader should be aware that developments in this area are very much still taking place.

One of the key features of visual cultures as a critical movement is its argument that the image has taken over the word as the primary source of information, and therefore analysis. Certain theories in visual cultures postulate that the world as written text is being challenged by the world as picture. The world as book is a theme that has dominated Western culture for many centuries, with its origins in the sense of the word as God, and the Bible as the text of the world. This is also the metaphor that has shaped the dominant theme of the author as a god-like figure. According to some theories in visual cultures, the word has given way to the image as a fundamental process in the representation of the world. This, visual cultures theorists argue, is because the postmodern world is one of visuals, of complex, rapid, and startling images that shape our consciousness, culture, and ways of making sense of the world. The image is not only a system of representation, but also a dominant mode of interpretation. This is certainly a controversial argument, but much of what is said in visual cultures functions, in part, to defend the discipline and, in part, to expand its critical rigour. This 'marking' of intellectual territory often occurs when new fields of study are being established, and it is interesting to observe such processes taking place firsthand.

There appear to be three waves of influence and sources for this emerging field of visual cultures. As with most simplifications, this description runs dangerously close to a generalisation of distinct lines of thought; but sometimes limited space necessitates brevity. The first source-pool is perhaps the most obvious. Much of the initial content of visual cultures came from the established fields of visual arts, notably painting, sculpture, and cinema, and then architecture, drama, television, media studies (including advertising), fashion, graphic design, and so on. More recently, developments in visual cultures have originated from endeavours as diverse as museum studies, anatomy and medicine, and internet design. This reflects the fact that visual cultures has moved from its traditional base of the visual arts to become a discipline that concerns itself with all aspects of the image, as it is constructed across different media. It is also developing theories that deal with the reception of such images and how they have such powerful effects in our lives. One of the results of this is that many of the topics and themes addressed by visual cultures take on much wider concerns than the visual. Themes such as the body, sexuality, power, ideology, cultural identity are all prevalent, and many more subjects are being drawn into this field of study.

The fact that visual arts was the first source for visual cultures tells us a number of things. First, it suggests that visual cultures as a critical movement has its origins not in a precisely defined field, but in a range of distinct disciplines with their own methodologies and systems of analysis. Visual cultures borrows, adapts, and alters these movements to produce a different set of ideas and issues. To analyse a film (or set of images from a film) as a process in visual cultures, for example, is to enact something intellectually different from what might take place in film studies. This is not to say that the two analyses would necessarily be antagonistic or incompatible, but it does suggest that the analysis of film in terms of visual cultures is a different intellectual process. This also suggests that visual cultures must develop its own set of critical tools, because it is engaging with the material in a different way. An examination of where such tools come from will enable us to identify another set of influences for this discipline. The variety of forms with which visual cultures concerns itself in turn produces new forms of the image. So, for example, we find visually rich films by Greenaway that draw on painting, or Warhol's paintings combining painting and advertising, or the fashion designs of Versace drawing on art from the Renaissance to subvert their function as images. In these sorts of cases what is produced is a new set of images that go beyond the mere combination of forms. Something that is not just a filmed painting, a stylised advertisment for soup, or an item of clothing. It is this combination of drawing different sources of the image together, engaging with new image forms, and attempting to produce new analytic methods, that gives visual cultures its identity as a discipline. A key aim of this critical movement has been to develop the analytic competence to address an increasingly image-driven world.

In its search for new analytic tools, visual cultures has used the work of radical theorists of painting and other visual art forms, theorists trained in the traditional methods of the academy who subsequently developed radical ways of rethinking both subject matter and processes of analysis. A good example is Norman Bryson, whose writings have had a major impact on the development of visual cultures. Bryson's works, particularly *Vision and Painting* (Bryson, 1985) and *Word and Image* (Bryson, 1981), demonstrate a solid grounding in one tradition and constitute the emergence of another, developed in order to overcome specific problems and issues. Bryson's subject is the study of painting and how it can be transformed through recent developments in critical theory. In *Vision and Painting*, Bryson tackles the thought of one of the key figures of art theory, Ernst Gombrich (whose book *Art and Illusion*, 1960, was highly influential), and produces a new way of thinking about painting and the act of looking. Bryson uses particular developments in other theoretical movements (notably discourse theory, psychoanalysis, and gender studies) in order to challenge the ways in which art theory has traditionally dealt with issues of representation and realism. In so doing he makes *Vision and Painting* a reworking of what painting itself is, and a treatise on how to read these images in different ways. While Bryson's writings engage with images that have traditionally been the subject of art studies (for example, nineteenth-century French painting and the Renaissance), he addresses them in the context of a different set of theoretical issues. His counter-reading of Gombrich points out that the dominant mode of thinking in art theory had turned what was essentially an interpretative gesture (by Gombrich and those who followed) into a form of naturalised thinking. In so doing, Bryson produces not only a new way of thinking about painting as a system of representation (and all the attendant ideological processes involved), but also how a study of a specific set of paintings can be used to discuss much wider issues, such as a crisis in subjectivity.

Another source for visual cultures theorists is poststructuralism. Below I map out some of the ways in which poststructuralism and postmodernism have formed the critical strategies of visual cultural theory. Given that some of these theories argue that the postmodern world is visually dominated, it follows that both the critical apparatus and the images themselves will draw on the same sources. This is important because the flow between theory and text is remarkable in much visual cultures theory. Often the image is the theory, and the theory is rendered as image. This is particularly striking in the works of Derrida, for example his books *Glas* (1986a) and *The Truth in Painting* (1987b), where the outline of the pages take on the visual shape of the arguments. In these books we find the format of the pages reflecting the analysis, with frames, mirroring pages, and even broken spaces.

Second Scene:

Disneyland Paris, like most theme parks, is laid out as different lands. Each one is visually striking and distinctive, and yet all are harmoniously blended so that the visitor can move seamlessly from one to another. In this way it is possible to be located in a Wild West town, and a few paces later in an African village. The images in these lands are curious in that they replicate a reality that is itself a replica. The Wild West town that leads up to the roller-coaster ride of Big Thunder Mountain is a replica not of a historical moment in American history, but of popular American culture's interpretation of the West; similarly, the African images are those of Disney's idea of Africa, via Kipling's Jungle Book. This is all taken for granted—the visitor is aware that what they experience is not the real thing, or even a faithful reproduction of another place and time. This is a Disneyfication process, a sort of extended willing suspension of disbelief, and it is one of the reaons we visit theme parks. Although operating on a level of education rather than entertainment, the Tropenmuseum in Amsterdam, functions in much the same way. It has recreated various third-world environments in such a way as to envelop the visitor with the sounds, smells, and images of Indian slums, African villages of mud huts, and so on. The Tropenmuseum is based on the Dutch colonial era, which means that what is experienced tends to be derived from a European culture's experience of Asia and Africa. Both this museum and Disneyland attempt to create a visually dominated environment that is more real than the reality, which is a real skewed with cultural investment. This is a 'real' that is not a part of reality, or even the environment of museum and Disneyland; rather it is a construction of a real beyond these.

In Disneyland Paris one of the most striking examples of this is the Swiss Family Robinson house. Derived from the story of a ship-wrecked family who survive on an island (and the Disney film version of this), the tree house is large enough for visitors to climb into and look in various rooms (for example, kitchen, bedrooms—complete with beds, toys, and books—and living areas). While we expect these rooms to look 'made up', part of the fantasy, it is the tree itself that is most striking. This structure has countless fake branches and twigs, and each of these has countless fake leaves that look so much like the real thing that leaves on trees seem somehow less real. The copy has overtaken the reality in its image of the authentic.

This second scene brings to mind Baudrillard's writings on simula-tion and simulacra, which have had a huge influence on the theoris-ing of the image in postmodernism. It is perhaps no surprise that the film *The Matrix*, so concerned with the falsity and production of the image, openly plays its postmodern sensibilities by having the pro-tagonist hide computer discs inside a false copy of Baudrillard's book *Simulacra and Simulations* (1981) (as well as quoting lines from it). In order to arrive at Baudrillard's position, which holds that simu-lacra dominate our world, I will sketch out more fully the theoretical trajectory that has taken place since Baudrillard (although the ideas stretch back at least as far as Aristotle in Western thought). The fol-lowing outline is by no means complete and the reader is encouraged to pursue the lines of thought more fully.

It is no coincidence that the opening scene of this chapter is an account of a visit to Freud's house. In many ways Freud has had a huge influence on the formation and direction of visual cultures. This may seem a little surprising, given that Freud's primary interest was psychoanalysis. However, many of the debates and ideas that are still in circulation today have a Freudian influence and backdrop. Freud did write on the visual, and scattered throughout his works are refer-ences to the gaze, image formation, and the role of the visual in the workings of the unconscious. Just a few short examples and refer-ences will suffice to illustrate this.

In *The Interpretation of Dreams* (Freud, 1986), Freud examines the processes that allow the repressed unconscious drives (stemming from the needs of the ego and id) to manifest in dreams. This is one of Freud's major contributions to studies in the humanities, because in working through this set of issues he offers a wider model for the interpretation of how meanings are formed and articulated. The movement from repressed drives to what we eventually dream is made up of a series of checks, each one building up a disguised version of the original material. One of the key moments in this movement is what Freud calls 'considerations of representability', which, along with 'condensation' and 'displacement', allows for 'the transformation of the dream-thoughts into the dream-content' (Freud, 1986: 459). Freud is explicit about the ways in which 'considerations of representability' is the rendering of ideas into images, and he sees it as a fundamental process in how the unconscious and conscious parts of the mind operate. What this offers the wider field of visual cultures is a model of the significance of the image in thought processes. We do not have to be Freudian to see the value of his interpretative gestures here—the attempt to describe the transformation of ideas into images marks a key point in the visualisation of modern culture.

The visual and image production are recurring themes in Freud's attempts to explain the mechanisms of the mind, the formations of subjectivity, and the idea of civilisation's impact on the human mind. We find these themes in, for example:

- his theories of sexuality (the phases of the act of looking in scopophilia and voyeurism (see Chapter 5 for further discussion of these terms))
- his ideas on the formation of the ego (his writings on narcissism are foundational to this)
- the continued theme of the visual in his writings on hysteria (from the works he co-wrote with Breuer through to his case study of the young woman who came to be known as Dora)
- the extended analysis of the visual in his theories on aesthetics (for example, such as his essay on the uncanny, with its analysis of writer E.T.A. Hoffman's (1776–1822) story of the Sandman and his analysis of Hoffmann's story of the Sandman).

Although there is not time to discuss these works fully here, it is possible to see from such a list that the visual is important to this branch of theory as both a theme and system of analysis.

From Freudian psychoanalysis, critical theory has developed a comprehensive and sustained set of theories on the visual (this is discussed in more detail in Chapter 5). Lacan, Kristeva, Cixous, and the film theorists Metz and Baudry have all extended Freud's writings on the gaze and the image to cover almost every issue of critical and cultural studies. Correspondingly, there has also been a set of theories and theoretical writings that have engaged specifically with the image, sometimes using psychoanalytic models, sometimes independent of them. For example, Bryson (1985) and Martin Jay (1994) have written books that engage specifically with the image as a conceptual process. It is clear that the visual has been (and continues to be) very important to intellectual developments in the humanities over the last 50 or so years. The following summary is a guide to this, and it also gives an idea of the range of issues involved. (Some of the ideas and readings referred to in this chapter are also discussed elsewhere in this book: for example, in Chapter 5).

Foucault's engagement with the visual takes place on at least two planes of analysis. He uses the image to work through the idea of 'epistemes'—units of meaningful utterances that cultures develop. From this, Foucault develops various points of analysis, including the famous power/knowledge idea, the formations of sexuality, and the processes of meaning as they inscribe the subject, history, and social institutions (including sexuality, madness, and punishment). Apart from the well-known case of the panopticon in *Discipline and Punish* (1977), the visual and the image are found elsewhere in Foucault's writings. It is significant that he opens *The Order of Things* (1970) with an extended analysis of the painting *Las Meninas*, using the theme of mirrors, which doubles as a platform for the ensuing discussion on how meaning functions in terms of power. This book is also concerned with the processes of forming and controlling subjectivity. Foucault introduces these themes through the visual (the idea of an absented site of viewing and the controlling devices of the gaze underpins the analysis of *Las Meninas*) in order to build a much wider set of issues and themes, closing the study with a section on doubles and the subject. The visual is also discussed (or used as a tool of analysis) in the volumes of *The History of Sexuality* (1980a; 1985), in the analysis of painting in *This is Not a Pipe* (1982), and in numerous essays and shorter pieces. There is, for example, something very image-driven about his debate with Derrida on madness. Commencing the finely argued analysis of the philosopher Descartes is the image of the body beside the fire. It is perhaps no surprise that another of his essays, 'Of Other Spaces', in which he introduces the idea of spatial realms marked by their visual otherness (what he terms heterotopias), is also informed by a sense of the visual in culture. Finally, consider this description of power from the first volume of *The History of Sexuality*: 'The pleasure that comes of exercising a power that questions, monitors, watches, spies, searches out, palpates, brings to light' (Foucault 1980a: 45). This represents how interwoven the qualities of the visual and power are in much of Foucault's writings.

If Foucault provides us with an example of a theorist who can be seen as working through some of his key points in terms of the visual, Barthes is another who demonstrates that an analysis of the visual is part of the whole agenda of theorising in poststructuralist terms. It is fitting that his final book, *Camera Lucida*, is a careful meditation on the photographic image, and reflects a 'translation' of many of his literary theories into the visual. One of the key ideas in *Camera Lucida* is Barthes's distinction between what he terms the *studium* and the *punctum*. The *studium* is the culturally derived image, the one that carries an intentionality of the photographer and is passive. As Barthes puts it: 'The *studium* is that very wide field of unconcerned desire, of various interest, of inconsequential taste: I like/I don't like. The *studium* is of the order of *liking*, not of *loving*' (Barthes 1984: 27). Against this is the *punctum*, which is the creative drives that the viewer him/herself brings to the image. It is the disruptive point in the photograph and it stabs at the viewer and disrupts him or her. It is a detail that, for a particular viewer, arouses interest and is often beyond morality (Barthes 1984: 43).

One of the striking aspects about the way in which Barthes speaks of the *studium* and *punctum* is how it parallels his other ideas on text and work, the death of the author (in this case the photographer's *studium*), and processes of desire in the distinction between pleasure and *jouissance*. It is not simply that Barthes is summarising his past ideas, or even going over familiar terrain; *Camera Lucida* marks a point at which Barthes organises his ideas around and through the image. As a text it signifies Barthes's critical movement from the word to the image.

There is no space here to further pursue ideas from Barthes (or indeed the other theoretical works so far mentioned) such as his essays in the collection *Image—Music—Text* (1977). However, it would be remiss of me not to refer to Derrida, who has also contributed a great deal of work in these areas. As with the other theorists discussed in this chapter, Derrida's works are not directly concerned with the visual, but some of his books are proving highly influential in the development of visual cultures. In passing, then, some works by Derrida that must be noted here are *Truth in Painting* (1987b) and *Memoirs of the Blind* (1993). (A third noteworthy text is the short work *Droit de regards* (1997), in which Derrida engages with the image, photography, and sexual identity. However, there is no space for summary of this here). These are large and complex works and the reader is urged to tackle them directly, for all that can be done here is to indicate certain directions.

Truth in Painting, like so much of Derrida's works, can be read at a number of different levels. One of its surfaces is a philosophical investigation of certain issues in painting and aesthetics, especially in terms of the philosophers Hegel, Kant, and Heidegger. Derrida works through and against certain key moments of Western philosophical thought, such as representation and reality, the artist as creator, and the role of the spectator. At another level, and this is one that is perhaps of greatest interest to the field of visual cultures, Derrida is applying extreme scrutiny to the whole process of 'framing'. The text is a series of frames within frames, with the opening section, entitled *Passe-Partout* (a technical term from the process of framing a painting), signaling Derrida's intent to pursue the mark of the frame, that is, the hermeneutic processes of frames as they shape how we produce meanings. One of the most significant parts of this discussion is the parergon, that which is neither inside nor outside the painting. This liminal space of the between is what interests Derrida here, for it signals all that is different from the included and excluded. As Derrida puts it: 'Between the outside and the inside, between the external and the internal edge-line, the framer and the framed, the figure and the ground, form and content, signifier and signified, and so on for any two-faced opposition' (Derrida 1987b: 12). In such a description we find similar interests to much of Derrida's earlier works, particularly his idea of the text as all-encompassing. Here issues of textuality and reading are translated into the issue of the frame and how it operates in the formation of the aesthetic.

Memoirs of the Blind is a record of an exhibition that Derrida organised for the Louvre Museum, around the theme of blindness[2]. Once more we find Derrida using a theme to examine a range of topics, including creativity and blindness across the arts. In *Memoirs of the Blind* Derrida works through his chosen paintings and images, examining the relationship between blindness and its causes and effects, such as love, punishment, and religion. This work is also about self-reflexivity, and Derrida spends time contemplating the relationship between mirrors and the blind gaze, which is, in part, the gaze as it is controlled and formed in various contexts. A particular moment of self-reflection is revealed as the initial stimulation for the theme of the essay: Derrida suffered a partial facial paralysis caused by a virus. Derrida reveals many of the issues of his analysis when he talks about the moment of his recovery: 'And so on July 11th I am healed (a feeling of conversion or resurrection, the eyelid blinking once again, my face still haunted by a ghost of disfiguration)' (Derrida 1993: 32). Here is Derrida framing himself (he goes on to describe the drive back from the Louvre and his revelation for the exhibition) as both blindness and insight.

The scene from Disneyland that opened this section, like the description of the Freud museum before it, carries a certain theoretical resonance. I have already made passing reference to Baudrillard, but a few further lines are needed on his contributions to the field of visual cultural studies. In Baudrillard's works we find not only

2 It is perhaps interesting to note that Derrida's exhibition in 1991 was followed, in 1992, with one organised by Peter Greenaway. A philosopher and filmmaker were thus important figures in a series about painting in one of the most famous art galleries in the world.

discussion of Disneyland and the wider scene of American culture, but also an analysis of the simulacra and simulation. Baudrillard argues, counter to the tradition in Western thought derived from Plato, that there can be no original point, no perfect form from which all else is a copy; instead everything is simulacra. The postmodern world, according to Baudrillard, is this world of unending copies. This is a fecund set of ideas and it is carefully detailed in his works *Simulacra and Simulations* (1981) and *The Ecstasy of Communication* (1996). He argues that there is a different sense of the real in postmodernism, that of the hyperreal: 'At the limit of this process of reproducibility, the real is not only what can be reproduced, but that which is already reproduced. The hyperreal' (Baudrillard 1983: 142). The hyperreal leads us to question not simply reality as it is formulated and represented, but the very notion of artifice. Baudrillard's point is that once we question the tradition of the real and the authentic, we also question meaning itself. This, he points out, is the road to psychosis.

These ideas recur in Baudrillard's work; his essay on the Gulf War (suitably entitled 'The Gulf War Did Not Take Place'), for example, is about media representation and the effacing of an event through simulacra. His essay on Disneyland works as a wider commentary on the simulation of cultural form and identity. In *Seduction* Baudrillard tackles psychoanalysis and feminism (at times using disturbing ideas, in that they appear to border on misogyny), and we discover further inflections on his approach to the visual. A core part of this book is devoted to mirrors, appearances, and the false image. Baudrillard's analysis of pornography as the 'disenchanted simulation' (Baudrillard 1990: 60) pivots on the idea of seduction as a visually driven process, constantly drawn back into a cultural atmosphere of restraint. The seduction discussed in this book thus connects with the simulacra of a Disneyland environment. From these ideas and analysis Baudrillard provides an essential paradigm for the development of the discipline of visual cultures.

Third Scene

The Notting Hill Carnival in London is a West Indian-based street procession of steel bands, extravagant costumes, and West Indian food and drink. It turns a small part of London into an exaggerated version of no place in particular from the West Indies. To attend the carnival is to be immersed in this sense of the hyperreal Island life, translated through London eyes. The visual effect of such a carnival is to jolt the spectators out of one type of existence and into another. The same can be said of the Gay and Lesbian Mardi Gras in Sydney, which is both a part, and an exaggeration, of homosexual life in that city.

Many carnivals cross our lives now. Hardly a major city in the world does not, at some point in the year, allow sections of itself to be turned upside down for this purpose, enabling overt manifestations of the carnivalesque to take place. The experience of attending these carnivals is strikingly similar—the tightly pressed crowds of spectators, the flow of particular types of food and drink (linked in some way to the event itself), noise as sensation, media coverage and packaging, music of an identifiable sort, the street procession (often staged as a competition of costumes), and so on. In these elements of the carnival, the juxtaposition of cultures (which are often defined through their 'fundamental' differences) is also an attempt to mesh them together.

The rushed tour I have provided through the origins and influences of visual cultures as an emerging area of study has left little space to explore the latest trends in this field. As research methodology emerges, it is possible to identify points that, at the very least, should give you an idea of what to expect from this area of study in the future. First, visual cultures has become both an area of study (with its own developing methodologies and texts), and itself a concept to be investigated. The latter point means that, like so much of critical and cultural studies, a certain degree of self-reflexivity is required to identify exactly what is meant by the term 'visual cultures'. Beyond this, there are four themes that seem to recur in recent developments of visual cultural studies.

1. The locating of the visual in a cultural sense and context

The key here is to identify how the visual has a particular power within cultural forms and contexts. This would include ideas such as the historical development of various visual forms (television in the twentieth century, for example); how the visual has been treated in different cultural contexts; the hierarchy of visual forms in cultures; the comparative study of the visual (how, for example, Picasso 'borrows' African art styles in the development of cubism).

2. The visual sense of a culture

This is related to the above point, the difference being that studies of this type are concerned with how cultures perceive, use, and read the visual. This approach investigates how the visual is related to the formation and preservation of cultural identity. Examples of this include:

- the ways in which subcultures use the visual (how street gangs visually display themselves)
- the sense of the erotic in a culture (this includes censorship—that is, what is seen as permissible as an image)
- the representation of a culture visually, and the ideological forces of such images (A flag, for example, is a culturally designed image that represents the ideological values of that culture. Another example is the sterotyping of gender to represent a culture—singlets and thongs for Australian men, and so on.)
- the creation of the star system (and the subsequent investment of cultural power in certain images—note the image of Bardot as a visual representation of French culture in the 1960s, and Pamela Anderson as a parallel representation of American culture in the 1990s).

3. The power of visual signs

Part of the effect of visual cultures has been recognition of the power of the image. Of course this in itself is not new; we have relied on the visual to represent ourselves for thousands of years (paintings on cave walls are often cited as examples of the visual record of history, aesthetics, culture, and science), and in so doing we have come to recognise the image as a site of power. Recent studies have shown just how much power is invested in images, and how important they are in shaping cultural consciousness. Subjectivity, ideology, and meaning, as well as the cultural, are formed within systems of the visual.

4. Visual and Culture

As a discipline, visual cultures emphasises, and allows for, the connections between culture and the image. As such, it presents us with a system of analysis for the study of how cultures represent themselves visually. This represents a movement between 'art' as the visual medium of culture, to culture itself as a visual form. For visual cultures, culture is image and image is culture. The study of visual cultures provides analytic tools for the 'and' in this formulation.

Further Reading

Apart from the texts mentioned so far in this chapter (which will provide a good sense of the background to visual cultures), a number of books and anthologies demonstrate the current state of this area of study. One of the best places to start is *The Visual Cultures Reader* (1998), edited by Nicholas Mirzoeff. The collection is divided into six sections (beginning with 'A Genealogy of Visual Culture' and ending with 'Pornography'), each of which contains a good mix of historical and current pieces on the visual. The collection also demonstrates some of the key areas of debate for visual cultures, including the body, sexuality, race, and class. Chris Jenks's edited collection *Visual Culture* (1995) is based more on various visual forms (including advertising, the city, cinema, painting, representations of history, television, and photography). For this reason, it is a good way to come to terms with the breadth of textual forms in visual cultures. Martin Jay's book *Downcast Eyes* is a very good survey of the influence of the visual in postmodernism and poststructuralism.

PART THREE

Contextuality

Introduction

In this part, we turn to the question of the relationship between culture, society, and politics. This has been the most important and controversial area of inquiry in the new humanities. This is partly because of the proliferation of material on the politics of culture from a wide number of viewpoints. It is also because of the growing importance of a political understanding of the nature of all cultural analysis. It is now more common than not for intellectuals to see their work as deeply implicated in the politics of their societies, and of the world in general. The definition of politics here is very elastic, covering all relationships between people and peoples that involve disproportions of power. Since it is hard to imagine human relationships unaffected by power, the range of material covered in this field is endless.

In order to make sense of this, we have chosen to limit our approach to an overview of the way in which the relationship between texts and society has been theorised in the present, postmodern era. Chapter 7 presents an introduction to the key theorists of postmodernism: Jean-François Lyotard, Fredric Jameson, and Jean Baudrillard. While this chapter provides a general overview of the broad historical context in which contemporary cultural politics is played out, Chapter 9 focusses on what has become the key debate in cultural studies: the face-off between identity politics and Queer theory. We have also included a chapter on feminism—the most influential cultural political movement in the last thirty years—particularly its poststructuralist version. We are unable to give more than a brief insight into a movement as diverse and important as this, so we have chosen the material most connected with the other issues surveyed in this book.

7

Contextuality: Postmodernism

If modernism means the commitment to the new and the now, as Ezra Pound said, how can it have come to an end? How can our present life be *post*modern? The simple answer is that the very principle of the new is now met with suspicion and the belief that the modernist principles of revolutionary change and thorough rationalisation, whether in social policy, architecture, politics, or the arts, have not fulfilled their utopian promise. Of course, there was always a resistance to modernism, usually in the name of older traditional social and cultural values. The rootlessness of modern life—caused by several centuries of industrialisation, urbanisation, migration, population growth, war, and genocide—is often interpreted as the loss of traditional, stable ethnic, community, and family structures. It has often been blamed on the growth of the mass media, changes in social and educational policy, and so on, although these developments were often a response to a perceived crisis, rather than its cause. Postmodernism, on the other hand, recognises the problems that modernism attempted to solve, and does not seek the rescuscitation of traditional values. It also sees modernism itself as part of the problem. If modernism was about a Western culture that had entered into crisis, and attempted to provide expressions of or solutions to that crisis, then postmodernism sees modernism as itself in crisis.

Modernism saw the rise of experimentation in the arts as a way of engineering new cultural values to replace inherited ones that were thought exhausted and discredited. It also saw such experimentation with large-scale change as a solution to problems in other areas. Decline in urban housing standards caused disease, crime, and social deprivation. Massive slum-clearance programmes and the building of high-rise public-housing estates were seen as possible solutions. Indeed, modernist architecture was pervaded by a sense of purposefulness, summarised in the slogan 'form follows function'. This slogan proposed a new aesthetic wherein the progressiveness, mechanics, and productivity of the modern age would be embodied, not just in the logic of buildings, but also in their cultural meaning.

In politics, however, the modernist project soon proved destructive. The rise of fascism and nazism represented an attempt to abolish the inheritance of evolving liberal democracy in the name of a primitivist cult of violence that would sweep away the perceived impurities brought to modern life by migration, racial cohabitation, and inter-marriage. The state and its leader were promoted as the expression of the unity and meaning of the national group, and the extermination of other ethnic groups was used to simplify and strengthen the myth of a racially defined solidarity. A very different political development like Stalinism also dreamed of the purification of the state, and the reduction of social life to a single historical purpose. The ambition of socialist theory was to produce meaningful social improvement, eventually on a utopian scale, and bring an end to the dislocation, instability and suffering that went to make up human history. An absolute intolerance of dissent developed in the Soviet Union, partly as a result of civil war and encirclement, but also because of authoritarian administrative and economic structures that produced a paranoid and vindictive leadership, and inflexible and repressive policing practices. The millions of deaths caused by Nazism and Stalinism dominate the twentieth century, and, more than any other single factor, have determined its gathering sense of bitterness and horror.

Other social developments, like the growth of the modern welfare state, also attempted to solve social and political problems by redefining the relationship between the state and its citizens. The provision of health services and welfare payments to the unemployed, sick, and aged was part of an attempt to guarantee that no one would be excluded from society, and that the dislocation and alienation that was considered part of the modern crisis would diminish. This kind of system has always been criticised by conservative commentators as encouraging dependence—and this view has been much promoted in the 1980s and 1990s. Even those who are sympathetic to the idea of a social 'safety net' have been critical of the development of massive social-welfare bureaucracies with impersonal procedures, and of their capacity to centralise information about welfare beneficiaries and indeed all citizens.

The distinction between these two criticisms of the welfare state is in some ways emblematic of the contrast between an antimodernism and a postmodernism. The antimodern reaction against the welfare state is critical of the very principle of welfare, and believes that there should be a return to the individualism and self-reliance that are seen as its forerunners. In a sense, the antimodern point of view does not recognise the problems of social alienation that modern policies sought to solve. The postmodern point of view, on the other hand, recognises the contribution made by the welfare state, but argues that alienation and dehumanisation have either not been solved, or have even been increased, by such social policies, which need to be administered in a more flexible and less authoritarian way.

The second half of the twentieth century, therefore, not only saw a deepening of the modernist crisis, but also a perception that the revolutionary changes proposed to deal with it have proven even more destructive. In the 1970s and 1980s, this view that there was not only a modern crisis, but also a crisis in modernism itself, came to be known as postmodernism. Postmodernism has been identified with a thorough scepticism, even negativity, and, in many ways, it has been hostile to what were thought of as the most enlightened and optimistic ideas and policies. On the other hand, by remaining implacably opposed to fixed and universal principles of meaning and value, postmodernism has encouraged the rise of a whole variety of cultural and political practices that promote diversity and improvement on a local, or molecular, scale. Postmodernity is, therefore, an era of scepticism, but also of plurality and difference. Now we will look in some detail at the three most important theorists of postmodernism—Jean-François Lyotard, Fredric Jameson, and Jean Baudrillard.

Lyotard published an important and influential book on postmodernism entitled *The Postmodern Condition* (1984)—its subtitle calls it 'A Report on Knowledge'. Lyotard set out to answer the question of how knowledge is produced in the contemporary world, and how it is validated. He argues that in the modern age (which he sees as beginning with the Enlightenment in the eighteenth century) the pursuit and production of knowledge is justified by being presented as part of a larger story—or narrative—of human development. A certain idea, piece of work, or social plan is justified by its contribution to larger principles of historical development, which have come to embody universal ideas of human progress and meaning. These principles arose to replace religious value systems that had lost their authority. The two narratives that have dominated the modern age are the Progress of Spirit and the March to Freedom. The first of these 'grand narratives', as Lyotard calls them, sees the human race as ascending towards the greatest possible understanding of itself, the purest possible self-consciousness of its inner value and potential. A work of art, an educational policy, or a political programme can be justified by how much it 'advances', 'frees', or 'fulfills' this human spirit. The second grand narrative assesses things according to how much they contribute to the eventual production of a society that is equal, just, and free. If an idea, text, or proposal elucidates present injustice and contributes to the minimisation of inequality and restriction, it is said to be aiding the process of social improvement. Behind this is the dream of a utopian society built on equal rights and opportunities.

These principles explain many of the positive developments in Western societies over the last two hundred years and, certainly, those suspicious of postmodernism dislike its equivocal attitude towards such achievements. Lyotard, however, sees the promotion of these principles as leading to a rigidity and purposefulness that may easily prove murderous:

> The nineteenth and twentieth centuries have given us as much terror as we can take. We have paid a high enough price for the nostalgia of the whole and the one, for the reconciliation of the concept and the sensible, of the transparent and the communicable experience. Under the general demand for slackening and for appeasement, we can hear the mutterings of the desire for a return of terror, for the realization of the fantasy to seize reality. The answer is: Let us wage a war on totality; let us be witnesses to the unpresentable; let us activate the differences (Lyotard, 1984: 81–2).

For Lyotard, the grand narratives tried to provide an overarching unity in which the abstract and the concrete would be perfectly co-ordinated, and in which meaning would be readily available and communicable. It is this desire to have everything explained by a single, universal theory that Lyotard sees as the source of the authoritarian systems that produced Nazism and Stalinism, the twentieth century's ruthless philosophies and regimes of terror. The present call—this part of *The Postmodern Condition* was first published in 1982—for the rescuscitation of such universal theories is decried by Lyotard as 'nostalgia' and 'the desire for a return of terror'.

Modernism, for Lyotard, is the era of the grand narratives, of systematic principles of thought and cultural production that do not realise total knowledge, but have established the forms in which such knowledge is conceivable. Talking of modern aesthetics, Lyotard writes: 'It allows the unpresentable to be put forward only as the missing contents; but the form, because of its recognizable consistency, continues to offer to the reader or viewer matter for solace and pleasure' (1984: 81). Modern paradigms recognise that there are things that they cannot make communicable and comprehensible. At the same time, they provide a logic, a system, a *form*, in which these unpresentable things would be located. The consistency and surety of this form, its confidence that at least the logic and purpose of truth are known, provide us with a reassurance that gives us 'solace and pleasure'. Modernist artists such as Joyce and Woolf believed that they had found the overall structure of narrative and form that could make the world meaningful again.

Postmodernism, on the other hand, does not see the unpresentable as a mere gap in our knowledge. Postmodernism is sceptical of grand narratives. The dreams of the progress of the human spirit and the march to freedom have been discredited as principles of truth and meaning. In this way, the pursuit of knowledge cannot be justified according to some previously existing principle that transcends the historical fluctuations of political and cultural change. The postmodern, therefore, sees a question mark hanging over the forms and purposes of knowledge: since there are no eternal principles, according to postmodernists, each new endeavour must discover its own principles—not in order to reinvent new grand narratives, but in order to explain and justify itself, just in the moment in which it is performed:

> The postmodern would be that which, in the modern, puts forward the unpresentable in presentation itself; that which denies itself the solace of good forms, the consensus of a taste which would make it possible to share collectively the nostalgia for the unattainable; that which searches for new presentations, not in order to enjoy them but in order to impart a stronger sense of the unpresentable. A postmodern artist or writer is in the position of a philosopher: the text he writes, the work he produces are not in principle governed by preestablished rules, and they cannot be judged according to a determining judgment, by applying familiar categories to the text or to the work. Those categories are what the work of art itself is looking for. The artist and the writer, then, are working without rules in order to formulate the rules of *what will have been done* (Lyotard, 1984: 81).

Postmodernism, then, is not simply an era after modernism, as the name would seem to imply. Instead, it is an attitude to modernism's faith in the grand narratives of historical meaning. Put simply, postmodernism does not recognise the grand narratives' claim to meaning or to a greater insight into what human beings are or what they need. Postmodern work is inherently unstable and problematic. It takes nothing for granted, always calling into question its own most basic principles and assumptions. Postmodernism is sceptical, even of itself. Whereas earlier cultural work had always relied on the assumption that it was contributing, no matter how indirectly, to one or other of the 'humanising' grand narratives, postmodern work should be rigorously self-critical. It should take nothing for granted, and be careful of never enlarging its sense of its own value into some general claim about human society or identity. This explains one of the most commonly recognised features of, for example, narratives deemed postmodern—their insistence on drawing attention to the conventions, structures, and clichés of narrative itself. The audience is constantly reminded that the very (postmodern) process in which it is engaged is not so much clarifying the world for them, as the realists had proposed, as much as immersing them in the problem of representation.

Lyotard's model of postmodernism sees itself as involved in the politics of the twentieth century, but it has been criticised for discrediting the very principles that show how political progress might be possible. Fredric Jameson's discussion of postmodernism in his article 'Postmodernism, or the Cultural Logic of Late Capitalism' is much more grounded in what we conventionally understand as history. To Jameson, postmodernism is not a theory of cultural work as it is for Lyotard, nor is it a fashion or style. Postmodernism is a 'cultural dominant', the most significant and telling aspect of cultural activity in our period. As such, it cannot be chosen or rejected. The role of the cultural critic is to recognise, understand, and historicise it. For Jameson, postmodernism is the third important cultural dominant in the history of capitalism. Mutations in capitalism, therefore, lie behind and explain the rise of postmodernism and its nature. Put simply, if realism was the dominant cultural mode of industrial capitalism, and modernism that of monopoly and colonial capitalism, then postmodernism is that of post-industrial or multinational capitalism.

What are the characteristics of postmodern culture, then, and what are their political meanings? Jameson compares Van Gogh's *Peasant Shoes* with Andy Warhol's *Diamond Dust Shoes* in order to illustrate the contrast between a work of the modern period and one of the postmodern period. He describes how Van Gogh's work captures both the hardship of peasant life and, by way of aestheticising it, an image of how that life could be transformed. Van Gogh's work engages directly with the social world around it by representing its hardships. But it does more than this. It replicates that social world's divison of labour in its own structure, and then uses a utopian explosion of colour as a way of signalling that it is subject to possible transformation. The work incorporates within itself the logic of the economic life of its society, and an idea of how that society could be changed.

Warhol's work, which concentrates on images from the world of consumerism, would be expected to produce the same sort of elucidation of the economic and social worlds, according to Jameson: 'Andy Warhol's work turns centrally around commodification, and the great billboard images of the Coca-Cola bottle or the Campbell's Soup Can, which explicitly foreground the commodity fetishism of a transition to a late capital, *ought* to be powerful and critical political statements' (Jameson in Docherty, 1993: 68). We are in the world of the consumer commodity in Warhol, but the artist's interest is not in presenting this 'fetish' object, as Jameson calls it, in its economic context, in order to elucidate the economic system of which it is a part. Warhol's work lacks any critical distance from the economy it is part of, and merely repeats that economy's logic. With Warhol we are in a world of 'superficiality' and 'depthlessness'. To Jameson, this is emblematic of the postmodern era. In the postmodern, there has been what Jameson calls a 'waning of affect' and an 'effacement of history'. By the former he means that in the postmodern era we no longer experience our lives with the same sense of intensity and individuality. We do not feel with the same depth. Instead, postmodern life is characterised by the quick transition of emotional responses that are themselves like commodities, not deeply felt, and not contributing to an intense individual response to the world. According to Jameson, we have lost our sense of ourselves as unified and meaningful, as full and coherent feeling, responding subjects:

> As for expression and feelings or emotions, the liberation, in contemporary society, from the older *anomie* of the centered subject may also mean, not merely a liberation from anxiety, but a liberation from every other kind of feeling as well, since there is no longer a self present to do the feeling. This is not to say that the cultural products of the postmodern era are utterly devoid of feeling, but rather that such feelings ... are now free-floating and impersonal, and tend to be dominated by a peculiar kind of euphoria (Jameson in Docherty, 1993: 72).

A related development sees the loss, or effacement, of the sense that we are moving meaningfully through time. History in the postmodern age, according to Jameson, is not a means by which we can connect events with one another and make sense of our society. History represents a mere resource of images that are plundered for purely decorative or recreational purposes. The past, therefore, no longer functions as a way of understanding ourselves, our politics, and how we can take charge of our destiny. There is no longer a feeling of an organic connection with the past. The past is simply a set of dead styles or images. The art form symptomatic of this development Jameson calls the 'nostalgia' film. His examples include *American Graffiti, China-*

town and *Body Heat*, amongst others: 'the nostalgia film was never a matter of some old-fashioned "representation" of historical content, but approached the "past" through stylistic connotation, conveying "pastness" by the glossy qualities of the image, and "1930s-ness" or "1950s-ness" by the attributes of fashion' (Jameson in Docherty, 1993: 75). This fashion may indeed involve reference to an earlier film style rather than just the attempt to reproduce commonly accepted images of an era. *Body Heat*, for example, is not set in the past, but merely attempts to recall the mood and stereotypes of the films of a past era.

The effacement of history, according to Jameson, robs us of our ability to understand where we are in time, and where we are going. It is emblematic of the postmodern contempt for time, which had been a preoccupation of modernist artists. Postmodern life is dominated by space, rather than time, and Jameson analyses in detail the architecture of the Bonaventura Hotel in Los Angeles as a way of providing an image of our location in postmodern space. The Bonaventura is designed in such a way that the individual never gets a clear sense of his or her location. There is no apparent structural logic built around a central lobby, a clear floorplan, or a simple sense of the building's interior as a defined space amidst the equally defined spaces of the other buildings in the city. To Jameson, the Bonaventura represents the new space of postmodernism, which he calls 'hyperspace':

> postmodern hyperspace ... has finally succeeded in transcending the capacities of the individual human body to locate itself, to organize its immediate surroundings perceptually, and cognitively to map its position in a mappable external world. And I have already suggested that this alarming disjunction point between the body and its built environment ... can itself stand as the symbol and analogue of that even sharper dilemma which is the incapacity of our minds, at least at present, to map the great global multinational and decentered communicational network in which we find ourselves caught as individual subjects (Jameson in Docherty, 1993: 83).

In the same way that an individual is adrift in the confusing corridors and arcades of the Bonaventura Hotel, we as human subjects, because of the loss of our sense of an intensely felt and critically located place in history, are unable to represent to ourselves the global economic networks that are our most important context. For Jameson, it is the gradual attempt to recover our sense of these networks and our position in them, starting with a 'cognitive mapping' of our immediate social position, that is the pressing task of artists and intellectuals.

For Jameson, then, images and representation in contemporary culture, such as Warhol's, do not give us an understanding of the deeper structures of our society and its development through history. Baudrillard, another prominent theorist of postmodernism, echoes this notion, but takes it further to argue that images are now completely dissociated from meaning, and from their ordinary 'common sense' task of representing the world. He writes that images have 'no other destiny than images' (Baudrillard in Docherty, 1993: 195), and goes on: 'if they fascinate us so much it is not because they are sites of the production of meaning and representation—this would not be new—it is on the contrary because they are sites of the *disappearance* of meaning and representation, sites in which we are caught quite apart from any judgment of reality, thus sites of a fatal strategy of denegation of the real and of the reality principle' (Baudrillard in Docherty, 1993: 194). Mass media, from cinema to infotainment, 'for better *and* for worse' (emphasis added), have relinquished the claim that they represent a world with its own objective existence, and now merely draw on an endlessly proliferating bank of images as the basis for their 'representations'. As a consequence, images are built on images. We live in a society of pure surfaces, where the dream of reconstituting the real is a mere fantasy indulged in by intellectuals and social planners, but scorned by 'the silent majority'.

This is one of postmodernism's most influential ideas: that in contemporary life we have abandoned the depth model. Put simply, the depth model assumes that the surface reality presented to us in our lives is a mere cover for or representation of a deeper structural truth within. The defining characteristics of that truth are unity and authenticity. In politics, superficial social practices are a mere trace of deeper structures of social organisation; the behaviour of an individual is a mere reflection of a deeper psychological reality, a deeper truth of the personality; images or words are the mere envelope or sign of a deeper more fundamental meaning. The depth model is assumed by almost all the conventional practices of Western culture. Baudrillard describes this model in the field of signs: 'All of Western faith and good faith was engaged in this wager ... that a sign could refer to the depth of meaning, that a sign could *exchange* for meaning, and that something could guarantee this exchange—God, of course' (Baudrillard in Docherty, 1993: 196). But what if God itself operated in the world as a mere image, another cultural artefact interchangeable with other cultural artefacts, and having to compete with them for attention: 'Then the whole system becomes weightless, it is no longer anything but a gigantic simulacrum—not unreal but a simulacrum, never again exchanging for what is real, but exchanging in itself, in an uninterrupted circuit without reference or circumference' (Baudrillard in Docherty, 1993: 196). What if the depth model itself is not a verifiable truth, but a mere article of faith, a cultural convention, not a transcendental explanation for reality, but another image of it, in circulation with thousands of images, as valid or invalid as any of them? If God and the depth model themselves are mere images, then the whole depth model collapses. It would be a mistake to see Baudrillard's view here as the result of a patiently argued philosophical position that we have to accept because it is more logical than all others. Baudrillard is not trying to argue a case we should believe in, but is merely asking us to recognise the way in which ideas and values circulate in the contemporary world. The depth model may be logically defensible, but this does not matter in a world where everything is the mere play of images on the surface.

This repudiation of a depth model of society makes Baudrillard's argument very different from Jameson's. Baudrillard's discussions of society go further in his controversial book *In the Shadow of the Silent Majorities* (1983). Here he argues that 'the masses' are constitutionally resistant to any meaning or meaningful activity selected for them by social élites, be they religious, educational, or radical-political. The masses are a void of meaning: 'this indifference of the masses is their true, their only practice ... there is no other ideal of them to imagine, nothing in this to deplore, but everything to analyse as the brute fact of a collective retaliation and of a refusal to participate in the recommended ideals, however enlightened' (Baudrillard, 1983: 14). According to Baudrillard, the legendary passivity of the masses is not the result of powerlessness or stupidity; it is a tactic, partly conscious, partly unconscious, whereby they resist, or at least remain outside of, attempts made to better them, convert them, give them a political role or place in history. The masses resist all these attempts at meaning. Instead of participating in the serious religious meaning that the Church tries to instil in them, the masses turn religion into a mere spectacle, enthusing over ritual and festivity. The masses scorn the political meaning constructed for them by the left, preferring to indulge in superficial social play rather than become subordinate to someone else's sense of what their historical meaning may be: they watch a football match on television, rather than attending a political demonstration. The masses do not merely accept gratefully social policies designed for their benefit. They turn universal health care into a sort of carnival, over-consuming until the system breaks down. This is what Baudrillard calls 'hyperlogic': 'They know that there is no liberation, and that a system is abolished only by pushing it into hyperlogic, by forcing it into an excessive practice which is equivalent to a brutal amortization. "You want us to consume—OK, let's consume always more, and anything whatsoever; for any useless and absurd purpose"' (Baudrillard in Docherty, 1983: 46). Baudrillard does not believe that a challenge can be made to the reigning world of postmodernism by recourse to older values—social and political theory, liberal democracy, socialist reform or revolution, and so on. The only threat to this system comes by a forced acceleration of its 'logic' into 'hyperlogic' till the system itself breaks down. The only way to thwart the world of images and the simulacrum is to produce ever more images till the whole process overloads. How this would look, and where it is supposed to get us, is not revealed by Baudrillard.

Perhaps the most significant idea to emerge from postmodernism and the reaction to it is the dismantling of any universal principles of truth. Attempts to define the ultimate truth of society and history, or the universal structure of individual or human nature are completely and thoroughly scorned. According to contemporary cultural theorists, there is no human nature, and attempts made in the past to define one usually represented an attempt on the part of one social or national group to impose its priorities on the world. For example, defining human nature in terms of an ambitious quest for truth and self-advancement reduces the infinite variety of human experience to the cultural and economic values of a specific class that dominated the West in its most world-dominating period—the European upper-middle class in the nineteenth century. Claims that human beings are all social or curious may seem inoffensive enough, but other universalist claims—that human beings are 'naturally' ashamed of their bodies, are irreducibly violent, or define themselves primarily by race, and so on, all represent attempts to universalise based on narrow, often extreme and ephemeral, beliefs.

Postmodernism in theory and practice is fundamentally committed to *difference*. In Derrida's philosophy, this comes down to an understanding of language as a field in which endlessly multiplying differences are produced. In social terms, ethnic, national, class, and gender groups, as well as those defined by sexual orientation, have seized the opportunity to express and theorise their difference from others, and especially from central, conventional, 'normal' value systems.

In Australia, these developments have been particularly dramatic. The study of both historical and contemporary Aboriginal culture has been fuelled by significant political and legal developments, such as the Australian High Court's Mabo decision, and recent historical research that demands a revision of the understanding of Aboriginal and non-Aboriginal relations. Adam Shoemaker's study *Black Words, White Page* (1989) detailed the long history of Aboriginal literature, and writers such as Oodgeroo Noonuccal, Mudrooroo Narogin, and others have co-ordinated their literary work with cultural and political theory. The commercial success of writers such as Sally Morgan, and of the rock band Yothu Yindi, shows the influence of their work as it takes advantage of the contemporary reinvigoration of the nexus between culture and politics. This activity has also led to a complete reinvestigation of the meaning of Australian literary history, particularly as it is defined by Aboriginal experience, in works such as Bob Hodge and Vijay Mishra's *Dark Side of the Dream* (1991).

Developments in the study and theorisation of postcolonial cultures have also been important in Australia. Writers and critics such as

Frantz Fanon, Ngugi wa Thiong'o, Wole Soyinka, and Chinua Achebe have produced in Africa a long history of reconsiderations of how the cultural and political landscapes, and even psychological experience, have been defined by colonisation and decolonisation. Australia, as a settler colony that established itself by the conquest and displacement of the indigenous population, does not neatly replicate the situation of other colonies. Yet the cultural dislocation, and the problems of identity and cultural authority, as manifested in the dominance of the colonial language, education system and cultural values, have been felt deeply here as well. The impetus of postcolonial studies is towards the disestablishment of the cultural place and authority of the ex-colonial power, and the promotion of diversity within postcolonial cultures. What has been traditionally perceived as the centre is challenged by the rise to confidence and prominence of the margins. This development may seem to be the simple replication of broader populist nationalist developments as played out in the public sphere, but postcolonial studies analyse the meaning of the colonial/postcolonial history as it underprops language, social, and political life at its historically most enduring, and constitutionally most fundamental, way. This can be seen in the work of critics such as Edward Said, Homi K. Bhabha, and Gayatri Spivak.

Another priority for postcolonial studies has been to resist the recolonisation that results from the globalisation of culture, the fragmentation of Cold War power blocs, and the spread of a centred information technology network. Postcolonial theorists have often seen postmodern theory as a version of this recolonisation, despite its claim to celebrate difference and abhor centred cultural and political systems. Indeed, in the academic community the authority accrued to a handful of European and North American theorists is more than just ironic. It is a challenge to its own radical pluralism, and to efforts on the part of previously marginalised cultures to represent themselves. Given the increasingly centred world of publishing, the conventional medium for academic debate, this has proven a practical as well as a theoretical problem. As we can see, many of these movements in literary and cultural studies are directly connected with political events outside of university life. Since the 1960s there has been a reconsideration of the function of academic work, and particularly its co-ordination with power and politics. The political work of contemporary cultural theorists has come a long way from the realists' belief that the political function of art was to represent the 'real' world of economic and social injustice. Instead of being a vehicle for representing the world, postmodernism sees cultural work as a way of transforming it, of seeing how the world, and the individual subjects within it, could be re-imagined. This nexus between postmodern culture and contemporary politics will be investigated in detail in Chapter 9.

One of the most influential contributions to this project has been the work of Donna Haraway, particularly her essay 'Cyborg Manifesto'. Haraway is committed to established political movements such as feminism, and to various struggles for the advancement of oppressed minorities. She attempts to situate these struggles in terms of the radical postmodern reconceptualisation of what human beings are. As a cybernetic organism, part animal and part machine, the cyborg crosses the traditionally impermeable frontiers between animality and humanity, and between humanity and technology. Haraway sees the cyborg not only as an image of contemporary human life, but of how we can control that life as society transforms itself 'from an organic industrialized society to a polymorphous information system' (Haraway, 1991: 161). According to Haraway, politics no longer functions on us as fixed and stable natural objects, but rather on the various connections and boundaries, the 'interfaces' that form between representations and bodies, social groups and institutions, machines and human networks. Her particular concern is imagining some new way in which women can re-think themselves in a world that has changed from what she calls 'the comfortable old hierarchical dominations to the scary new networks called the informatics of domination' (1991: 161). She writes: 'If we learn how to read these webs of power and social life, we might learn new couplings, new coalitions ... The issue is dispersion. The task is to survive in the diaspora' (1991: 170).

Haraway looks to 'women of colour', a social group that is doubly marginalised, as a model of how such new coalitions could be rethought. Women of colour are marginal to a debate about gender dominated by White women, and a debate about race dominated by

Black men. Because of this, they have had to discover a specific political identity that cannot be reduced to any one 'natural' defining factor: they are not simply 'women' or 'coloured', but exist on the dynamic 'interface' between the two: 'This identity marks out a self-consciously constructed space that cannot affirm the capacity to act on the basis of natural identification, but only on the basis of conscious coalition, of political kinship' (1991: 156).

The shifts in understanding of the political function of narrative and representation reflect changes in the nature of politics: from the nineteenth century's preoccupation with money and class to the postmodern concern with sexuality, gender, and ethnicity. As a result, works of art and literature have shifted from being representations of the world, to being attempts to reconsider and remake human beings in that world. It is to the question of subjectivity—what does the word 'I' mean, where does what it refers to come from, and how does it connect with politics, society and culture?—that these changes inevitably lead. This issue, in turn, will be investigated in detail in Part 4.

Further Reading

Much of the material on postmodernism is difficult to read. An introductory guide such as Madan Sarup's *An Introductory Guide to Post-structuralism and Postmodernism* (1993) may be the best place to start. John Lechte's *Fifty Key Contemporary Thinkers: From Structuralism to Postmodernity* (1994) has good sections on Lyotard and Baudrillard, and on many of the other important theorists treated in this book. Other useful starting points are Steven Connor's *Postmodernist Critique: An Introduction to Theories of the Contemporary* (1997) and Stuart Sim's *Routledge Critical Dictionary of Postmodern Thought* (1999). Lyotard's *The Postmodern Condition: A Report on Knowledge* (1984) is short, but difficult, and his *The Postmodern Explained to Children* (1992) doesn't always live up to its name. Jameson's essay 'Postmodernism, or the Cultural Logic of Late Capitalism' is published in a book of the same title (1991). The version used in this chapter is from Thomas Docherty (ed.), *Postmodernism* (1993: 62–92). The excerpts from Baudrillard's work here are from the articles 'The Evil Demon of Images' and 'The Precession of Simulcra' (Docherty, 1993: 194–200), and from *In the Shadow of the Silent Majorities* (1983). If you are interested in postcolonial studies, one of the most popular places to start is W.D. Ashcroft et al., *The Empire Writes Back* (1989) and *The Post-Colonial Studies Reader* (1995). There is an important consideration of postmodernism's own cultural imperialism in Ziauddin Sardar's *Postmodernism and the Other: The New Imperialism of Western Culture* (1997). Issues of Aboriginality in Australian cultural history are dealt with in Bob Hodge & Vijay Mishra's *Dark Side of the Dream: Australian Literature and the Post-Colonial Mind* (1991). Writing by Aborigines is surveyed in Adam Shoemaker's *Black Words, White Page: Aboriginal Literature 1929–1988* (1989), and the standard study of the representation of Aborigines in literature is J.J. Healy's *Literature and the Aborigine in Australia 1770–1975* (1989). Donna Haraway's article 'A Cyborg Manifesto' appears in her collection *Simians, Cyborgs, Women: The Reinvention of Nature* (1991).

8

Contextuality: Feminism and the Fluidity of *Noir*

The issue of feminism is complex in itself, but once we introduce the aspect of texts the complexities multiply. However, it is precisely this combination of textual systems and the political strategies of feminism that has produced a new and radical set of ideas on ways of approaching the text. This chapter will consider the place of feminism in relation to other theories (particularly poststructuralism) and how some ideas from feminist theory can be applied to textual analysis. The idea of a new humanities is impossible without reference to feminist theory, because this has been one of the most influential developments. The challenge that feminist theory brings covers all disciplines and all textualities. As such feminism is very much a system of thought within its own right, and one that has impacted on other hermeneutics. To illustrate the relationship between feminism and other theoretical paradigms, and to consider how feminism can operate as a model for textual and cultural analysis, this chapter will also consider the issues of morality and ethics, in particular transgressive morality.

We can begin by asking what is perhaps an unanswerable question: is feminism a poststructuralist theory? This necessarily carries the inverse question: how much has poststructuralism been shaped by feminism? One of the main difficulties in answering these sorts of questions is that feminism is far from homogeneous. The split that has dominated the movement since the 1960s has been defined as a division between the Anglo-American and Continental.[1] It now seems that such a division cannot really be sustained in a theoretical sense. While there is still a great deal of difference between these cultural types and methods, the trend more recently has been a form of conflation of the different feminisms, with a growing influence from French feminism in particular. This may well be a third form of feminism, rather than simply a negation of the other two. Certainly the cultural sensibilities that caused this split are still apparent in many cases. This postulating of a third type of feminism partly answers our initial question. The relationship of feminism to poststructuralism reflects the former's dynamism and its impact on a wide range of ideas.

It is always difficult to encapsulate such vast and complex issues, but essentially the principle difference between these two historically defined schools of thought lies in their relationship to systems of knowledge. The French/Continental feminist movement tended to draw on systems and issues from areas such as philosophy, psychoanalysis, and semiotics. Anglo-American feminism during the same period was more antagonistic to these fields (arguing that they were male-dominated and historically aligned with patriarchy), and instead tended to be more sociological and linguistic based. In some ways the emergence of cultural studies and the growth of critical theory in the humanities (which crossed over so many of the disciplinary boundaries) allowed for the development of a new type of feminism in the Anglo-American cultures. This new feminism demonstrates a strong influence from the key French feminists, particularly Kristeva, Irigaray, and Cixous. Of course, it must once more be acknowledged that the development of these areas of critical theory and cultural studies in themselves owe a great deal to feminism, and it is through the works of Kristeva, Cixous, and Irigaray that these developments can be best understood.

We will now focus on four points that will allow us to examine the nature of the relationship between feminism and poststructuralism.

---

1 The 1960s is a fairly arbitrary time frame, although it can be justified because feminism was marked by the social and cultural revolution of 1968 in France, which saw a subsequent rise in a new wave of feminist thinkers—a type of post-de Beauvoir phenomenon. In Anglo-American circles, one of the most influential books of the time, Kate Millet's *Sexual Politics*, was published in 1969. For a dated, but still excellent summary of the split between Anglo-American and French feminism see Toril Moi's *Sexual/Textual Politics* (1985).

Method and Critique

It can be argued that what poststructuralism has done in all of its interdisciplinary fields is provide a critique of ideas and issues that have become historically established as truth. Poststructuralism is concerned both with the ideas themselves, and how they become established and validated as ideas. So, for example, Foucault examines systems of value in order to expose the very nature of value as a social process; Derrida deconstructs the notion of centres and origins in order to problematise the act of thinking from a point of certainty; Lacan communicates like the unconscious in order to grasp the unconscious as a discourse, and so on. The new forms of feminism do very similar things, often with an emphasis on gender and sexuality. The value of masculine sexuality, the centres of patriarchy, and the discourse of masculine unconscious are all themes that feminism has taken up and critiqued in a powerful and highly effective way. In doing so it has produced insights into both the poststructuralist concerns and its own interests in sexual politics.

The Meta-Discourse

Part of the processes of critique in poststructuralism and feminism has led to a questioning of the discourses of their disciplines. Derrida must always write with one eye on the language and technique of philosophy because ultimately he is attempting to write outside of it, or rather inside of it to expose it. Similarly, Foucault shifts his whole enterprise from an archaeology (a type of history and critique of ideas) to a genealogy (an investigation of the relationship between ideas and power) because he realises that he is in danger of producing, and therefore becoming a part of, a discourse he is attempting to expose. And this is what feminism has also tried to do. By writing outside the established phallocentric discourses it seeks to distance itself from and dismantle those very systems of thought. Both poststructuralism and feminism seek to create a meta-discourse (a discourse about discourses) in order to think outside of the dominant forms. In a truly reflexive turn, both poststructuralism and feminism have examined themselves and each other as (potentially) dominant discourses.

Production of New Ideas

Much more than being concerned solely with ideas and discourses as they currently exist (as the above two points might suggest), both poststructuralism and feminism are invested with the production of new ideas and concepts. There is a problematic relationship between the questioning of systems of thinking and the thinking through of ideas (as noted above with Foucault), but there is also the very necessary requirement that the systems of thought of poststructuralism and feminism produce ideas within themselves. This is precisely what has happened, and the emergence of this vast array of material has seen one of the most innovative and explosive periods of critical thought. In a moment we shall consider some of the ideas that have developed out of feminism.

The Investigation of Common Material

Partly because of the influence that feminism and poststructuralism have had on each other many of the issues examined by them have a common ground. There has been a radical and profound examination of issues such as subjectivity, meaning and interpretation, culture, and textuality. Once more the emphasis in a feminist analysis on these sorts of concerns is based on gender and sexual politics, on the interplay between (sexual) power and its institutionalisation, and on attempts to produce differences and subversions. In this common material lies the greatest cross-over between feminism and other recent theoretical developments. This is a good point at which to introduce some of the ways in which these feminist thinkers have tackled such ideas.

Kristeva draws on at least four major disciplines to construct a complex and sustained analysis of areas such as subjectivity, meaning, and the text. Her early work is dominated by linguistic theory, semiotics, and philosophy; while her later work is informed by psychoanalysis and, again, philosophy. Of all these disciplines, the psychoanalytic theories of Freud and Lacan have had the greatest influence. For an illustration of how Kristeva has blended so many theoretical models, and developed a unique type of feminist theory, consider how she approaches the subject's relationship to language.

Kristeva investigates the Freudian idea that the subject is split from itself and from its social contexts. One of the major contributions to these investigations is her idea of the subject that is never fixed and settled. For an exposition of her idea of the subject in process/on trial, read her *Powers of Horror* (1982) and *Revolution in Poetic Language* (1984b), which both, in different ways, explore the theory that the subject is in a state of constant developing. Kristeva sees this process of the subject (that which enforces the trial) as deriving from the subject's own interplay with language. In her schema there are primarily two sources or receptacles of language—the 'symbolic' and the '*sémiotique*'. (The *sémiotique* is usually translated as the semiotic, but to avoid confusion between this specific use and the more general sense of semiotics as a discipline we have left it untranslated here.) The symbolic corresponds to Lacan's conceptualisation of the domain of social discourse. As in Lacan's theory, the subject is caught in a continuous effort to become part of this order, to be accepted into it, in effect. However, this is an impossibility—we can never possess the signifier—and so, Kristeva asserts, we are always in the process of becoming such a subject, without ever actually achieving it. The *sémiotique*, on the other hand, operates outside of (perhaps *beneath* is a better metaphor) this symbolic order. If the symbolic is structured, ordered and directed towards communication, the *sémiotique* is unstructured, free-flowing, and chaotic. It opposes the symbolic, and continually tries to disrupt it. In this way it parallels the operation of the unconscious.

This dynamic model of the subject in process, the social fabric of the symbolic and the anarchic, poetic *sémiotique* forms a key part of Kristeva's theories on language, discourse, and subjectivity. Its most obvious feminist connection is when the symbolic is read as part of the phallogocentric order, and the *sémiotique* as alternative practices of language (such as those of women, or even those that are culturally based, such as postcolonial languages against the colonising voice). If we inflect these in a different way and consider the issue of morality, then these terms can be seen to hold an even wider set of implications and possibilities.

In *Powers of Horror* (1982) Kristeva develops the idea of abjection, which she defines thus at one point: 'The abjection of self would be the culminating form of the experience of the subject to which it is revealed that all its objects are based merely on the inaugural *loss* that laid the foundations of its own being. There is nothing like the abjection of self to show that all abjection is in fact recognition of the *want* on which any being, meaning, language, or desire is founded' (Kristeva, 1982: 5). In this succinct description Kristeva lays down many of the central points of her interpretation.

It is significant that Kristeva correlates abjection with the self. It is a relationship that she continues to explore throughout her book, and one that is central to the psychoanalytic model on which it is premised. Kristeva's point is that abjection may well be a cultural construction, but we relate to it through our sense of the self. Horror is at its most powerful—most abject—when we align it to the self. This construction of the self is a specific one, again derived from the psychoanalytic theories of Freud. In this model the self is based on loss and fragmentation. However, abjection emphasises this loss even more than usual, and it is a loss that draws attention to the foundations of the cultural and psychic self. In other words, abjection produces an awareness of the self in its relationship to the self, to others, and to objects. This is why Kristeva emphasises so strongly the issues of loss and want. This is the dual play of the horror—the fear of the loss of the self, and the fear of the loss of those foundations of the self. When Kristeva lists meaning, language, and desire she is constructing abjection as part of those systems so essential to social and cultural fields. If we follow Kristeva's line of thinking then, when abjection is formulated, it is done so through language, meaning, and desire.

One of the most significant ways in which Kristeva speaks of the relationship of the subject to language is her use of the term 'syntactical passivation'. This term describes the situation where the subject, positioned in the place of the object, loses the interplay with language. Because the subject is denied access to language (that is, an active part in discourse) he or she is essentially silenced and objectified. This line of argument is comparable to the way in which some feminists have argued that women have become silenced through patriarchy, or the way postcolonial theory has examined the denial of the voice of the colonised culture. This is the horror to those groups. Once access to the systems of language/discourse is denied, then subjectivity is lost and people become like objects. This is one of the sites of abjection, both for the individual and for cultural groups.

The abjection of the body leads Kristeva to postulate the idea of the *corps propre*—the clean and proper body, which is 'pure' and whole—as distinct from the abject body. The *corps propre* is an ideal form; it is a body that cannot exist except as an abstraction. This does not, however, stop it from having a powerful presence and influence in our lives. The concept of the body's ideal form has produced, in recent times, anorexia nervosa, silicon implants, and steroid-based body building, as well as having an influence in the constant and dynamic changes in fashion. We are continually asked to measure our own (imperfect) bodies against this ideal form (and, of course, must always fail in the comparison). In this failure is abjection and, consequentially, the production of the abject body. This form of the body is what Kristeva terms the 'deject', which illustrates once more the relationship of the self to abjection. In such a context we are forced to deject. Significantly, versions of both the deject and the *corps propre* must always shift across time and cultures, even if what remains constant is their presence. This suggests that the formulation of what is abject or beautiful in the body is strongly connected to, perhaps wholly determined by, other cultural forces and influences.

One of the major productions of abjection in the body is the sense of the loss of the *corps propre*. Of course the curious thing about this is that the *corps propre* has never been possessed, or even experienced; it is a *false* loss that produces this abjection. This complex relationship is bound up with the idea that the body is both apart from and a part of the world external to it. The abject is developed and sustained in those parts of the body where the internal (body) and external (world) meet and exchange signs; where the internal is made external (blood, vomit, excrement, sperm, discharge, pus) and the external is made internal (penetration, absorption, inhaling). The idea of the body as *corps propre* is broken down through these holes, gaps, and absences, which in turn emphasises the breaking down of intactness and wholeness. An interesting point for comparison here is that both Foucault (in, for example, *Discipline and Punish* (1977) and *The History of Sexuality*, volumes 1 and 2 (1980a; 1985)) and Lyotard (especially in *Libidinal Economy* (1993)) analyse the subject's position in culture through the body, but often focusing on skin. However, even though each theorist is concerned with similar ideas, their approaches and conclusions are not necessarily the same. What we witness in such a comparison is the border of the subject in the social order, defined and derived through skin.

So the whole gives way to the hole, and in so doing the margins of the body become the sites of both abjection and pleasure. They also become the sites through which subjectivity is defined, determined, and disputed. They are the areas of contestation because they cannot be comfortably located in an established signifying practice. It is the margins of the body and the holes that define them that determine the issues of subjectivity. This is the complexity of the relationship: both pleasure/desire and abjection are often located in the same sites of the body, and so are, psychoanalytically and culturally speaking, bound up with one another. The eyes, sexual organs, mouth, ears, and so on all occupy a strange position of both abjection and pleasure because they formulate the *corps propre* and dissolve it. They are the points at which the subject's body interacts with the world and others, and so become the defining aspects of subject and object, internal and external.

If morality is a social convention, which is defined, articulated, and sustained within the cultural world order, then, according to feminist theories, this morality must reflect a patriarchal bias. It will also operate largely within the symbolic realm, through laws, taboos, and regulations. Transgressions against this moral structure can take place in the *sémiotique*—which leads to the difficult question of whether this order is potentially immoral or amoral, or offers a different type of morality altogether. A few examples will not resolve this, but will demonstrate some of the issues at hand.

Kathy Acker's writing (for example, *Blood and Guts in High School* (1984)) goes against two of the moral structures of the symbolic: her overt sexual descriptions have all the trappings of what might be considered pornography; and her pilfering of literary texts with little or no regard to the originals goes against the morality of authorship and ownership. But these moral structures rely on certain ideological premises—the first defines sexuality through a masculine perspective, the second defines ownership through the ideology of capitalism. Without such contexts of privileged phallic sexuality and of possession and control such texts would not be read as in any way transgressive. Similarly, some of Robert Mapplethorpe's photographs have been defined as pornographic (leading to the famous recent legal battle in the United States for an art gallery to be allowed to show his works). The 'offence' to the symbolic order here is most likely to be the overt homosexual and sadomasochistic depictions in his work. The defence of Acker and Mapplethorpe are the aesthetic contexts—Acker's literature is found in bookshops not sex shops, Mapplethorpe's photographs are exhibited in art galleries. But, if we use this defence, can we still argue that Mapplethorpe's 'Self-portrait with Bull Whip' is part of the *sémiotique* if it is viewed in prestigious art galleries? Is it still transgressive? We can turn to another concept of Kristeva's to address such questions.

Rather than a binary system of either the symbolic order or the *sémiotique*, Kristeva often speaks about the liminal areas of these orders, and of the dynamics of the flow between them. It is at the margins, Kristeva argues, that the challenges and disruptions take place. Her subject position/type of the 'borderliner' is crucial to this, as is her theory about textual spaces called the 'chora'. (For discussions on the borderliner see her *Powers of Horror* (1982), and on the chora see her *Revolution in Poetic Language* (1984b). These are the two most significant texts on these issues, but similar ideas are to be found throughout Kristeva's writings.) A theme of marginality runs throughout Kristeva's works, informing a wide range of topics, including subjectivity (the borderliner), textuality (her theories of poetic language), the sociocultural (her discussions on love, motherhood, abjection). What this theory of marginality provides is a way to understand issues such as the politics of transgression and morality. These are empowered, and empowering, sites of subjectivity and textuality. For Kristeva, the repressive devices of the (masculine) symbolic affect not only different ways to desire, but also different sites of subjectivity. Mapplethorpe's marginality is sustained (and empowered) because within current moral codes his work is marked as difference. This difference is derived precisely because it locates itself outside of the established codes of the symbolic. So the reader must confront his or her own position. At its most effective the image forces readers to acknowledge their own marginality.

Similar, yet in some ways markedly different, issues are found in the works of Cixous. Once more there is a strong influence from the ideas of Freud and Lacan, and a concern with the feminist implications of them. In many of her works Cixous focuses on the relationship between the body and the unconscious as they are positioned in terms of pleasure. For her, pleasure is a political issue, and women's pleasure is something that has been controlled, denied, and repressed in patriarchal structures. She attempts to develop systems of thinking and ways of writing women's pleasure outside of the restraints of the phallocentic order. One of her key strategies in this is the idea of *écriture feminine*, or women's writing, although, interestingly, Cixous argues that this is not necessarily gender specific and cites Jean Genet as an example of a male writer who produced *écriture feminine*. This type of writing/thinking and the force of female *jouissance* work counter to the male-dominated orders that determine a phallogocentricism.

Cixous argues that there is a direct link between forces of *jouissance* and formations of knowledge. She takes this relationship in two ways: how *jouissance* formulates types of knowledge and sense-making paradigms; and how these hermeneutic processes shape structures of *jouissance*. Clearly this is a complex line of thought. In the first configuration we need to contend with the issue of *jouissance* as it might somehow constitute an interpretative field; while in the second we need to consider how two seemingly divergent orders can be reconciled. This is precisely what Cixous wants readers to come to terms with. The various relationships between what constitutes knowledge and how this relates to the politics of pleasure and its enactment are vital to her writings. It is also important in other feminist writings, as well as in the works of Foucault.

One of the main ways in which Cixous explores these ideas and relationships is through the body and the unconscious, and how these forces might constitute a new language system. Cixous argues for the centrality of the body in all these concerns, because it is in the body that *jouissance* is articulated, and knowledges are formulated and argued through. Once more we find parallels with Foucault in his aim to explore the connections between bodies and knowledge in prisons, medicine, and sexuality (see, for example, his *Discipline and Punish* (1977), which investigates the body and prisons; *The Birth of the Clinic* (1973), which looks at the body and medicine; and *The History of Sexuality* (1980a; 1985; 1986)). For Cixous the body is a semiotic system that speaks and has its own language; it is a political site where knowledge, power, presence, and subjectivity are formulated and negotiated. The significance of this is that women's bodies are immediately set against the phallocentric order by their very difference. As we find with Irigaray, Cixous's version of the body is one that defines subjectivity and not simply gender. Irigaray argues, for example, that women are denied articulation of their pleasures and must develop auto-affection—that is, pleasure of/for their own bodies. (One of Irigaray's key texts on this subject is *This Sex Which Is Not One* (1985b), which contains an essay of the same title.) This makes sexuality and desire particularly important as they are seen as political processes in their own right. A concept and practice such as *écriture feminine* makes sense and operates only within a highly political (and often subversive) atmosphere. It is *jouissance* against the symbolic.

Irigaray has a similar concept to *écriture feminine* with her idea of *parler femme*, or women's speech. Although there are differences, both Cixous and Irigaray are primarily concerned with developing a language system that will allow women to express their subjectivity, as well as exposing the inadequacies of masculinised discourses. The initial premise is that a phallogocentric language will always restrict those outside of its identifying practices the capacity to 'speak' and be heard, and so deny subjectivity. The recent interpretations of this conflation of the formation of subjectivity and access to language systems (including the written, spoken, visual, etc.) owe a great deal to feminist theories, as well as the Lacanian blend of semiotics and psychoanalysis. To illustrate how Irigaray inflects such discussions in a different direction we will look at her theories of fluids. This is both a theorising of women's position in a phallogocentric world order, and a strategy for changing not only such a position, but the situation itself.

The idea of fluids recurs in Irigaray's works: we find discussions of it in her *Speculum of the Other Woman* (1985a) (especially the section entitled 'Volume-Fluidity'), *Marine Lover of Friedrich Nietzsche* (1991), and *This Sex Which Is Not One* (1985b). In these discussions some of the topics examined elsewhere in this volume occur, notably the defining of subjectivity through the body. The idea of fluids in Irigaray's thought is tied to her examination of women's position as it is determined through and in patriarchy. One of the central premises on which *Speculum of the Other Woman* is based is the relationship of masculine knowledge and the feminine body, and the subversion of this type of knowledge through the fluids of the body. Just as Kristeva speaks of the abjection of the bodily fluids in a phallocentric context, Irigaray seeks to examine the convolution of fluid and resistance (and so uncertainty). This is why she argues that 'woman is neither open nor closed. She is indefinite, in-finite, *form is never complete in her*' (Irigaray, 1985a: 229). Irigaray also uses the idea of fluids to point out the failings of masculine sciences (see, for example, Irigaray 1985b: 106), as well as becoming a defining point for why women are excluded from a phallocentric world order. It is the fluidity of woman that defines her and sets up a contestation of knowledge.

To illustrate how these sorts of ideas can be used in terms of textual analysis we will consider two examples: the first focuses on a genre of cinema, the second on some paintings. The discussion below considers concepts such as the subject in process/on trial, *écriture feminine*, and the theory of fluids in order to better understand how different aspects of recent feminist theory have developed.

Film noir was a form of cinema that developed during the 1930s and 1940s in Hollywood. It demonstrated a strong European influence, however, borrowing heavily from German expressionist cinema in particular.[2] Running counter to the popular musicals of the time, *noir* cinema, as its name suggests, explored the shadowy and sinister side of human relationships. The plots often involved an innocent man being drawn into a violent world, usually with little

---

2 Examples include John Huston, *Key Largo* (1948) and *The Maltese Falcon* (1941); Michael Curtiz, *Mildred Pierce* (1945); Tay Garnett, *The Postman Always Rings Twice* (1946); Billy Wilder, *Double Indemnity* (1944); Jacques Tourner, *Out of the Past* (1947); Edward Dmytryk, *Murder My Sweet* (1944); Jules Dassin, *The Naked City* (1948); Howard Hawks, *The Big Sleep* (1946).

understanding or control of the situation. One of the more subversive aspects of these films was the challenge to many of the values inherent in capitalist, conservative Hollywood. Many of the films tried to escape the strong moral codes of the time, and one that was most strongly enforced was that any transgression of the laws (including ethical and moral prescriptions) must be punished. This is most apparent in terms of women.

One characterisation of women in *film noir* is the sexually active vamp; but rather than being a positive attribute, this always involved a transgressing of society's moral and ethical codes and, almost inevitably, punishment. These women characters were powerfully drawn with strong libidinal urges, a politicised passion, and a willingness to lead men astray. In a sense they were the elements of fluid within the rigid, male-orientated society. Irigaray's idea that fluids have an uncontainable (read subversive) aspect to them fits in with the sexualised and disruptive nature of women characters in *noir* films. When Irigaray states that all this is 'feasible by virtue of her "fluid" character, which has deprived her of all possibility of identity with herself within such a logic' (Irigaray, 1985b: 109), this can be read as a description of women operating outside of the logic of the social order in *noir* films. The significance of this is that even though these women were ultimately portrayed negatively, or as deserving of punishment (even if the audience's sympathy had been elicited), there was at least an acknowledgment that women had desires and passions. What is fascinating about many of these films, and the tenor of the form overall, is that the questions of morality and of women's sexuality are raised in such a way that the former is scrutinised (and perhaps questioned) while the latter is merely acknowledged.

The *film noir* form has been revived in recent years, with many of the elements, except for the inevitability of the punishment of the women, being retained. Films such as the remake of *The Postman Always Rings Twice* (Bob Rafelson, 1981), and *Body Heat* (Lawrence Kasdan, 1981), present strong, sexually aggressive women characters who actually succeed in transgressing masculine moral codes. They are active agents because of their sexual power, and part of their sexuality is this power. It is important to acknowledge that more recent *noir* films also demonstrate marked differences in style. *Blue Velvet* (David

Lynch, 1986), for example, problematises sexual power so that for every character's seeming position of power there is a corresponding position of victimisation and entrapment, which the character at some point occupies. This, in itself, is a recurring motif in *noir* cinema. Another difference is that some films use the *film noir* form, but challenge the content. *Blood Simple* (Joel Coen, 1984) (and *Seven* (David Finche, 1995), to give another example) looks '*noir*ish' because of the lighting, camera angles, and multiple twists in the narrative. However, it ultimately becomes a homage to and parody of the style, distancing itself through the humour evoked. Similarly, *Blade Runner* employs all the stylistic devices of *film noir*—including themes of the detective genre—but is a science-fiction film set in the future.

It is difficult to say why this revival of the form has taken place. Two possible influences have been the rise (and in some ways popularisation) of feminism and a foregrounding of certain sexual politics. The rise of feminism into popular consciousness has led to the development of a number of textual forms—not all as sympathetic or revolutionary as they make out. *Noir* cinema occupies a deeply ambiguous relationship to feminist politics because although it allows women a space for power and desire, it still operates within a masculine perspective, and often represents this space in a negative context. None the less, there does seem to be a correlation between this textual form and feminism. Whether or not it is possible to go as far as describing certain texts of *film noir* as versions of *écriture feminine* is difficult to say, but this certainly constitutes an interesting interpretation.

A second possible reason why there has been a revival of *film noir* is a corresponding foregrounding of sexuality and morality. With the increased awareness of Aids and the accompanying discourses (medical/scientific, sociological, mass media, religious, sexual), the 1980s and 1990s have seen a renewed interest in sexual and moral issues. *Film noir* was originally produced in a social climate concerned with the inseparable nature of passion, danger, and morality. In its return we see a similar conflation of sexual power and threat to life—*film noir* has, after all, always been concerned with the issues of safe and unsafe sex! This raises another set of questions, not the least being how do we read such a configuration in terms of the growing prominence of feminist politics?

Women in *noir* films demonstrate the subject in process/on trial. Their subjectivity (through a foregrounding of gender and the body) is constantly in view as they move against the restrictions of moral codes. Given that so much of the material in these films is based on a challenge to legal systems, these subjects are both quite literally on trial, as well as being on trial in Kristeva's sense of the status of subjectivity being in question. The women in these films challenge the social institutions (such as the legal system, the family, marriage) in the process of becoming subjects. They also operate very much within the sense of the borderliner, refusing to occupy a masculine construction of female personality and sexuality. Once they move outside of such categorising they operate socially in a liminal zone. This liminality is precisely what a great deal of feminist theory has dealt with. They argue that if women are denied systems of pleasure and desire within phallogocentricism they must either change the system, or operate outside of it to create a new one.

As Cixous has theorised, there is a connection between the body and the unconscious with its drives and desires. We see an illustration of this in *film noir*, although what is perhaps most interesting is how this filmic form actually shapes the relationship. Cixous's premise is that the body is crucial to the articulation of the unconscious and its desires and drives. Women in *noir* are very much models of unrestrained unconscious feminine wishes. Interestingly, it can be argued that what they represent and signify alters with gender. To the feminine these characters demonstrate a way of desiring differently; to the masculine they are mostly seen as the unknown and unknowable, for the interpretative systems available are unable to make sense of them. This raises the issue of the interrelationship between the text, its cultural contexts, and the act of reading. Part of the very politics of feminism must be concentrated on reading acts. That *film noir* was a form made by male directors in a male-dominated context (both socially and aesthetically), means that if we are to read such texts in terms of the politics and strategies of feminism, then we must be equally, if not more, concerned with the creative act of reading. In this sense, the feminist politics of a text may well be formed in the reading rather than in the creation. In this way a concept such as *écriture feminine* can be understood as an act of reading as much as an act of writing. Just as Barthes speaks of the writerly text as one that the reader actively constructs and creates, so a feminist text can be devised through the activities and politics of the reader.

This is a difficult terrain to negotiate. In some ways there is a very compelling argument to be made along the lines that certain discourses must be 'written' from particular agents (such as women, Blacks, gays and lesbians) whose desires are negated or ignored by the dominant forms. The Black director Spike Lee insists that the reader must be Black to understand his films. However this leads to the idea that there must be a textuality, identifiable in its own right, that declares such politics. In such a scenario the author once more becomes the defining point for interpretation. If, however, the reader is seen as a creative agent who shapes the politics of the text, then there is less need to investigate the background of the author, or defend the reading by looking for certain qualities invested in the text by the author. At the heart of the question of where the feminist element exists in a text (the author, the text, or the reader), the answer, as unsatisfying as it may seem, would appear to be a dynamic and heterogeneous one, shifting depending on the force of each of the elements. We would, for example, feel far more comfortable arguing that Jeanette Winterson and Virginia Woolf write texts with feminist politics more apparent than those of the masculine-dominated westerns of John Ford. In doing so we attach those elements to a type of authorial force. Yet there is something to be said in analysing a Ford western through feminist criticism. The absolute celebration of masculinity to the point of the exclusion of women in these films can only be fully understood by employing feminist analysis. This does not make Ford's *The Searchers* (1956) a feminist text, but it does mean that the film can be examined to reveal aspects about the culture that produced it, especially its sexual politics—just as can Woolf's *To the Lighthouse* (1977) or Winterson's *Oranges Are Not The Only Fruit* (1985). The difference in the texts is not necessarily a political (authorial) intent, but how the analysis is constructed and directed in the act of reading and subsequent analysis. The focus shifts from the idea of feminist texts to feminist readers, or sites of readership informed by feminism. The very generic structure of the western has always resisted a feminist politic, which is precisely why so many slide between parody and celebration of the form.

The complexity involved with this set of issues is revealed here. Analysis, interpretation, and textuality are knitted together because each one is part of the formulation of the others. A feminist reading of a text cannot simply be a search for the positive portrayal of women, for its range of texts and interpretative positions must be wide. A feminist analysis must be able to deal with feminist and non-feminist texts alike. To understand this better, we can consider a number of Dutch paintings from the seventeenth century as a second example. These paintings have been chosen precisely because they have no declared feminist politics about them.

If we take the initial point as bodies within the text and the constructed point of the gaze we very quickly enter a well-documented and analysed set of ideas. (John Berger's *Ways of Seeing* (1972) is an early example of this type of analysis. Similarly, Laura Mulvey's essay 'Visual Pleasure and Narrative Cinema' (1975) details the relationship between the power of the active, masculine gaze and the passive objectification of the woman.) Rather than discuss this particular aspect, we would instead like to consider the ideas raised earlier (the subject in process/on trial, the idea of *écriture feminine*, and the theory of fluids) in relation to a number of paintings. In doing so we can continue to bear in mind this issue of the power of the gaze and the negotiation of women's subjectivity.

The first example is Jan Vermeer's *Soldier and Laughing Girl* (1657). What is initially striking about this image is that spatially the canvas is dominated by the masculine (the male figure in the foreground, the map that was commonly used as a symbol of male exploration and adventure), yet it is the woman we experience as a subject. The male figure is dark and obscured—we only have a slight sense of his facial features—whereas the woman is in full light and animated. This raises the question of which world we are experiencing here—the masculine or the feminine? One reading might stress the active male and passive female idea. By positioning the woman against the same wall of the map she becomes part of the territory to be explored and conquered, and the facelessness of the male figure enables the male viewer to occupy this powerful site. There is also the dominance of masculinity in terms of space, themes, and the gaze. In this sense he acts as a shadow for an intended male gaze. But what if we reverse the reading, arguing that the subject in process/on trial is the male who lacks any semblance of subjectivity? The woman's smile is more powerful, knowing, and dominant in such a reading. Her hands hold the vessel (a signifier of the feminine) in a gesture of control with the possibility of the gift, rather than a loss. Importantly, the space in which this takes place becomes one dominated by the woman, and the map and the man hang there as alien. Compare this painting to Vermeer's *The Art of Painting* (1665), which has a very similar structure. The woman in this second painting is much more the alien within the artist's studio, and even though once more we see her face and not his, her expression is more closed and passive, while the male figure is creative and active.

This idea of certain spaces being feminised recurs in other Dutch paintings of the time. Individual women were often depicted in either the bedroom or kitchen, and rarely outdoors. One of the more extreme examples of this is Samuel van Hoogstraten's peep-box (1678), which has an expanse of space, but represents the figure of a woman tucked away in a far corner (watched by a man through a window!). The complete domination of the architecture, rather than the human figure, is curious as the image is ultimately about the construction of realism and perspective in painting. The subject becomes ancillary to the space (significantly, a domestic one), and her location is politicised by this. It is important to note that this is not a fate suffered only by women depicted in such paintings.

Pieter Saenredam's *Interior of the St Laurens Church at Alkmaar* (1661) shows two male figures in the bottom-right corner, completely dominated by the church interior. The difference, of course, is that humanity is supposed to be dominated by the power of the Church and God—that is one of the points of such representations. This is masculinity represented on a larger scale of things! The same reading furthers the politics of Hoogstraten's peep-box. Space defines the body and subjectivity, and in turn the viewer is enmeshed into the politics of positionality. As he or she stoops to look through the 'keyhole' the act of voyeur is conflated with the perspective of the feminine and masculine.

Further Reading

The following are representative texts for the three theorists discussed in this chapter. They will provide a solid grounding in the philosophies of the women, as well as giving a sense of their style of writing.

Hélène Cixous

Two essays that were crucial in the development of this area of feminist thought are 'The Laugh of the Medusa' (1976) and 'Castration or Decapitation' (1981). 'The Laugh of the Medusa' is interesting to read against Derrida as it offers a counter-argument to his ideas of the gift. Cixous's novel *Angst* (1985) provides a good example of how her writing style allows theory to fold into narrative, and vice versa. Perhaps one of Cixous's most influential works, and an excellent place to begin looking at her ideas, is her and Catherine Clément's *The Newly Born Woman* (1986).

Luce Irigaray

Speculum of the Other Woman (1985a), is one of Irigaray's earliest and most influential works. Many of the ideas can be seen developing in later works by her so it is a good place to begin reading. In *This Sex Which Is Not One* (1985b), as in *Speculum of the Other Woman*, Irigaray examines the relationship of psychoanalysis (particularly the ideas of Lacan and Freud) and philosophy to feminism. Many of the articles provide an excellent introduction to Irigaray's ideas on the feminine and its political agenda. In *Elemental Passions* (1992), Irigaray engages in the relationship between philosophy and feminism. *Sexes and Genealogies* (1993) is a collection of essays and lectures based around the theme of gender(s) and their historical processes. Many of the works produce a meta-discourse on the acts of thinking-as-feminine, which, in turn, is partly a result of Irigaray's concerns with an ethics of sexuality.

Julia Kristeva

Powers of Horror: An Essay in Abjection (1982) and the essay 'Ellipsis on Dread and the Specular Seduction' (in P. Rosen (ed.), *Narra-*

tive, Apparatus, Ideology (1986: 236–43)) are key texts in Kristeva's ideas on horror, culture, and the subject. For her theories on literature, the arts, and language the two best works to look at are *Desire in Language: A Semiotic Approach to Literature and Art* (1984a) and *Revolution in Poetic Language* (1984b). For a consideration of Kristeva's writings on psychoanalysis, texts, and culture an interesting work is *Tales of Love* (1987). Her commentary on this work in 'Histoires d'Amour—Love Stories' and 'Julia Kristeva in Conversation with Rosalind Coward' (in Lisa Appignanesi (ed.), *Desire* (1984: 18–27)), is also useful.

Film noir

There are many books on *film noir*, and its recent revival has led to a number of new works being published. Of these one of the most interesting is Joan Copec's *Shades of Noir* (1995).

9

The Cultural Politics of Postmodernism

Contemporary critical and cultural theory does not believe it is possible to view textual practices in isolation. This is in stark contrast to the approaches and values of modernist thought. To modernist thought, texts were usually viewed in a double-sense: a cultural product was the result of a specific act of creativity, but only in relation to a context. This relationship between work and context could be viewed in a variety of different ways. The work could *represent* its context, according to the logic of social(ist) realism, getting to the heart of social relations and giving its audience a clear understanding of the economic and political arrangements in their society, thus educating them in a revolutionary ideology. Here, the work is the transmission of one set of political values from one mind to another. A related but significantly different approach sees the work as the exhibition of artists' involvement in the political or collective psychological structure of their world. Here, the work is a transmission of unconscious social or psychological meanings. Third, the work could be seen as an artifact of the human imagination, worthy of attention, even fascination, in itself, as an image of a possible transcendence or reconfiguration of the mundane world. Here, the work inducts its audience into a domain of higher aesthetic, and usually moral, sensibility. All these approaches rest on at least a notional separation of work and context. This separation can be defined in a number of ways, each of which outlines a type of relationship, usually one in which the world either justifies or explains the work, or is spurned by it.

Postmodern criticism and theory, on the other hand, sees the situation of the text as much more complex and fluid. The very concept of "the text" as we have encountered it in the work of Roland Barthes and Jacques Derrida does not accept the neat separation of word and world, even allowing for modernism's complex theories of how the two could be re-joined. Whereas, for modernism, the political appeared in the relation between the work of art and its context, for postmodernism, politics develops within textuality itself. As we recall from Chapter 4, this textuality is not merely a sophisticated model of how writing works. It structures all the processes of representation, identity, and communication that constitute human interaction. Thus, textual politics defines the kind of relationships we have in the world and, as we shall see in Part 4, the kinds of thinking, feeling, experiencing people or 'subjects' we are able to be. The aim of this chapter is to give you an understanding of how postmodern thinkers understand the relationship between text and politics. The key terms discussed are otherness, difference, identity politics, and the performative.

Because they see textuality and politics as so inseparable, many postmodern theorists see *identity* as the key issue for contemporary culture. Identity is indeed the public face of much contemporary political activity. We 'identify' ourselves as members of knowable ethnic, national, gender, religious, and sexual groups. In turn, the identifications we make position us in relation to other social groups, sometimes in terms of alliance (if our needs and goals can be brought into alignment), sometimes in terms of conflict (if we see ourselves competing with or obstructing one another). Inevitably, these groups are separated by power. Society is not pluralistic or egalitarian in any simple way. There are dominant and subordinate social groups. No demarcation between identities seems possible without one identity being positioned as central, and others as marginal.

It is important, however, to remember that an identity is also an image, or signifier. Our identities are not spontaneous or the result of our own personal will or imagination. They spring from an already existing history of narratives, slogans, and styles with which we choose to connect or in which we are educated. No matter how intensely or spontaneously we connect with them, these identities have a history that is made up of both political entanglements and textual practices. The development of recent cultural politics turns on the twin themes of identity: its delineation of society into knowable groups and its inevitable implication in the volatility of contemporary understandings of signifiers, images, and texts.

Otherness

The first key point to be made about this kind of politics is that it understands that identities can only be made in relation to one another. To identify oneself as masculine, for example, is only possible in a context that divides the human population into knowable and mutually exclusive gender groups. To be masculine is more to be not-feminine than it is to be the bearer of absolutely certain qualities and essences. When we try to determine what these qualities may be the same process recurs: masculine love is distinguished from feminine love; masculine entertainment is distinguished from feminine entertainment and so on. Jacques Lacan has gone further to argue in a memorable phrase 'The subject is the discourse of the other'. According to Lacan, and the philosophy of Jean-Paul Sartre that influenced him, we only exist in the world in the terms offered to us by other people, whether these people are conceived of as our intimates, or as the collectivity given form in language and culture.

Put simply, therefore, we define ourselves in relation to other people. The identities we fight over are produced in what contemporary theorists have understood as an economy: a shifting interchange of meanings and desires, a perpetual give and take of values and images. In this way, the relation between self and other is itself highly charged and volatile. When we represent ourselves, we inevitably, even if tacitly, represent others. Since, in fact, the politics that positions one group in relation to another is always mediated by identities, it is always caught up in a second economy: the economy of images. Texts do not merely represent the interaction between social groups. Such interaction is always textual. In turn, texts always deploy the people, and social groups they represent, according to the logic they inherit from the relationships of self-definition, distinction, and contrast that operate in the world. This is the way in which textuality is inevitably politicised, and politics inevitably textualised.

How does this politics of identity manifest itself in texts? The most important way in which this is done has come to be known as 'othering', or self/other relations. One social group identifies itself in contradistinction to another. This second group is positioned on the outside of the identifying one. Its attributes are understood purely in contrast to the latter's. The identifying group, if you like, consolidates its sense of collective selfhood by nominating and defining what is other to it. The identity thus created inscribes two kinds of possible selfhood, therefore: the identifying self, and the counter-identified other. This does not simply mean that in texts authors are preoccupied with defining themselves, and stereotype other people in order to do so, although this is indeed one straightforward version of how self/other relations develop. Texts are not merely positioned in the world as a way of exhibiting their authors' perspective. They do, however, constitute different positions that define distinct ways of being inside—or relegated to the outside of—social identities and formations. It is not that these positions are a reflection of the author's priorities. Indeed, authors define themselves by occupying the position of selfhood that an already established textual politics offers them. The text is not merely a fully imagined and fully controlled product of its author's mind. The nature and identity of the author is constructed within the text. For example, newspaper columnists who comment on weekly affairs in national politics may project themselves as independent and idiosyncratic opinion-makers. Yet this very role, the sort of opinions that are available to it, are determined by this author's very need to validate and promote this image of their work. They cannot be in two minds; they must have outrageous or judgmental views of the world; they must project themselves as having inside knowledge, a maverick indifference to offending the powerful, and a colourful writing style. Such journalists, therefore, are not just individuals expressing their opinions. Their writing is highly structured by their need to make an impact and to court controversy. No matter how they like to present themselves, the subjectivity of such writers is controlled not by their fearless determination to make their opinions count, but by a whole conventionalised ritual of self-promotion and pontification. The identity of such writers is constructed within the conventions of this specific style of writing.

Similarly, texts anticipate a certain type of audience, with a certain level of education, a set of previously existing knowledges to which the texts can refer, and usually a predictable and assumed gender, class and ethnic identity. In the mainstream press in Western countries, the expected audience of the newspaper columnist is almost the definition of the brokers of the mainstream: White, middle class, middle aged, male. Texts thus *invite* or, in the words of French political philosopher Louis Althusser, *interpellate*, a certain type of author and audience. This already complex situation is complicated further by the presence in the text of other possible figures, who may be neither author nor audience but become the subject matter of the writing.

The relationships between these different possible positions that the text offers are not equal, however. The text constructs a hierarchical relationship between them, in terms of the self/other dichotomy outlined above. It is not a simple case of the author occupying the position of self, and the audience or subjects discussed the position of other, although this is often the case. The text usually produces one set of identities that are considered normal and substantial, and another that is marked off as different or inferior. One set of attributes is validated and another treated sceptically. Usually the position of author is affiliated to the dominant and accepted identity; identities that are 'written-about' are treated disdainfully and reductively, and the audience is invited to dissociate itself from the latter and approve the former. In other words, two rival sets of identities are constructed, one of which presents a complex and dynamic position in the world, and the other a simpler, more debased one. The former (the self) is given a full and rich interior perspective. The latter (the other) is almost invariably seen from the outside.

This sort of politicised structure emerges in even our simple day-to-day social encounters: gossip, for example. In gossip, two speakers construct a sort of shared authorship that validates their own sense of themselves as thinking, fluid individuals at the expense of an absent other who is treated as a mere object of scandal and judgement. The shared self the speakers construct for themselves usually has complex motives and acts correctly. The absent other usually has simple questionable motives and acts in an indefensible manner. The behaviour of the self is open-ended and creative; the behaviour of the other, in contrast, is predictable and limited. A more complex example would be, say, a government report on homeless teenagers. The position constructed for the authors and audience of such a report is usually one of objectivity, detachment, breadth of perspective, and open-mindedness. The youth taken as the topic of the report, however, are treated as objects: their motives are knowable, their behaviour is uniform and predictable, and subject to ultimate explanation *on the authors'/audience's terms.* The behaviour of the self producing the report is not to be explained, and is not even seen as behaviour; the behaviour of the other, in contrast, is always seen as closed in on itself, quantifiable and reducible to a single or simple explanation: young people are undisciplined, victims of unemployment or family breakdown, and so on.

Here then is a list of the contrasting attributes of self and other:

self	other
speaking	spoken about
active	passive
strong	weak
owns language	object of language
subject	object
free	bound
complex	simple
controlling	controlled
varied	uniform
agency	predictability

Thus, if the identity of the self only becomes possible in relation to the other, it automatically constructs a complex set of political relationships that, in turn, become an inevitable strand in any textual process. The values and practices of the other become subordinate to those of the self and vulnerable to judgement and condemnation on their terms. This inevitable subjection of one set of behaviours to the world-view of another means that the other is never seen on its own terms. It always appears as a deficient or inferior version of the self. The most notorious example of this is Freud's definition of gender, in which gender identity is determined by ownership (or lack) of the penis. Women are defined not in terms of their own bodies, but as castrated men. In this way, the feminine is understood purely in terms of masculinity and is thus seen as implicitly lacking.

This process is commonly described as *the reduction of the other to the same (or self)*. The other loses its independence and becomes merely an inferior version of the dominant self. In broad social and historical terms, in Western countries at least, this has usually meant that dominant social groups judge and determine the value of marginalised ones. Historically, the self in the West has been White, middle class, male, and heterosexual. Marginalised social groups have been objectified and silenced by the process of othering. Homosexuality, for example, has been seen a distorted version of heterosexuality such that homosexual couples are divided into butch and femme roles, imitating the conventional sexual polarity of heterosexuality. Homosexuality, futhermore, has been deemed in need of explanation while heterosexuality has not.

Postmodern politicial activism fiercely contests the reduction of the other to the same. As mentioned in Chapter 7, postmodernism believes that difference needs to be recognised and respected at all levels of culture. For poststructuralist language philosophy, this difference inhabits language itself, which is always and everywhere unstable and fluid. In political terms, there is a developing divide between two conceptions of how difference operates in relation to identity. The first concentrates on the differences between various social groups as defined by identity. These differences need to be respected and never subordinated to a single, reductive and skewed principle of judgement. This approach is commonly understood as 'identity politics'. The second approach acknowledges the diversity of social practices, but is influenced by the poststructuralist theory of the instability of any sign or image. In these terms, identities are unstable, assumed rather than spontaneous, and cannot be used to rigidly distinguish social groups. Instead of drawing attention to the differences *between* social identities, this approach acknowledges the difference *within* them. This development has been most closely associated with the Queer theory movement, which is discussed in Chapter 12. I will now discuss these rival approaches in terms of identity politics, on the one hand, and the theory of performativity on the other.

Identity Politics

The politics of identity has been one of the defining features of Western political life since the 1960s. The first half of the twentieth century was dominated by the politics of the grand narratives: class or national groups were seen to have arrived at a critical historical moment when either decadent class structures or inferior races would be either annihilated or subsumed into a massive historical momentum that would result in a fuller or purer future, an ultimate arrival at a utopia of racial purity or ideal social arrangement. As we have seen in Chapter 7, it is these historical ambitions that Lyotard has identified as the cause of the horror that dominated the twentieth century and tipped Western culture into the period of necessary scepticism that we know as the postmodern.

From the 1960s onwards, there has been the growth of an alternative social politics that has emphasised the rights of suppressed or minority groups. These groups are defined by the gender, ethnic, or sexual identities that have traditionally been used to deny them equal access to social rights. These struggles are not simply alternatives to earlier models of political activity. They have often been coordinated according to the civil philosophy of traditional Western liberalism or the material politics of Western socialism. Yet these two philosophical traditions have limitations in addressing the question of the place of minority identity groups in society. Liberalism promotes individual choice in terms of a doctrine of universal human rights. In this way, differences in values, practices, and representations are respected only in so far as they do not contradict general liberal understandings of the common humanity that binds us together and must be respected. It might be possible for liberalism to respect indigenous art, for example, but not traditional indigenous punishment practices. Similarly, a socialist politics almost invariably subordinates the issues of minority ethnic or sexual oppression to a larger class politics, thus silencing those who may seek liberation from homophobic persecution but not the overturning of a liberal democratic social and economic order.

Thus both liberal and socialist politics repeats the logic of the reduction of the other to the same. Minority rights are fine as long as they do not go too far or see themselves as part of a larger process. This inevitably repeats the problem of marginalisation that gave the original impetus to the struggles of identity politics. We can see then that the issue of minority rights returns inevitably to the problem of representation. The drive towards universal statement, whether it be in the hands of psychologists searching for the truth of human interior life, political theorists seeking to outline an ultimate model of social structure and destiny, or those in the culture industries seeking to appeal to, and flatter, dominant values and stereotypes, inevitably de-emphasises or under-represents positions perceived to be minority ones. This is then experienced as a kind of erasure or silencing. The title of Ralph Ellison's novel *Invisible Man* (1948) identifies the social position of African-Americans as one in which they are not merely treated with indifference, but are not even seen. This can be confirmed in street scenes in American films of the first half of the twentieth century, in which African-Americans rarely, if ever, appear. Similarly, poststructuralist theorists have likened the traditional image of the feminine in Western culture to a kind of 'dark continent', in Hélène Cixous's famous phrase. The other, in both these cases, is represented as a sort of blind spot, an invisibility in the standard economy of representation.

Given this invisibility, a key aim of identity politics is to make social groups appear. Minority and immigrant ethnic groups have laid claim to the street as a legitimate forum for the promotion and exhibition of traditional dress, food, and culture. For 1970s feminism, publishing and documentary making were crucial to the uncovering of female experience and perspective. Similarly, festivals such as the Sydney Gay and Lesbian Mardi Gras insist that sexual identities and cultures outside the heterosexual mainstream must not just be allowed freedom from persecution but also equal rights to appearance, on their own terms.

The politics of identity, therefore, is a politics of visibility and invisibility. Because it must deal with a tradition of representation that insists on subsuming varied social practices to a standard norm, its struggle is as much on the page, screen, and website as it is at the barricade and in the parliament, traditional forums of political intervention before the postmodern. Similarly, the domain of cultural theory has seen an intense struggle over identity and definition. For those seeking to assert the validity of marginalised viewpoints, universities have become important contexts. Courses in indigenous, women's, and gay and lesbian studies have drawn attention to the hidden history of cultures that have had to spurn and conceal their diversity.

Thinkers coordinated with these developments have also analysed the reduction of the other to the same not only as a useful strategy for dominant social groups, but also as a way of understanding the function of culture. We noted above that in Freudian psychoanalysis, for example, the reduction of the feminine to a masculine principle constructs the phallus as the crucial arbiter of gender definition. As Luce Irigaray has consistently noted, this idealisation of the phallic unquestioningly results in the Western fascination with unity, consistency, and purity, and produces a hostility towards ambiguity, contradiction, and open-endedness. Art critics fetishise an artwork's structural unity; politicians call for us all to subordinate our diverse needs to a single national purpose, and our bosses want us to pull together. The price to be paid for this drive towards homogenisation is that hierarchies of the more or less purposeful, the more or less unified, and the more or less meaningful map out dividing lines that not only set off one activity against another, but also one social group against another. Marginalised social groups not only contest the material ascendancy of the mainstream, therefore, but also challenge its cultural logic. The reduction of the other to the same can be seen as both the tactic and the faith of the dominant. Plurality, diversification, and irresolution can often appear to this culture as first steps towards social breakdown and chaos.

Performativity

Identity politics has been very successful in liberal democratic societies in the last quarter of the twentieth century. Although prejudice, hostility, and violence remain, and the cultural mainstream continues to fiercely 'other' minority groups, progress has been made in terms of government policy and institutional practice. It is in this success, and the ongoing need for more to be done, that identity politics finds its justification.

Recently, however, there has been a dramatic problematisation of the whole notion of identity. When we review the various strands of the argument as we have outlined them above, we can see how this has emerged. If identity politics defines us in relation to other people, it may be very successful in mapping out distributions of power, resources, and visibility amongst different social groups. Yet, by defining us in relation to one another, it inevitably implies that our identities are not an expression of our real or essential nature, but distinguishing marks that only have meaning in a specific context and a specific economy of representation. Rather than being fixed or true in any simple sense, they are the result of a complex and contingent historical process that has come up with a particular set of ethnic denominations, sexual classifications, and gender practices. If I am Australian, American, or Filipino, I only take on this identity as a result of an almost unimaginably complex and barely coordinated set of historical events that have set national boundaries in certain places, demarcated states one from another and attributed certain names to them, and so on. Much as I might like to see this identity as a product of my own nature as it conjoins with all others who seek to claim it as well, it is really the crystallisation of a set of impersonal historical developments. In order to appear in the social world, we conflate ourselves with these identities. Yet inevitably, because they can never be authentically or completely our own, a gap or disjunction appears between us and our identities.

The identities themselves are also unstable. What it means to be a man or a woman, an Australian or an American, gay or straight is also constantly undergoing transformation. Identities calcify into stereotypes. New identities challenge and subvert them. Men cease being impassive and are called upon to express their feelings. Women cease being the guardians of sexual modesty and are called upon to express their desire. Australians cease being rough and rustic and are called upon to be cosmopolitan and multicultural, and so on. These transformations and the inevitable backlashes against them are all accompanied, even policed, by a subtle yet unavoidable pressure for us all to present ourselves, to *be,* in specific ways. For example, men will be ridiculed for being unemotional in one context, and too emotional in others.

Thus there is an arbitrary quality to the way identity groups separate from one another, and there is also a forced conformity within each group. We must act as if we know what it is to be one thing and not another, where the dividing line falls between us and those who are different to us. Judith Butler, the American cultural theorist who has been most influential in analysing identity in this way, describes the identifications we make as 'imaginary . . . phantasmatic efforts of alignment [and] loyalty' (Butler, 1993: 105). This is not to say that we simply invent our identities in some make-believe or idle way. Butler's understanding of the function of identity here draws on psychoanalytic theory to see the process of self-identification as part of the complex way in which we seek to make ourselves in the world. We use these identities as a way of stabilising our experience, of making ourselves into something that will not only become secure but will be continually validated by the world around us. We seek the other's recognition, even approval. When we appear to be something, it must be something that has meaning to the other, and the massive, impenetrable social forces the other represents. By assimilating ourselves to known and recognised identities we become someone.

This understanding of identities and the patterned behaviour that proves our connection to them is known as 'performativity'. We do not express our inner nature in our identities so much as we perform identities in order to give the impression that we have a recognisable, orthodox, acceptable inner nature, even if it is a radical or marginalised one. It is important, however, to distinguish performativity from mere performance. We do not put on our identities the way an actor puts on a costume. We are not free and unique selves that then choose an identity that suits or amuses us. We can only appear in the social world by adopting a recognisable identity. Our selfhood depends on our doing this. The repetition of certain acts—certain styles of dress, speech, and gesture—is what allows us to be recognised as men or women, a distinction that has to be made clearly in order for us to appear in the regular social world. This repetition is demanded of us. We cannot simply decide whether we want to collaborate with it or not.

The purpose of drawing attention to the constructed, even enforced, nature of identity is not part of a backlash against the achievements of identity politics, although many of the proponents of the latter are highly suspicious, even hostile towards these insights. Identity politics activists see them as undermining the political progress that has been made by marginalised groups, fearing that the very terms by which they define themselves are being invalidated just as they are securing some sort of social place. On the other hand, theorists of performativity such as Butler argue that identity inevitably creates hierarchies within each identity group: the more or less feminine, the more or less authentically gay, and so on. To be accepted one must conform to some set of recognisable practices and appearances. This undermines the rhetoric of identity politics, which validates self-expression, coded as liberation. Similarly, it misrepresents the nature of our interior lives, which remain irreducibly diverse, ambiguous, and unstable. Our desires, for example, continually contradict and subvert one another in a way that defies the easy categorisation that distinguishes the few acceptable identities our culture allows us.

The conflict between proponents of identity politics and the theory of performativity is not easily adjudicated. This can be seen in a recent controversy about the 'male lesbian'. In the economy of sexual identities that we have inherited from the nineteenth century, a male lesbian is a contradiction in terms, an impossibility. The logic of identity politics sees lesbians as an oppressed group of women who desire other women. However, to the theory of performativity, gender and sexual identities (like maleness or lesbianism) are historical constructs that deny the complexity of subjectivity and desire: why is it not possible for a person whose body is biologically male (as defined by the structure of their genitals) to imagine themselves a woman who loves women, whose desire for other women repudiates the conventions and logic of heterosexual practice? We do not have to reflect long before we can see our desire as this fluid, obscure, and complex, and the identities we impose on it as reductive and restricting. On the other hand, women who have been abused and attacked for identifying themselves as lesbian and for living a lesbian lifestyle may feel aggrieved that their hard-fought-for identity can be taken over by men who have not experienced the same degree of risk in association with their sexuality. This controversy has a long way to run. As we can see from the examples given in this chapter, the debate about performativity has been most dramatic in the areas of gender and sexuality, and it is a major contribution to the burgeoning field of Queer theory, which will be discussed again in Chapter 12.

In sum, postmodern cultural politics has not seen culture as a mere reflection or by-product of political activity being played out elsewhere. For modernism, there is a knowable political context that develops according to its own momentum. A cultural product, like an individual work of art, merely reflects that context. The artwork might need its context, but the context is where the main action is. For postmodern cultural politics, the relationship between cultural practice and politics is far more complex. The shifting and volatile play of identities opens up the material world to the interactions of textuality and meaning, to the point where the two become inseparable. No cultural activity is absolutely distinguishable from politics, and no politics can separate itself completely from cultural and textual determinants and structures. This results in a politics that is far more complex, unstable, and obscure, a politics that defies the grand narratives' clear (and, if we are to believe Lyotard, murderous) sense of absolute right and wrong, and a fixed and final destiny.

Further Reading

There is a huge amount of material on the cultural politics of postmodernism. Most of the chapters above include references to books on the politics of culture and textuality, or on the key issues of identity politics: race, gender, and class. The best place to start is with one of the anthologies of essays and articles, such as the influential collection of conference papers edited by Laurence Grossberg et al, simply entitled *Cultural Studies* (1992) or Simon During's *The Cultural Studies Reader* (2nd edn, 1999); or an overview treatment of recent cultural politics such as Glenn Jordan and Chris Weedon's *Cultural Politics: Class, Gender, Race and the Postmodern World* (1995). Judith Butler has been the most influential theorist of performativity. Her key works are *Gender Trouble* (1990), *Bodies That Matter* (1993) and *The Psychic Life of Power* (1997). An important collection on the crisis in identity politics is L. Nicholson and S. Seidman's *Social Postmodernism: Beyond Identity Politics* (1995).

PART FOUR

Texts and Subjects

Introduction

This part covers one of the most important recent developments in the new humanities: subjectivity. Put simply, theories of subjectivity analyse what is referred to by the word 'I'. Where does it come from? What is its structure? How does it relate to language, texts, and representations? How does it fit into the politics of gender, ethnicity, race, and class? It has become a truism of the humanities that the human individual was once (wrongly) thought of as whole, single, and naturally occurring, but that recent theories present it as split, multiple, and implicated in the complex processes of culture and politics.

Chapter 10 outlines the main psychoanalytic theories of subjectivity, from Freud and Lacan onwards. The rejection of the psychoanalytic tradition by poststructuralists presents subjectivity as a construct of the relationship between power and knowledge (in the work of Foucault), while in Deleuze and Guattari the subject is seen as produced from the multiple and dynamic energies of desire and possibility. This alternative to psychoanalysis is explained in Chapter 11. This part concludes with an introductory survey of some recent discussions of sexuality. From Freud to Queer theory, modern understandings of subjectivity have emphasised the place of sexuality as a focus of personal definition, social administration, and cultural work. Here we present this issue as a way of understanding the interrelationships between culture, textuality, politics, and subjectivity that have been the emphases of this book.

10

The Edge of the Mirror: The Subject and the Other

To demonstrate how the concept of subjectivity has been radically rethought in the second half of the twentieth century, we will focus on a number of different, but often interconnected, models. Although there are certain antagonisms between these systems of thought, there is also a sustained and well developed set of common features. It is the shared features that we will concentrate on here, rather than the differences. What is important to note at the outset is that many of these background perceptions are derived from the challenges to a certain history of subjectivity. In the eighteenth century there were a number of developments in the sciences, philosophy, politics, and humanities, which became known as the Enlightenment. Driven by a desire and (for their philosophy) need to see human subjectivity as utopian, complete, whole, and secure, Western thought since this time has been dominated by models that celebrate the achievements and potential of humanity. However, in the excesses of this humanist movement the celebration became orgiastic and self-congratulatory. These extremes led writers, such as Voltaire (1694–1778), to pen biting attacks and satires on their own times. Whatever well meaning and positive plans the Enlightenment had for human society, there was equally a blindness and narrowness of vision. Fundamental to this were the theories of subjectivity, for they informed almost every facet of social consciousness, including cultural identification, religion, systems of analysis, and developments in the arts and sciences. One of the foundations of this interpretation of subjectivity is the set of ideas developed in Descartes's theory of the *cogito*.

Although Descartes (1591–1650) predates the Enlightenment, his influence was so great that he is often seen as a precursor to the period and its philosophies. When Descartes strove to determine a site of certainty, and declared that this is to be found in human consciousness (the famous dictum of *'cogito, ergo sum'*—'I think therefore I am'), he marked a phase in history that would dominate the production of ideas for the next 200 years. It is important to realise that developments in the sciences gave rise to a sense that everything could be known and explained. Part of this certainty of knowledge was on defining human existence and social life. This interpretation of subjectivity as knowable and definable was challenged most directly, and quite specifically in a number of cases, in the developments of poststructuralism, and what has been termed here as the new humanities. To consider how this has happened we can turn to some illustrative ideas from psychoanalysis and deconstruction.

Psychoanalysis and the Subject

In many ways Freud played a key role in the formation of the new theories of the subject in the twentieth century. In total opposition to the idea of the complete and whole subject, Freud postulated that the subject was fragmented, split, and often at odds with itself and its social surroundings. We only have to consider his topographic, economic, and dynamic models of the mind to see how significant rupture and division is to the definition of subjectivity in psychoanalysis. These three models, which Freud described as a metapsychology of the mind, are related in that they attempt to provide an overall structure to explain how the subject is formed through the layers or divisions of the mind.

The topographical division is that of the conscious, preconscious, and unconscious. The conscious mind, that which is most familiar to us, allows the subject to operate in a social context. The preconscious lies just below the surface of the conscious, almost as a buffer zone. The unconscious is a repository of all those drives and desires deemed unsuitable by the highly censored conscious mind. In the economic model Freud argues that the mind is determined through the management of energies and their flow. This is strongly connected to his ideas on repression. Basically Freud argued that the mind operates in terms of balance and imbalance, with various mechanisms of the psyche trying to control and regulate thoughts, desires and passions. This is connected to the third model, that of the dynamic. The unconscious constantly attempts to manifest itself in the conscious. However, because it is devised and constituted by anti-social desires (dominated by the id with its sex drive and death drive) the conscious mind, through the super-ego, represses these thoughts. They are never forgotten, but instead return in disguised forms, such as dreams and slips of the tongue.

Even in so short a summary, what becomes obvious is that in the Freudian model the subject is far from whole, either within itself or its environment. Instead there are a series of competing forces and energies, of potential imbalances and disruptions. The subject, for Freud, contains within itself ideas and feelings that it could never consciously understand or come to terms with. There are parts of the psyche that are totally antagonistic to other parts, as well as having a disregard for others in the social world order. Even within the internal workings of the mind itself there is conflict where each part has little regard for the others. Consider Freud's theory of the pleasure principle and reality principle. The pleasure principle is based on the premise that certain desires demand immediate and total fulfillment, regardless of the consequences either to others or even to the subject himself or herself. It presents a very real danger to the self because any sense of preservation of the self is ignored. To balance this, the reality principle continually seeks the deferral of such desires. Such a situation produces a constant interplay of conflict between the drives for pleasure and the self-preservation of the subject and the social world order. Freud is careful not to privilege either of these processes, and make one seem more appropriate or valid as a state of mind. In doing so he acknowledges that such internal conflict is a necessary part of subjectivity. Such a model is a long way from the Enlightenment's view of the complete person.

Lacan takes up the Freudian model and extends it in a number of directions, one of the most significant being the subject's relationship to others and the self in discourse. Lacan uses Freud's interpretations of the *Ichspaltung*—the split subject—to examine the multiplicity of ruptures that define subjectivity. Central to this is the negotiation of the social world, Lacan's symbolic order, by the subject. This is where Lacan draws on both psychoanalysis and semiotics to devise a theory that encapsulates the subject's relationship to the signifier. To understand some of the ways in which Lacan develops this idea we need to return to one of his earliest theories—that of the Mirror Stage—and consider how it relates to his ideas of the 'symbolic', the 'imaginary', and the 'real'. Here we will be concerned with the implications of these terms in the study of subjectivity in this poststructuralist and postmodern context.

One of Lacan's most famous theories was written early in his life, which is significant because it informed so much of later Lacanian theory. The theory is well known by now, but worth a short summary here. Lacan argued that at around the age of eighteen months the child goes through a sort of self-reflexive and revolutionary development. He or she becomes aware of the inadequacies of the self (whereas prior to this there was a feeling of complete and whole subjectivity, dominated by an egocentric view of the world), and of the lacks that define its existence. It is especially the lack of speech—that is, in effect the signifier—and the inability to communicate with others competently that compels the subject to enter into the symbolic. This order is dominated by the social constructions of knowledge and the power of the signifier and, because it exists prior to the subject's entry, is always seen in terms of otherness. It is also important to note that in this theory the Mirror Stage also marks the beginning of the Oedipal complex. Without going too far into this, the Oedipal complex is significant in Freudian and Lacanian theory, not simply because of its sexual politics, but also because it is a determining development in the sexualisation of the subject. In other words, the Oedipal complex is when the subject becomes gendered and social attitudes are imposed on it. For Lacan this also marks the point of the subject's defining relationship with the signifier, and so with power.

Lacan argued that the subject spends the rest of his or her life striving to possess the signifier and gain acceptance in the symbolic—which is always an impossibility. In doing so the subject becomes defined through a series of desires that can never be satisfied, and absences that compel many actions and thoughts. Once more we witness a model of subjectivity predicated on conflict and rupture, rather than on closure and certainty. What we must be careful of is seeing such descriptions in a totally negative light. Both Freud and Lacan argue that this subjectivity is as creative and fecund as it is negative. For them one of the key roles of psychoanalysis is to understand such psychic structures and mechanisms. Later we will see how such theories have become inflected in different ways through a number of critical concerns.

We have already encountered Lacan's idea of the symbolic, but we also need to grasp his concepts of the imaginary and real in order to understand better this model of the split subject. The imaginary is a fundamental part of the Mirror Stage, because it is this dominance of the visual—the image—which leads the subject into self-reflection. In this sense the imaginary is about the formation of the subject in terms of the self. It is partly because of the centrality of the imaginary field in this crucial early development that the visual is so significant in the formation of the subject. One of the theoretical consequences of this has been a proliferation of Lacanian-based film theory. Indeed, Lacan's theory of the gaze has had one of the most powerful impacts on the humanities, not only in the visual arts (cinema and painting), but also on the literary and dramatic.

If the symbolic is the social order, and the imaginary is the subject's sense of the self in relation to this order, to others, and to itself, then the real can be defined as neither of these. What is left is, in effect, the unconscious. Lacan's use of the term real to define aspects of the unconscious is quite startling and provocative. What he is suggesting is that what is normally seen as the real/reality—the everyday and its objects—is only a (social) construction. The real for the psyche will always be the demands, desires, and drives of the unconscious, for these never leave us, continually influence us, and determine our actions and reactions.

The combination of these orders of the symbolic, imaginary, and real, as well as the foundational premise of the *Ichspaltung*, inflects Lacan's works into many fields. It is partly because of this that his work has proven to be so instrumental in the development of poststructuralism and the changing of studies in the humanities. Before we move on to an example of how we might employ some of these Lacanian concepts in the analysis of texts we will introduce some related terms. This is because one of the issues at stake here is how these theories discuss the relationship of subjectivity to the other.

Lacan (1977) constructs the following formula to examine how the subject, driven by insatiable desires, operates in a relationship to the other:

Before we go any further with this formula it is important to understand what the other means in Lacanian theory. Lacan describes two orders of otherness—the *grand Autre* (the 'big' Other, hereafter designated with a capital O) and *objet petit a* (the object of the little other). The Other is the realm of otherness, containing all the variations and permutations of that which is not the self. The *objet petit a* is the various range of objects of desire that come to stand in for the realm of otherness. So, we desire the Other, but because it is so impossible we invest objects of otherness with the same type of desire. In the above formula the 'a' represents the *objet petit a* and the '$\emptyset$' represents the split subject. Between them lie alienation and aphanisis. It is through these latter two that the split subject enters into a relationship with its objects of desire. Alienation is clear enough—it marks the distance that is always there between the subject and such objects. Aphanisis is a little more complex. Lacan argues that we are compelled by that which we desire to the point where we actually invest certain signifiers with a sense of representing our own subjectivity. Aphanisis is the fear of the loss of such signifiers. To give a simple example: after writing words for this book the authors sometimes sit at a café on the street, drink coffee, and watch the cars go past. A common pastime for some young men is to drive their much-loved cars (sporting a great deal of chrome and loud music) up and down the road past the cafés. These cars are much more than vehicles, they are objects of desire for the men (and, it is hoped by these same men, in this curious ritual for mating, the women). The relationship they have to them is one of aphanisis and alienation: they invest their subjectivity into the objects, but must also harbour fears about this representation (other men's bigger,

faster cars with louder music, and of course the fear of breakdown).
As with all forms of desire, there is always a lack and a fear of loss.

Deconstruction and Subjectivity

As with psychoanalysis, it is impossible to summarise all the features
of how deconstruction has engaged in the issue of subjectivity. What
we can do is illustrate how this branch of philosophy has engaged in
some of the issues. Philosophy itself has always been concerned with
the subject, its formation, and the critical methodologies developed to
understand it. What deconstruction does is actually look at the very
system of philosophy as it has tried to do this. One of the main ways
it has done this, particularly in the work of Derrida, is to focus on the
issues of self-consciousness. For its entire history, Western philosophy
has attempted to define what makes human consciousness unique.
One of the main arguments has been that it has self-consciousness—
that is, that it can be, and is, aware of its own sense of existence. Derrida is not so much concerned with what self-consciousness is, or how
it is achieved (two aspects central to many areas of Western philosophy), but instead concentrates on the very models, tropes, and mechanisms that philosophy has devised to investigate these issues.

Part of this issue for Derrida is the idea of subjectivity as presence.
Derrida argues that one of the dominant models in philosophy has
been to privilege certain sites of subjectivity as being more legitimate
and valid. In his deconstruction of this metaphysics of presence Derrida is devising a series of analyses against the sense of privileged presences, and the philosophical methodology of metaphysics.[1] This is a
complex and sustained project, with consequences for many different
fields of study. For although Derrida is primarily concerned with philosophy and its texts, his challenge to the systems of analysis are
applicable to most, if not all, interpretative systems. In fact Derrida
has always had a strong literary inclination, arguing that he writes the

---

1 Metaphysics is a diverse set of inquiries, varying in definition depending on the line of
 philosophy taken. In the most general sense it is that branch of philosophy that is primarily concerned with being, usually in conjunction with knowledge. It is also concerned with configurations of existence in terms of the whole, rather than a set of
 parts. Significantly, the term is derived from the works of Aristotle.

literary as much as he does the philosophical,[2] so that his style reflects an interdisciplinary interest. An example will help to illustrate this.

One of the most sustained discussions by Derrida on this issue of subjectivity and presence is in his analysis of *ousia* (Greek for 'substance') and *parousia* (Greek for 'arrival'). These are very old terms, dating back to Aristotle's *Categories*, which relate to the concept of being as presence. Derrida attempts to show how these terms have become invested in Western thought so that they have passed from speculation to the status of truths. That is to say, philosophy has lost the capacity to recognise its own biases and blindspots. It cannot see its own metaphors in analytic techniques and methodologies, so that a concept such as 'truth' or 'subjectivity' passes beyond the analysis at hand. Derrida explores examples from many different philosophical sources, including Aristotle (in his *Margins of Philosophy* (1986b)), Plato and Socrates (in his *The Postcard: From Socrates to Freud and Beyond* (1987a)) Rousseau (in his *Of Grammatology* (1976)), Freud, in effect, as philosopher, Hegel and Nietzsche (in his *Writing and Difference* (1978)). It is this weight that constructs what Derrida describes as a will to *parousia*.

The difficulty lies in how such centrality and presence is defined and determined. In the early and highly influential essay 'Structure, Sign, and Play in the Discourse of the Human Sciences' Derrida (1978: 278–93) analyses the constructions and privileging of centres and margins, arguing that the idea of a centre is only possible through an artificiality. As with concepts such as origins or presence, the centre has nothing inherent within it that positions and defines it as such. Rather it is a set of forces and interpretations that sustain the pretence. In this sense deconstruction must examine, and ultimately challenge, systems that produce ideas of centres, origins, and the privilege of presence as truths rather than metaphors.

There are a number of significant aspects to this. In terms of a feminist politic, for example, it is very important that the structures that position masculine sexuality as the centre be revealed for what they are;

---

2 See, for example, 'Derrida l'insoumis' (*Le Nouvel observateur*, 9 September 1983), where he talks about being drawn to the literary rather than the philosophical. Derrida's writing is very much literary, playing with meaning, polysemes, and puns.

in terms of postcolonialism, the ideologies of cultural centres can be revealed if such centres are seen only as constructs; the idea of an author who creates an original work is much more problematic in a deconstructionalist analysis because the very notion of origins must be scrutinised. All of these examples feed back into the processes of subjectivity—sexuality, culture and ideology, and the origins (and originality) of thought (invested in an individual) become sites of subjectivity that must be understood in themselves as well as their manifestations.

One of Derrida's strategies against the will to *parousia*, the foregrounding of centres and presence, and so on, is his concept of *différance*. This concept includes, but goes far beyond, the common interpretations of meaning, being based on acts of difference and deferral (hence Derrida's neologism), rather than being a fixed and knowable structure. For in *différance* Derrida encapsulates this whole issue of Western thought, focusing on a resistance to the fixing of meaning and the reliance on established systems of analysis. Against, for example, the idea of a privileged, centred site of subjectivity invested in sexuality (phallocentrism) a reading of *différance* will produce a reading of the sexual subject that is multiple, unfixed, and capable of aberrations. What is at issue is not heterosexuality, homosexuality, and bisexuality, but a relationship between gender and subjectivity that goes beyond, and resists, such categories and possible centres.

To illustrate better these ideas from psychoanalysis and deconstruction we will now turn to a specific example. This text—John McTiernan's film *Die Hard* (1988)—is selected partly because initially it would seem to be a highly unlikely candidate to illustrate such concepts. By applying them to such a film we can investigate how such concepts might be applied to a wide variety of texts and concerns. Rather than choose a text that in itself explores issues of subjectivity (as, for example, de Beauvoir's *All Men Are Mortal*, Kafka's *Metamorphosis*, or Shakespeare's *Hamlet* can be said to do), *Die Hard* has been selected so we can focus on the ideas themselves. Implicit within a choice of such an example is that we can use with great effectiveness an example such as *Die Hard* to discuss the issues of subjectivity, and not rely on declarations of art or the canon.

It is important to recall that for Lacan certain foundational relationships of subjectivity are based on the operation of the symbolic—

that is, the signifier in its social and cultural contexts, and the subject's interaction within them. Subjectivity, in this sense, is formulated through the psychic apparatus (the unconscious, the drives, etc.) and social forces. Once the subject engages in the symbolic he or she is constructed by that very order. There are, for example, issues of gender, race, class, and language that shape the subject's position in the symbolic, and its psychic responses. Within these interactions is the play of the subject and the objects of desire and the other. The *objet petit a* can be the object represented by the signifier, or the signifier itself, or a combination of the two (it is this final permutation that is the most common). By engaging in the cultural *objet petit a* subjectivity is actually formed in a social context. Because of the dangers, errors, and problematics of this relationship, however, subjectivity for Lacan is almost always devised through variations of alienation and aphanisis.

If we evoke Lacan's model of the split subject's relationship to its objects of desire in terms of the main character (John McClain) in *Die Hard*, it is possible to see how aspects of subjectivity are formulated through these paradigms. The *objet petit a* can be read in a number of different ways and contexts—four will suffice in this discussion. These four—his wife, moral issues, other people (that is, the socialised world order), and freedom—also illustrate how the splitting of the subject takes place in the symbolic. This can be represented as follows:

$$\text{\$} \qquad \diamond \qquad\qquad a$$

(McClain)   (wife, other people, morality, freedom)

McClain is constantly positioned as split from the three social groups portrayed—the social world order of 'everyday' people, the 'terrorists'[3], and his wife (who stands metonymically for concepts such as social stability, marriage and family, social responsibility).

---

3 It is important that there is some ambiguity about the group of men that takes over the office block and holds the workers hostage. For the majority of the film, all the other characters, as well as the reader, are kept in the dark as to what they actually want. The criminals themselves feign terrorist aims and objectives to the police. When it is revealed that the true aim of their violence is theft, the textual intent is to make them seem less worthy—that is, it is not a political struggle, but rather a crime of robbery.

His alienation from them represents a seemingly irreparable split within McClain towards the symbolic. He is always located out-side—as the other—of social relationships and cultural contexts. This is the first order of McClain's *Ichspaltung*, a subject split from the regularities of social bonds. Even the terrorists are depicted as having a sense of community and order within their own social struc-ture. This is a fairly common representation of the protagonist in this genre—the outsider whose bonds to social order are at best fragile, and usually absent. One of the consequences of this is that the for-mation of subjectivity resists many of the symbolic restrictions, not the least being the capacity to kill. This death drive is possible only because the subject is not restricted by social repression. Compare this to Hamlet, who demonstrates many of the same splits, and is constantly aligned with death, but who has an incapacity to act.

The vel (the diamond that joins the split subject to his/her objects of otherness and desire) is constructed in terms of life and death. Under 'life' we would also list emotive and ideological constructions such as morality, freedom, American (as opposed to foreign); while under 'death' these same aspects take on a negative inflection. McClain's subjectivity is tied to 'life' through aphanisis, so it becomes more than an issue of mortality. The fact that he can choose to escape, and yet doesn't, invests the signifiers of the *objet petit a* with aspects of his own idealised subjectivity (that is, American, moral, and free)—hence the processes of aphanisis. Similarly, the relationship to 'death' is for-mulated around alienation, but it is still a part of his split subjectivity.[4]

Reading these same issues through Derrida's deconstruction of *ousia, parousia* and *différance* we can examine constructions of subjectivity from a different, yet often compatible, angle. In terms of self-reflexivity, *Die Hard* uses soliloquies to humanise McClain. Throughout the film he continually talks to himself, commenting, explaining and making jokes. This has a certain narrative-driven function, but one of the consequences is that it establishes his

---

4 See also Lacan's discussion of the vel, where he discusses the relationship of life and freedom to the choices made by the subject. In this example it is significant that of all the characters only McClain actually has the choice of this vel. See Lacan's *The Four Fundamental Concepts of Psychoanalysis* (1977), especially the section entitled 'The Subject and Other'.

subjectivity for the reader. The hostages are largely undeveloped as characters, and the terrorists demonstrate a subjectivity that is dehumanised and alien. In other words, it is the self-reflexivity of McClain that enforces and confirms his subjectivity for the reader. The monologues explain and give reason, whereas the actions of the terrorists are not explained until near the end. Because we experience his fears, plans, and tribulations, McClain's subjectivity is foregrounded and so elicits more sympathy.

A further consequence of this foregrounding of McClain's subjectivity is that it is represented through the body and under constant threat. In other words, its presence is always threatened with absence (of a conflict in *ousia* and *parousia*). However, his presence is a mistake and is continually represented in liminal areas. We encounter him in elevators (both in and on top of), in air-conditioning shafts, in stairwells, on the roof top, in the basement, in the unfinished rooms of the building, in bathrooms—all spaces that are not part of the usual presences of office buildings. McClain's subjectivity is formulated outside of the symbolic order of terrorists/criminals, hostages, office workers, and police. It is a subjectivity of *différance* because it belongs to no other social group (in a sense the symbolic) and is continually under threat (that is, his existence is deferred and differed rather than assured).

The subject positions within the film contest with one another for the privileged presence of Western thought. The will to *parousia* operates through a violence of 'beingness' more than any single crime. The threat of death is constantly evoked through this struggle for presence. This is why when the motives for the crime are revealed the subjectivity of the criminals is brought even further into question. The object of desire for the criminals is money rather than an ideological cause, whereas McClain's actions are motivated by the care of others rather than himself.

Further Reading

In one sense this chapter tries to illustrate some of the ideas from Derrida and Lacan. So to remain true to this aim this list of suggested further readings will focus on them rather than on the impossible task of texts on subjectivity.

Derrida is a prolific writer, and how one approaches his work will depend largely on what one wants to do with it. To come to terms with Derrida himself the best place to start is Derrida's own introduction to *Positions* (1981b). This is Derrida's early attempt to set the scene for his critical methodology. To witness the deconstructionalist method in action, his collection *Writing and Difference* (1978) is a good place to begin. Two essays in particular are good starting points: 'Structure, Sign and Play in the Discourse of the Human Sciences' is an early conference paper given by Derrida, and it was instrumental in the formation of what we now know as deconstruction; 'Cogito and the History of Madness' is Derrida's response to Foucault's *Madness and Civilization* (1967). Read in conjunction with this book (and Foucault's own response to this), the essay provides a good example of the sorts of issues at the core of poststructuralism. For a sustained set of (deconstructional) analyses, Derrida's earlier *Of Grammatology* (1976) is also useful. (Spivak's introduction is a lengthy and often insightful guide.) *Margins of Philosophy* (1986b) is essential for anyone interested in positioning Derrida within a larger history of philosophy; just as *Dissemination* (1981a) allows us to see Derrida examine one of his favourite areas—language and discourse. His *The Truth in Painting* (1987b) is a fascinating study on the visual. Finally, for anyone interested in Derrida's interpretation of Freud and Lacan, the best place to start is *The Postcard: From Socrates to Freud and Beyond* (1987a).

Apart from the two often-cited works by Lacan—*Écrits: A Selection* (1985) and *The Four Fundamental Concepts of Psychoanalysis* (1977)—other key works on his theories of subjectivity include *The Psychoses* (1993), which investigates one of Freud's case studies, and in doing so seeks to explain the relationship between subjectivity and knowledge; and *The Ethics of Psychoanalysis* (1992), with its concerns with the sociocultural relations of the formation of the subject. For those feeling inspired (and with a knowledge of French!) two essential works that have yet to be translated are *Encore* (1975), which contains Lacan's curious ideas on *jouissance* and women, and *L'envers de la psychanalyse* (1991), which has the most beautiful discussions on systems of discourse, formations of subjectivity, and the force of the hysteric.

11

Making and Unmaking the Subject

Psychoanalysis does not represent the only attempt at theorising subjectivity in the postmodern era. Alternative theories have arisen, especially in the work of Foucault, and Deleuze and Guattari, some of which take as their starting point a rigorous and thorough-going attack on the assumptions and claims of psychoanalysis. Foucault has indeed argued that theories that claim, implicitly or explicitly, to offer an explanation for diverse phenomena across the breadth of the social and cultural field, that claim in effect to be what he calls 'totalitarian theories', have proved to be more a hindrance than a blessing. Theoretical projects, such as Marxism and psychoanalysis, which see everything as repetitions or fulfillments of a single set of models, distract us from the instability, obscurity, and contingency of historical events.

This is not to say that history is without pattern and cannot be described. Rather, Foucault, like Nietzsche before him, has chosen to see history as what he calls 'genealogy'. Writing on Nietzsche, Foucault states: 'In placing present needs at the origin, the metaphysician would convince us of an obscure purpose that seeks its realization at the moment it arises. Genealogy, however, seeks to re-establish the various systems of subjection: not the anticipatory power of meaning, but the hazardous play of dominations' (1977: 148). The argument here contrasts two views of history—the metaphysical, which understands history as an implicitly meaningful process, and the genealogical, which sees history in terms of contingencies, provisionality, and discontinuity.

To the metaphysician, the present is the fulfillment of a meaningful purpose, which has sought this moment of its realisation from its very beginnings. The present, according to this logic, is always the product of a meaningful destiny. The past is itself made meaningful as the process by which this destiny has sought to evolve and deliver itself. Foucault is sceptical of this model of history because, in his words, it places 'present needs at the origin'. By this he means that our preoccupation with present concerns will always construe the past as the mere anticipation and production of ourselves, and what is important to us. We do not produce a model of history according to its own priorities and the structures it itself throws up. Instead we define history always according to our own needs, and ourselves as some sort of point of arrival. In this way, history is seen as *teleological*, fulfilling and completing a meaningful design. As in the grand narratives, analysed by Lyotard, metaphysical history selects events and themes that advance the idea that humanity is moving collectively on an ascending path through time.

Genealogy, on the other hand, seeks to recover the complex exchange of sometimes random, sometimes obscure, dominations and subordinations that constitute history. Instead of discarding or patronising events that fall outside the pattern of ascent inserted retrospectively into history by the metaphysician, the genealogist seeks to know how at any time power has been deployed, and the sort of life this power has made possible. What is important to Foucault, then, is not the rise of certain social classes, such as the rise of bourgeois parliamentary democracy at the expense of the aristocracy; nor things such as the gradual consolidation of the nation-state as the fundamental unit of collective organisation in the world. Understanding history in terms of these sorts of developments is metaphysical history to Foucault—it sees our present systems and structures as the cause and destination of historical evolution. Anything that did not contribute to these and like developments is no more than a curiosity or epiphenomenon to metaphysical history. Instead, Foucault is interested in the way individuals have been administered and the varying structures of power that have organised lives in the most banal and invisible way. Instead of the French Revolution, Foucault is interested in the daily timetable of the reformatory at Mettray, because it is emblematic of the rigorous discipline—the strict segmentation of time and separation of bodies and body parts—that has come to characterise how we are able to move, speak, and live.

The focus of this research is what we have traditionally called the individual, yet the model of individuality in question here is not the conventional one. The important thing, for Foucault, is that we do not see our individuality as naturally occurring, as something that arises spontaneously, and that society, coming to it from the outside, either cultivates or represses. Our individuality itself is a product of our relationship with power. Foucault writes:

> The individual is not to be conceived as a sort of elementary nucleus, a primitive atom, a multiple and inert material on which power comes to fasten or against which it happens to strike, and in so doing subdues or crushes individuals. In fact, it is already one of the prime effects of power that certain bodies, certain gestures, certain discourses, certain desires, come to be identified and constructed as individuals (Foucault, 1980b: 98).

The contrast here is between two models of individuality—one that idealises the individual by seeing it as something that exists in contradiction to power, society, and culture. Power, according to this alternative, is fundamentally alien to the individual, and an imposition on it. If left alone, the individual would be able to develop its natural potential. Power acts to limit and restrict this natural potential, subduing or crushing the individual. This model of the relationship between the subject and power has been a popular one in Western culture from Rousseau to the counter-culture of the 1960s. Foucault, however, does not agree with it. Instead, for him, one of the primary operations of power is to define individuality in certain specific terms. Out of the amorphous and open field of possibility, power selects certain types of behaviour, certain arrangements of the body and bodies, certain emotional states, and identifies them as the fundamental constituting parts of what is called individuality. The individual is not just the point of application of power—our definition of ourselves as, for example, sick or well, mad or sane, homosexual or heterosexual, male or female, turns us into a manifestation of social and political processes that are both the routines of administration, and the result of the quest for knowledge of social researchers. For Foucault such categories do not represent the truth of humanity as much as modes of knowledge that replicate and facilitate the operation of power by turning our interior life, our subjectivity, into material for analysis and transcription. In turn, this analysis defines what it is possible for us to be as subjects. We are to be made well, and kept sane and law abiding. We are to see the categories of gender and sexuality as impermeable and naturally occurring.

Towards the end of his career, Foucault argued that all his work, even that in the field of intellectual history, had had the subject as its primary focus. Summarising his work for a book published in 1982, Foucault wrote: 'My objective ... has been to create a history of the different modes by which, in our culture, human beings are made subjects. My work has dealt with [the] modes of objectification which transform human beings into subjects' (1982: 208). Now let us consider some of Foucault's major works in order to get a clear understanding of what they can contribute to our understanding of subjectivity.

The 1966 volume *Les mots et les choses* (literally, 'Words and Things'), translated into English as *The Order of Things: An Archaeology of the Human Sciences*, traces the transformation of various intellectual disciplines from the Renaissance to the modern era, analysing the varying philosophies of language on which they depend. The study concentrates on the way specific disciplines mutated in this period—why general grammar became philology, natural history became biology, and the analysis of wealth became political economy. The most famous and important theme of this work is that the nineteenth century saw the rise of a certain construction of humanity as an object of analysis and research. This version of humanity is the one chosen for study by the human sciences, including those just listed, but extends to psychology, sociology, criminology, and so on. The human being that is the object of this analysis is not a naturally occurring phenomenon, but something that has been constructed by, in broad terms, culture, but, more specifically, by the manoeuvrings of power and the methods of systematic research. Put simply, this version of 'man', the creature that lives, labours, and speaks, is a *historical* product to Foucault, one that arose at a certain time, as a result of the needs of certain power formations, and one that will also pass away. In fact, what distinguishes our present time for Foucault is that it seems to be the moment when this version of 'man' is reaching its end, and is beginning to disappear:

> Strangely enough, man—the study of whom is supposed by the naive to be the oldest investigation since Socrates—is probably no more than a rift in the order of things, or, in any case, a configuration whose outlines are determined by the new position he has so recently taken up in the field of knowledge. Whence all the chimeras of the new humanisms, all the facile solutions of an 'anthropology' understood as a universal reflection on man, half-empirical, half-philosophical. It is comforting, however, and a source of profound relief to think that man is only a recent invention, a figure not yet two centuries old, a new wrinkle in our knowledge, and that he will disappear again as soon as that knowledge has discovered a new form (Foucault: 1970, xxiii).

We can see here another version of the two views of history outlined earlier—what we have called the metaphysical and the genealogical. Metaphysical history sees the 'man' that has become the object of study in the modern era as a consistent issue and concern for intellectuals and cultural work from the foundation of Western intellectual history (conventionally identified with Socrates) to the present. This 'man' is a stable phenomenon, about whom universal truths can be formulated. What is important to metaphysical history is the sense that there is a consistent thread of development and ascent in the quest to understand man, and that our work in the present can be seen as both a significant contribution to it, and almost its end-point.

Genealogical history, on the other hand, is not satisfied by this romantic view of historical progress. To the genealogist, history is made up of discontinuities and inconsistencies. Man is a formation of recent arrival, one that represents a radical disjunction with what preceded it, and that will itself probably be abandoned in another similar event. Rather than being a continuity of progression, this history is a conformation of accidents. This is not to say that it is random and unknowable. It is, rather, turbulent and disproportionate, subject not to the clarification of meaning, but to the instabilities of politics.

Before we leave this phase of Foucault's work, it is worth identifying exactly what is meant by the 'man' that is the object of study of the human sciences, and how it relates to subjectivity. Foucault concludes that

> man for the human sciences is not that living being with a very particular form (a somewhat special physiology and an almost unique autonomy); he is that living being who, from within the life to which he entirely belongs and by which he is traversed in his whole being, constitutes representations by means of which he lives, and on the basis of which he possesses that strange capacity of being able to represent to himself precisely that life (1970: 352).

To theorise 'man' automatically means that the human body, that 'special physiology', is seen as an insufficient definition of the human. There must be something more essential, more abstract and universal that is seen as the necessary defining attribute of the human. This separation of the essentially human from the incontrovertibly biologically human has such a long history in Western (and other) cultures as to be almost uncontroversial. It underprops much of our ethical vocabulary—from the *human*itarianism of philanthropy to the in*human*ity of atrocity. Yet, Foucault's work implies, these definitions of what is essentially human are unstable and obscure. What is more they are in an endless process of change, which their attempted formulation in universalising maxims, and in legal and scientific generalisations, consistently seeks to deny.

What is distinctive about the human sciences' definition of humanity? First, this humanity is self-identical and single. What this means is that the human being conceives itself as a unified and coherent phenomenon, one not in contradiction with itself, and with all its parts coordinated with one another. If the model of the human we adopt is the individual body, this unity and coherence seem obvious enough. Yet, when we start to venture further into the domains of personality and interpersonal behaviour (from sexuality through economics to collective class, ethnic, and national identities) this coherence is harder to maintain. What is our economic self, where does it come from and how does it relate to the self that loves, fantasises, or goes mad? How does it relate to other selves as patterns of behaviour cross and recross one another? Are our national self and our sexual self the same? Critiques of universalising models of humanity draw attention to the overlaps, inconsistencies, and contradictions that map out our human life, and that consistently frustrate generalisation. These contradictions are what general statements about humanity have to reconcile by acts of either theoretical insistence or rhetorical extravagance.

The second important aspect of this definition of the human is its model of representation. The self-identical human fulfills the image of its own unity and coherence by representing itself to itself, and using these representations as a sort of currency for the stabilisation and continuity of social practices, and for the construction of cultural meanings. Again, this aspect of the human seems obvious enough, but one of the primary goals of Foucault's work here has been to emphasise the importance of different theories of language and representation for different formations of human history. The human being of the human sciences organises life around a set of representations of greater or lesser significance and authority, which plot norms of behaviour and possibilities of being. It is at this level that the work of radical intellectuals can intervene, showing how such representations affect our lives, and how by manipulating them we can imagine living otherwise.

In his essay 'What is Enlightenment?', published posthumously, Foucault outlined the logic behind the sort of critique he was already undertaking in *The Order of Things* (1970). He describes it this way: 'criticism is no longer going to be practiced in the search for formal structures with universal value, but rather as a historical investigation into the events that have lead us to constitute ourselves and to recognize ourselves as subjects of what we are doing, thinking, saying' (1984: 45–6). Formations such as the human sciences do not only have effects in an abstract theoretical or academic field, according to Foucault. The way knowledge locates, defines, and maps human behaviour has consequences for the way we live. In Foucault's terms, it plots out the possible ranges of behaving and being of which we can become subjects. If psychology and psychiatry map a range of possible behaviours on a line whose poles are sanity and insanity, we must position ourselves accordingly, reproducing behaviour already considered and reconsidered for us. If criminology already distinguishes between legal and illegal behaviour, we are always careful to present ourselves, even to think of ourselves, in these terms. We internalise, and in the end mimic, even become, the representations of possible human behaviour that the human sciences circulate around, between, and within us. Sanctions like institutionalisation exist to orient our behaviour towards one pole rather than another, and any attempt to live life without these alternatives is abominated. In the era of the human sciences and the mass administration of populations, it is impossible to imagine life outside of these polarities. Indeed such behaviour is always reduced to the negative end of the scale: claiming that there is no such dichotomy as that between sanity and insanity is replotted as insane or at least irrational behaviour. Claiming that there is no dichotomy between acceptable and illicit behaviour is impugned as clearly amoral, and therefore aberrant.

It is at the level of subjectivity then, the level at which individual interior experience is constructed and felt, that the human sciences have their greatest impact. Foucault goes on to say that criticism, as he describes it, is the place where the limitations of subjectivity can be challenged and transgressed. He continues:

> it will not deduce from the form of what we are what it is impossible for us to do and to know; but it will separate out, from the contingency that has made us what we are, the possibility of no longer being, doing, or thinking what we are, do or think. It is not seeking to make possible a metaphysics that has finally become a science; it is seeking to give impetus, as far and wide as possible, to the undefined work of freedom (1984: 46).

The contrast between metaphysical and genealogical history was discussed earlier. Here we have a refined version. The work Foucault seeks to promote will not outline a universal definition of what is true and untrue about humanity, which he characterises here in negative terms as constructing limits, deducing for us 'what it is impossible for us to do and to know', and making possible a 'metaphysics that has become a science'. Instead its role is to allow us to imagine our lives as other than they are, outside of the rigidly defined and policed alternatives that are presented to us in our particular moment of history. Foucault's analyses of the co-ordinated operations of institutions of social administration and the sets of writings that cluster around them constitute his most famous work. The combination of institutional practice and the writings of the human sciences Foucault characterised as discursive formations of the simultaneous operation of power and knowledge. In fact, the operation of power and knowledge here is considered one thing, which Foucault writes as 'power/knowledge', a single word. His first major work was *Folie et déraison: Histoire de la folie à l'âge classique* (1961), abridged and translated as *Madness and Civilization* (1967). The scope of this work does not lend it to easy summary, but suffice it to say that it traces changing perceptions and definitions of madness from the Renaissance into the Age of Reason, and beyond to the institutional practices of the eighteenth and nineteenth centuries. In this period, madness was transformed from a continual accompaniment, even inspiration, to social life, into a focus of psychiatric intervention and institutional administration. The mad ceased to be literal and metaphorical wanderers in the social landscape and became a marginal form of being, a danger to themselves and to society in general. They were categorised into specific types, based on theories of moral, physical, or sexual normality, and became subject first to policing, and second to medical intervention and research. This process gave birth both to a new type of institution—the asylum—and to a new type of knowledge—psychiatric therapy.

Here we see two things consistent with Foucault's larger project. The first is an elucidation of historical development in terms of sudden ruptures and discontinuities, such as that between the Renaissance view of madness as a kind of alternative insight, and the Classical eighteenth-century view that it is unreason, and therefore properly outside of any meaningful mode of understanding and communication—in effect, no better than a form of silence. The second is the early version proposed here of the co-ordination of institutional practice and scientific knowledge. Indeed, the study here presents a model of the historical processes that made this co-ordination a cardinal factor in modern life.

The other major study of power/knowledge Foucault provides is that which deals with prisons and punishment. *Surveiller et punir: Naissance de la prison* appeared in 1975, and was subsequently translated as *Discipline and Punish: The Birth of the Prison* (1977). One of the important themes of this work is to distinguish between two forms of punishment graphically described in the book's opening pages: the savage dismemberment of the body by torture and ritual public execution, and the systematic and routine monitoring of the institutionalised body, according to a rigorous timetable. The transition between these forms of punishment, which spans the eighteenth century, summarises the transition from a model of power that is centred and authoritarian (imaged in the body and prerogative of the sovereign) to one that is dispersed but immanent in every facet of social life. The image Foucault develops for the latter depends on a metaphorical adaptation of Jeremy Bentham's panopticon, a model prison in which the greatest number of prisoners could be supervised by a single guard in a central observation post. Indeed the panopticon works by making prisoners feel permanently watched according to strict regimens for the disposition of their bodies and the use of their time. As a consequence the prisoners internalise the surveillance, perpetually monitoring themselves according to received notions of normal and acceptable behaviour. This system is proposed by Foucault as a model of the way all institutions operate in modern Western life—not only the prison and the reformatory, but also the school, the armed forces, and the factory. All imitate one another in their strict rules about the presentation of bodies in rigidly delineated timetables. This is the beginning of the disciplinary society, in which the subject is not merely placed in relation to an external power that attempts to dominate and repress it, but, instead, becomes a form of the operation of that power, the point where the dividing line between acceptable and unacceptable, normal and abnormal behaviour operates and is policed. Foucault writes:

> it was no longer the offense, the attack on the common interest, it was the departure from the norm, the anomaly; it was this that haunted the school, the court, the asylum or the prison ... Replacing the adversary of the sovereign, the social enemy was transformed into a deviant, who brought with him the multiple danger of disorder, crime and madness. The carceral network linked, through innumerable relations, the two long multiple series of the punitive and the abnormal (1977: 300).

By way of this new and decentred operation of power, subjectivity itself becomes the site of social administration and, eventually, of political resistance.

The final phase of Foucault's work concentrated most explicitly on the issue of subjectivity, this time as it was felt in the domain of sexuality. We study this writing in detail in Chapter 12, which concentrates on sexuality as an issue. Suffice it to say here that one of Foucault's interests in *The History of Sexuality* (1980a; 1985; 1986), was to define subjectivity in terms of a possible 'aesthetics of existence', wherein the subject would perpetually re-imagine itself in an act of dynamic self-recreation. In the final volume, *The Care of the Self,* Foucault goes further to adapt the ancient ethos of sexual and bodily self-discipline as a possible model of an ethics of subjectivity, where a rigorous self-consciousness on the part of the individual subject allows him or her to perceive their location in cultural and political history, and inflect it towards the maximisation of a creative and political self-discipline.

The second important and related theory of subjectivity that we want to deal with is that developed in the collaborative work of Deleuze and Guattari, especially their *Capitalism and Schizophrenia.* Before embarking on an outline of their work, it is worth noting that subjectivity is only one of its dimensions, even though it is the one that interests us here. Their studies traverse the fields of anthropology, psychoanalysis, and political theory, as well as aesthetics, science, and numerology, to mention only a few. The work of Deleuze and Guattari constitutes one of the most monumental and ambitious cultural projects of the postmodern era, spanning a vast array of disciplines, huge blocks of history and a great variety of social and cultural practices, from nomadism to chaos theory.

Capitalism and Schizophrenia is comprised of two volumes: *Anti-Oedipus*, originally published in French in 1972, and *A Thousand Plateaus*, originally published in 1980. The former is a rigorous attack on psychoanalysis as it had been developed by Freud and Lacan, while the second is a collection of interconnected essays on a diverse range of cultural, philosophical, and aesthetic topics.

One of Deleuze and Guattari's fundamental projects is to reconsider the nature of desire. According to psychoanalysis, desire is understood as lack, the mythical depletion of the self experienced by the subject as it splits into conscious and unconscious dimensions. At the centre of the psychoanalytic subject is the experience of split, of incompleteness, of the loss of an imaginary unity that we always aspire to recover. To Deleuze and Guattari, this is a false and negative model of desire, imprisoning us in an experience of subjectivity as isolated and inadequate. Desire, instead, should be imagined in terms of a highly energised, dynamic, and open-ended series of interconnected possibilities—what they call 'producing-machines' or 'desiring-machines'. What we are presented with then is two competing models of the self: the psychoanalytic, which understands the subject as built around a central core of lack; and the anti- or schizoanalytic, which sees the self as the mere accidental or contingent collection point of myriad intersecting possibilities.

Deleuze and Guattari are absolutely and rigorously opposed to any conventional idea of the subject as an individual unity. This image of the self denies the dynamic interconnections that make up our relationship with the world around us. The radicalism of this thought and its challenge to conventional common sense cannot really be overstated. Something as simple as a person opening a door, to Deleuze and Guattari, is not a stable and consistent self performing an act on the inert material world, so much as the creation of a production machine that links the differing surfaces and bodies in an ephemeral co-ordination, a sort of door-opening production machine. Our relationship with the world is made up of this sort of situatedness, where the simple definitions we make between ourselves, each other, and the world around us no longer operate. They write: 'There is no such thing as man or nature now, only a process that produces the one within the other and couples the machines together. Producing-machines, desiring-machines, everywhere, schizophrenic machines, all of species life: the self and the non-self, outside and inside no longer have any meaning whatsoever' (1977: 2). The model of the self as a unity, even the Freudian model of the self as internalised loss, divides the world into artificial fixities built around the dream that within each there is a stable and recoverable essential truth. In Deleuze and Guattari, this idea of stable interior truth gives way to an imagining of dynamic and provisional interconnections, of a world in a vast web of endlessly multiplying changes, across a field of ever new interweaving surfaces, what they call, in a phrase adapted from Antonin Artaud, 'the body without organs'. They write: 'The only subject is desire itself on the body without organs, inasmuch as it machines partial objects and flows, selecting and cutting the one with the other, passing from one body to another, following connections and appropriations that each time destroy the factitious unity of a possessive or proprietary ego' (1977:72).

The contrast betwen the two sorts of subject they are outlining can be captured by a closer look at this phrase 'the body without organs'. The anatomical model of the body, favoured by the Western scientific tradition, imagines the body as an internally co-ordinated set of interdependent, purposeful, and functioning parts. The truth of the body is in this hierarchical and functioning structure. This image of internally interdependent meanings summarises the Western sense of internal structure. The body without organs does not refuse to recognise the obvious existence of the anatomical body, but it rejects it as preliminary to our understanding of what human subjects are. The encounter between different subjects is not the meeting of separate unities, but the interpenetration of dynamic and changing surfaces. As they assert in *A Thousand Plateaus* (1987): 'It is no longer a question of organs and functions, and a transcendent Plane that can preside over their organization only by means of analogical relations and types of divergent development. It is a question not of organization but of composition; not of development or differentiation but of movement and rest, speed and slowness' (1987: 255). The mission of the subject, according to this model, is an echo of that outlined in Foucault: a recognition of the complex cultural, political, and material forces that have produced it as and at a particular moment, and subsequently, its radical orientation towards change and the open-ended field of possibility. Although the final volumes of Foucault's work became interested in a more serious model of self-discipline, there remains an echo in the phrase 'aesthetics of existence' of the dynamic and outrageous Deleuze-Guattari image of the self as a fragmented and spirited field of change, energy, and subversion.

Further Reading

Foucault's work, like that of many other post-structuralists, is often quite difficult. A good place to start is *The Foucault Reader* (1984).

This provides some important extracts from the major works as well as some essays not found elsewhere. His *Discipline and Punish* (1977) and *Madness and Civilization* (1967) are relatively accessible, and quite compelling, given how broad are the ramifications of the issues dealt with. The same can be said of *The History of Sexuality*, especially Volume 1 (1980a). The more theoretical works *The Archaeology of Knowledge* (1974) and *The Order of Things* (1970) are dense and difficult, but do repay hard work. Some interesting essays and interviews are collected in *Power/Knowledge* (1980b). Simon During's *Foucault and Literature* (1992) is one of the best overviews of Foucault's contribution to intellectual history. Deleuze's *Foucault* (1988) is of significance both to those interested in its subject and in its author. There have been some important discussions of the relationship between Foucault and feminism. See Lois McNay, *Foucault and Feminism* (1992) and Caroline Ramazanoglu, *Up Against Foucault: Explorations of Some Tensions Between Foucault and Feminism* (1993). Other significant work on Foucault includes Gary Gutting's *The Cambridge Companion to Foucault* (1994), Mitchell Dean's *Critical and Effective Histories* (1994), C.G Prado's *Starting with Foucault* (1994) and Jim Jose's *Biopolitics of the Subject* (1998).

There have been fewer studies of Deleuze and Guattari's work. *Capitalism and Schizophrenia* is in two volumes: *Anti-Oedipus* (1977) and *A Thousand Plateaus* (1987). It is worth looking at some of the chapters of *A Thousand Plateaus* for an introduction, especially 'Rhizome: An Introduction'. There are some excellent essays on their work in *Gilles Deleuze and the Theater of Philosophy* (Boundas and Olkowski, 1994). Also see Phillip Goodchild's *Deleuze and Guattari: An Introduction to the Politics of Desire* (1996).

12

Deconstructing Sexuality

The cultural and political structure of human sexuality has become one of the most dynamic and provocative fields in contemporary cultural theory and cultural studies. This is largely because recent theorists have presented sexuality as spanning issues of individual subjectivity, academic investigation, political manipulation, and collective cultural identity. Sexuality plots out the most intimate of our investments. Yet it also makes us subject to medical intervention, even institutionalisation. It defines the way we relate to each other both on an intimate one-to-one basis, and and also as publically identified subgroups of different sexual orientations. It influences the way images and ideas—particularly those about the body and gender—circulate as both media of communication and funds of entertainment. Politicians target specific sexual identities as a way of courting particular constituencies. Indeed, across the broad spectrum of social and cultural life, many of the most public debates focus—covertly or overtly—on sexual orientation and behaviour.

More than any other single work Foucault's *The History of Sexuality, Volume 1: An Introduction* (1980a) helped promote the idea that sexuality is itself not a naturally occurring phenomenon that social structures then attempt to organise and control. To Foucault, the very fact that we separate out various of our inclinations and desires and co-ordinate them precisely with parts of our bodies and the real or imagined bodies of others, and call this complex our 'sexuality', is a specific historical and cultural event, not a simple state of affairs that nature, however we define it, maps out for us. Why are certain desires and pleasures called sexual? Why are they identified with genital reproduction? Why have our individual sexual prefer-ences come to be seen as a key to our psychology, or a badge of our social subgrouping, or even as a single thing? Why, in short, do we take sex so seriously?

> Sexuality must not be thought of as a kind of natural given which power tries to hold in check, or as an obscure domain which knowledge tries gradually to uncover. It is the name that can be given to a historical construct: not a furtive reality that is difficult to grasp, but a great surface network in which the stimulation of bodies, the intensification of pleasures, the incitement to discourse, the formation of special knowledges, the strengthening of controls and resistances, are linked to one another, in accordance with a few major strategies of knowledge and power (Foucault, 1980a: 105–6).

Sexuality here is not the truth of human nature that we struggle to keep under control, and that scientists and psychologists have to excavate. It is 'not a furtive reality that is difficult to grasp', in Foucault's terms. Rather, it is the pretext, the theoretical assumption necessary for a whole set of complex cultural and political developments. Foucault lists them. They range from particular types of pleasures promoted and triggered by culture; through specific academic inquiries that turn sexuality into something to write about and to theorise; and finally, to particular technologies of power that monitor the way we relate to each other's bodies, and to our own. Sexuality and sexual pleasure are not spontaneous things. They are systems of behaviour that individuals act out under the influence of historically conditioned forms of knowledge and deeply ingrained techniques of bodily organisation. In the end, these knowledges and techniques define the sort of subjectivity that it is possible for us to have—the sort of people we are able to be in the particular time and place that is our historical context. It is this relativity of sexuality—its different nature and function in different contexts—that Foucault goes on to analyse in the second and third volumes of the *History of Sexuality*. Volumes 2, *The Use of Pleasure* (1985), and 3, *The Care of the Self* (1986), study sexual discourse and its relationship to the construction of subjectivity in ancient Greek and Roman culture respectively.

To the modern world, sex then has been taken to be not just the way certain types of living organisms reproduce. Nor is it considered simply one form of pleasure amongst all the pleasures available to human beings. Sexuality has been defined as the behaviour through which is revealed the most fundamental secrets of the individual. Foucault writes: 'The essential point is that sex was not only a matter of sensation and pleasure, of law and taboo, but also of truth and falsehood, that the truth of sex became something fundamental, useful, or dangerous, precious or formidable: in short, that sex was constituted as a problem of truth' (1980a: 56). So familiar are we with this idea that sex holds the key not only to our individual psychology, but also to our social identity, that it is very difficult for us to respond to Foucault's challenge—to see sexuality as, at most, a shorthand term for a particular combination of sensations and practices. In sum then, sexuality is not something society encounters as naturally occurring in individuals, which it then seeks to repress. Instead, the very fact that certain tastes and behaviours are seen as sexual, or that certain individuals are seen as constituted sexually, is part of the positive or constructive operation of power. Power does not operate to repress our naturally occurring selves, according to Foucault. Instead, it maps out whole sets of actions and characteristics in taxonomies of possibility in which we as individuals are to be located. Counter-cultural movements for sexual liberation in the 1960s and since have usually promoted the idea that human sexuality is a naturally occuring, incontestable force that society has sought to keep in check. This view is called the 'repressive hypothesis' by Foucault. It is an idea he disputes.

This rejection of 'the repressive hypothesis' is one of the most famous and influential recent descriptions of power. Society does not augment its power by repressing sexuality, as much as by creating it as a method of identifying and classifying human subjects in the first place. What this means is that what were identified by nineteenth and early-twentieth-century science as 'perversions' (from homosexuality to foot fetishism, voyeurism, and masochism) were not scientific discoveries about the repressed nature of 'sick' sexual subjects. Instead, scientific knowledge and institutional practice sought to organise individuals across a range of known and precisely plotted categories. This distribution of individuals is the mode of operation of power in modern society, a power that does not operate either by repression or by way of ideals like justice and freedom, but by detailed isolation of individuals and their measurement against set norms of behaviour. Wanting to have sex with someone of the same gender is not just something people want to do, and that the law for some reason wants to outlaw. Instead, the identification of people with this want as a class of sexual subjects ('homosexuals') allows them to be measured against a standardised norm. They are 'perverse'. They are then easily vulnerable to clinical intervention and social administration.

> At issue ... is the type of power [society] brought to bear on the body and on sex. In point of fact, this power had neither the form of the law, nor the effects of the taboo. On the contrary, it acted by multiplication of singular sexualities. It did not set boundaries for sexuality; it extended the various forms of sexuality, pursuing them according to lines of indefinite penetration. It did not exclude sexuality, but included it in the body as a mode of specification of individuals ... Modern society is perverse, not in spite of its puritanism or as if from a backlash provoked by its hypocrisy; it is in actual fact, and directly, perverse (Foucault, 1980a: 47).

Perversity, then, is not something knowledge and power seek to control, but a means of control they use to manipulate and isolate sectors of the population. The logical consequence of this suspicion of sexual identities is that oppressed groups must be aware that the loud proclaiming of sexual orientation may result in them unwittingly co-operating with the power that is the oppressor in the first place. For this reason, political groups resisting homophobia, for example, which are organised around the definition of homosexuality as naturally occurring, may not always find Foucault's model helpful.

On the other hand, Foucault's work on sexuality has had a huge imact on the burgeoning Queer theory movement, which arose in the late 1980s and early 1990s as a response to the limitations of a civil-rights approach to the social position of homosexuals in Western countries. Queer theory aims to go beyond merely lobbying for the respect and equal treatment of gays and lesbians. It aims to problematise a social system built around a heterosexual norm. As Cherry

Smith has put it, queer 'activists are not interested in seeking acceptance within an unchanged social system, but are setting out to '"fuck up the mainstream" as visibly as possible' (Smith, 1996: 279). Queer theory challenges the identity-politics approach to sexuality, arguing that categories of sexuality aim to stabilise a highly mobile desire that challenges our conventional ways of relating to our bodies, our subjectivities, and each other. Where identity politics fixes homosexuals as a knowable social group ('gays and lesbians'), Queer theory takes on what was once a term of abuse as a way of problematising the socially monitored patterns of who we are supposed to be. As Michael Warner puts it, Queer 'rejects a minoritizing logic of toleration or simple political interest-representation in favour of a more thorough resistance to regimes of the normal' (Warner, 1996: 289). Queer activists and theorists confront social norms on a number of levels. They have mounted direct action campaigns against homophobic violence. They have broadened their attack on socio-sexual normalisation to take into account other forms of difference, particularly in terms of race, class, and gender. They have fiercely contested attempts made by liberal gay and lesbian activists to promote ostensibly 'correct' forms of sexual relationship and identification, embracing condemned forms of sexual practice such as sadomasochism and fetishism. Above all, they have critiqued and deconstructed the whole politics of identity dominant in Western countries, developing the theory of the performative (see Chapter 9) to argue that identities fix already oppressive categories and typologies in the service of a conservative phantasm, or the ruthless politics of power/knowledge, as Foucault identified them. Queer theory's defining characteristics are its attempt to problematise gay and lesbian activism by drawing attention to the way it has been affected by the inequity of power between men and women, and between dominant and minority ethnic groups; the thoroughness of its critique of sexual and political structure; and the intensity of its determination to re-imagine completely what new and different subjectivities could be made possible by radical cultural work.

Thus, one of the most important things that Foucault's work establishes is that sexuality has become so central in Western science and culture that it is impossible to treat it as simply the domain of either automatic natural drives or individual preference and choice. What is at issue when we talk about sexuality is at least the structure of knowledge and power as it organises our subjectivity. Other theorists have gone a lot further, indicating the centrality of sexuality to issues of gender, history, and even the distribution of wealth and material power in society. One of the most influential writers in this field has been Eve Kosofsky Sedgwick, whose two major works in this field, *Between Men: English Literature and Male Homosocial Desire* (1985) and *Epistemology of the Closet* (1990), were among the most influential in the early development of the Queer-theory movement. It is worth looking in some detail at Sedgwick's argument in *Between Men*, to understand how a Queer approach can develop a critique of the interrelationships between sexuality and other forms of power.

The problem with feminist research into the relationship between sexuality and power, according to Sedgwick, is that those feminists who are most successful in dealing with economic and political power (Marxist feminists) are unable to deal with the significance and meaning of sexuality; on the other hand, those feminists who best analyse sexuality (radical and French feminists, such as Cixous, Irigaray, and Kristeva) seem unconcerned by questions of material power. Some way of dealing with these questions together has to be developed, and Sedgwick's book is an attempt to do so. If we are unable to find an analysis that can deal with gender, sexuality, racism, and economic power, then we give in to the individualist ethos that wants to see these categories as separate. Nothing could be further from Sedgwick's position.

> The historical manifestations of [the] oppression of homosexuals have been savage and nearly endless. Louis Crompton makes a detailed case for describing the history as genocidal. Our own society is brutally homophobic; and the homophobia directed against both males and females is not arbitrary or gratuitous, but tightly knit into the texture of family, gender, age, class, and race relations. Our society could not cease to be homophobic and have its economic and political structures remain unchanged (Sedgwick, 1985: 3–4).

And elsewhere, Sedgwick writes: 'the placement of the boundaries in a particular society affects not merely the definition of those terms themselves—sexual/nonsexual, masculine/feminine—but also the apportionment of forms of power that are not obviously sexual. These include control over the means of production and reproduction of goods, persons, and meanings' (1985: 22). Again, according to Sedgwick, the present relationship between power and homophobia is part of the specific political and cultural structure of our society. In ancient Greece, to use a much quoted example to which Sedgwick also refers, power did not necessarily abominate homosexuality. Instead, male homosexuality at least was co-ordinated with systems of education and induction into membership of particular cultural élites, at the expense of women and the enslaved, of course. In modern Western society, the situation is quite different, and it is the structure of this power that Sedgwick hopes to reveal by a close reading of certain English literary texts.

From this aim is developed Sedgwick's use of the term 'homosocial'. The homosocial does not refer specifically to the homosexual, although it may include it. It also may include, importantly, homophobia. In fact, it may be simultaneously homosexual and homophobic. Homosociality refers to the relationship between men that mediates and determines the status and identity of others in society, specifically women. The idea is developed from René Girard's book *Deceit, Desire and the Novel: Self and Other in Literary Structure* originally published in French in 1961. Sedgwick says of Girard: 'What is most interesting for our purposes in his study is its insistence that, in any erotic rivalry, the bond that links the two rivals is as intense and potent as the bond that links either of the rivals to the beloved: that the bonds of "rivalry" and "love", differently as they are experienced, are equally powerful and in many senses equivalent' (1985: 21). In other words, the position of women in Western society is often determined by relationships between men, in which women are reduced to a means of exchange between colleagues or rivals. According to Sedgwick 'the status of women, and the whole question of arrangements between genders, is deeply and inescapably inscribed in the structure even of relationships that seem to exclude women—even in male homosocial/homosexual relationships' (1985: 25). What it is important to remember is that the goal of this analysis is not to understand how individual men and women relate to one another. This study is not about the literal relationships between the sexes, nor even how such relationships have been represented in literature. Sedgwick's goal is to reveal the structure of power in modern Western society, and how that structure is perpetuated: 'in any male-dominated society, there is a special relationship between male homosocial (*including* homosexual) desire and the structures for maintaining and transmitting patriarchal power' (1985: 25). Sedgwick's work reminds us that issues of gender, and the distribution of power that feminists analyse, are inalienable from discussions of the social and cultural meaning of sexuality.

Jonathan Dollimore's *Sexual Dissidence* (1991) continues the argument that homosexuality, or what has been called 'perversity', is neither socially nor culturally marginal. By analysing the way political and literary structures attempt to deal with perversity, we can go a long way towards understanding the nature of those structures. Again, in the study of the cultural meaning of homosexuality, it is not just the freedoms and rights of a certain social group that are at stake. Foucault had argued that a study of the rise of sexuality as a field of human study, and the taxonomy of perversities that it generated, held the key to transformations in the nature of power in the modern world. Sedgwick had argued that representations of male homosexuality may sometimes provide a key to the unequal distribution of power between genders in modern society. Dollimore argues that the identification and isolation of perversity is absolutely central to the way dominant political and social groups define and perpetuate themselves—that the norm needs the perverse, in other words.

Dollimore's study of modern treatments of homosexuality in theory and literature is pretty exhaustive. All we have space to do here is to summarise some of the key points of his theoretical argument. His aim in writing this book, he says, was 'to see why in our own time the negation of homosexuality has been in direct proportion to its symbolic centrality; its cultural marginality in direct proportion to its cultural significance; why, also, homosexuality is so strangely integral to the selfsame heterosexual cultures which obsessively denounce it' (1991: 28). Here we see echoes of an argument Foucault may have made, and indeed Dollimore acknowledges some of the similarities between his work and Foucault's. Yet, there are several key distinctions between the conclusions of the two theorists. Where Foucault sees perversity as a category contrived by power in order to administer the human population, Dollimore allows it to maintain some of its sense of danger and threat to the social order. Perversity is still subversive, according to Dollimore, not because it is completely alien to the social order but because it is so integral to it.

> If perversion subverts it is not as a unitary, pre-social libido, but as a transgressive agency inseparable from a dynamic intrinsic to social process. Provisionally then, this concept of the perverse dynamic denotes certain instabilities and contradictions within dominant structures which exist by virtue of exactly what those structures simultaneously contain and exclude. The displacements which constitute certain repressive discriminations are partly enabled via a proximity which, though disavowed, remains to enable a perverse return, an undoing, a transformation (1991: 33).

If perversity were truly something alien, unnatural, or unnecessary, it would not so obsess the upholders of sexual normality. It would be something more or less detachable from social life, a curiosity at most. Yet the very fact that perversity is seen as so threatening to the sexual and indeed the social order, and that it is treated so obsessively by artists and theorists alike, demonstrates that it may indeed indicate the artificiality of both sexual and social structures; in Dollimore's words, perversity may 'inspire recognition ... that the injustices of the existing social order are not inevitable—that they are, in other words, contingent and not eternal' (1991: 89). Again, what we are dealing with here is not merely the social position of a minority group, and its need for autonomy and freedom from persecution. In the same way that Sedgwick could read the social and political position of women in the structure of relationships between men, Dollimore can generalise from a discussion of perversity to the politics that form around it, and again, to the distribution of power across gender lines: 'political and social ordering is always internally disordered by the deviations it produces and displaces and defines itself against. This is one reason why patriarchy might imagine the greatest threat to it erupting from within that, and those, which it most powerfully controls: the household and women; the foreign erupts within the domestic' (1991: 160). Here we have an answer to the question of power's obsession with perversity. Perversity is a displacement of the dominant order's fear of its own possible queerness. The enemy must always be found within the gates.

There has been a proliferation of writings in the last ten years that use the issue of sexuality to provide startling and crucial insights into culture and power. The work of Teresa de Lauretis (especially her *The Practice of Love* (1994)) and Leo Bersani (especially his article 'Is the Rectum a Grave?' (1987) and *Homos* (1995)) stand out in this field. To conclude, however, let us look at an article from a collection of essays de Lauretis has edited, the Queer theory issue of the feminist cultural studies journal *differences*. The article is by Sue-Ellen Case and it is entitled 'Tracking the Vampire' (1991). The reason we have chosen this is because it shows how the detailed analysis of a specific cultural phenomenon in this field can lend itself to the broadest and most provocative conclusions. Case uses a widespread motif in popular culture—vampirism—to show how 'queerness' subverts the history of Western ontology. Ontology is the philosophy of being, in modern times, most closely associated with the work of Martin Heidegger, especially his *Being and Time* (1926). Basically, ontology asks the question 'what does it mean to say that something *is*?' Case argues that fundamental to our culture's ontology is the contrast between life and death. In what way do vampirism and queerness challenge this ontology?

Case argues that the vampire transgresses this very frontier: vampires are the 'undead' or 'living dead'. Traditionally, Western culture has transmitted ethnic identity and the ownership of property by way of blood. Blood is a term commonly associated with ethnicity— people are termed 'full-blood' or 'part-blood'—according to their ancestry. Similarly, lines of descent 'by blood' are a metaphor for family relations that involve the passing down of property from one generation to another, particularly between men. Blood therefore stands for doctrines of ethnic purity and private property that are still the mainstays of Western culture. Case quotes the racist writing of Adolf Hitler's *Mein Kampf* to highlight the historical significance of the blood metaphor. Then she writes: 'Such discourses invented the vampiric position—the one who waits, strikes and soils the living, pure blood; and it is against this bloody discourse that the queer vampire strikes, with her evacuating kiss that drains the blood out, transforming it into a food for the un-dead' (Case, 1991: 6). By turning what is a symbol of racial purity and ownership into food, the figure of the vampire threatens not only the personal safety but the cultural logic of his or her victims. Indeed, the threat and fascination the vampire represents to modern culture (no figure recurs more often in film and fiction) exemplifies widepread cultural sensitivity to the loss of both bodily and ethnic integrity, and the material social conditions that are linked to them.

What is the connection between this vampirism and queerness? Case shows how in classics of the vampire tradition, such as Sheridan Le Fanu's story 'Carmilla', and countless film versions, there has been a strong association between vampires and lesbians. Case proposes that lesbians and vampires in fact represent similar things to the dominant sexual discourse. In the same way that vampires threatened the processes of human procreation by defying both ethnic continuity and the transmission of property within the family to a man's biological descendants, lesbians, and same-sex couples in general, challenge the claims to priority of heterosexuality. Heterosexuality defines human life in terms of its own model of sexuality and human reproduction. Speaking of the slogan adopted by anti-abortionists, Case writes: 'the right to life was a slogan not only for the unborn, but for those whose sexual practices could produce them. In contrast, homosexual sex was mandated as sterile—an unlive practice that was consequently unnatural, or queer, and, as that which was unlive, without the right to life' (1991: 4). It is the heterosexual bias that lies at the heart of traditional Western ways for defining what life is that the queer is able to attack. Case writes: 'Striking at its very core, queer desire punctures the life/death and generative/destructive bipolarities that enclose the heterosexist notion of being' (1991: 4). In other words, those who choose to have sex with others of the same sex as themselves are not just acting out a personal preference. By standing outside of the logic that normally defines ethnicity and property they propose a new way of understanding what life itself may be, beyond the simple logic of heterosexual reproduction:

queer theory ... works not at the site of gender, but at the site of ontology, to shift the ground of being itself, thus challenging the Platonic parameters of Being—the borders of life and death. Queer desire is constituted as a transgression of these boundaries and of the organicism that defines the living as the good. The Platonic construction of a life/death binary opposition ... is subverted by a queer desire which seeks the living dead (Case, 1991: 3).

In this passage, we can see the measure of the radicalism of Queer theory. Adopting a traditional term of abuse of homosexuals, the 'queer' self-consciously places itself outside of what Case calls 'the rather polite categories of gay and lesbian' (1991: 3).

The aim of Queer theory, therefore, is not to promote the civil rights of a sexual minority, nor to plead for tolerance. The queer seeks to 'identif[y] with the insult, the taking on of the transgressive' (1991: 2). Nowhere does writing like Case's seek to make peace with the dominant sexual order. Queer theory aims to remain endlessly provocative and problematic, not to imagine an ideal social or sexual order of absolute freedom and equality, but to remind us that heterosexuality itself is a historically conditioned form of sexual orientation to which our subjectivity must be adjusted, often forcibly. The construction of a social world in which homosexuality would be unhesitantly accepted is a long way off. Even if it were here, the history of a culture that has adopted a genocidal approach to homosexuals would still need to be discussed. No crime of such magnitude has ever been forgotten, nor should mainstream politicians' promises of 'tolerance for alternative lifestyles' count for much as an end to the history of (public and private) crime and punishment, violence, dislocation, and intimidation that still defines Western sexuality for everyone everywhere.

Further Reading

One of the best places to start reading in this field is *The Lesbian and Gay Studies Reader* (Abelove et al., 1993). This includes important essays by leading figures such as Sedgwick, Dollimore, and Case, as well as Monique Wittig, Teresa de Lauretis, Judith Butler, and

Douglas Crimp. Foucault's writing can be approached by way of many introductions already mentioned. *The History of Sexuality* (1980a; 1985; 1986) is more readable than some of Foucault's early work, and the influential overview provided in *Volume 1: An Introduction* (1980a) is probably worth approaching directly. Sedgwick and Dollimore's work is challenging, but relatively accessible. It is of value for people studying the texts that are read in detail (which range from Shakespeare's sonnets to the writings of Oscar Wilde and Marcel Proust), but, at the same time, the introductions provide a good insight into the ideas. The details of these books are as follows: Jonathan Dollimore, *Sexual Dissidence* (1991); Eve Kosofsky Sedgwick, *Between Men: English Literature and Male Homosocial Desire* (1985) and *Epistemology of the Closet* (1990). Case's article appears in the Queer theory special edition of *differences* (1991). Many of the articles included there are important and informative, especially Teresa de Lauretis's introduction. For those interested specifically in lesbianism, de Lauretis's *The Practice of Love* (1994) is a detailed study of the issues of lesbianism, gender, and subjectivity. Elizabeth Grosz's work provides lucid overviews of poststructuralist and psychoanalytic treatments of gender, sexuality, subjectivity, and the body. See her *Volatile Bodies: Towards a Corporeal Feminism* (1994b) and *Space, Time and Perversion* (1994a). Other important work on Queer theory includes Annamarie Jagose's *Queer Theory* (1996), Donald Morton's *The Material Queer: A Lesbigay Cultural Studies Reader* (1996), and Alexander Doty's *Making Things Perfectly Queer: Interpreting Mass Culture* (1993).

Conclusion

Within the confines of a book of this size, we have not been able to offer any more than a sample of some of the assumptions and preliminary arguments that lie behind the recent explosion of productivity in the fields of cultural theory and cultural studies. Whole categories of investigation have been omitted, simply because this book must function as a starting point for, rather than a complete survey of, current discussions. Yet we hope we have provided some insight into the sort of interconnections and cross-fertilisations that have come to define this important growth area. It is this wealth of interconnections and the diversity of material that provide both the most exciting and the most intimidating aspect of such recent developments. For academics and teachers in mid-career, who have dedicated years to either researching or developing teaching resources in an area defined by the older paradigms, it is confronting to be told that cherished assumptions about culture, texts, and meaning are now considered superseded or, worse, implicated in a retrograde cultural politics. It is hard to be told that a profound knowledge of, for example, the canon of English literature, no longer equips someone to deal with the most vigorous debates in the field of culture. It is now important to know a range of theoretical materials, and indeed an almost completely open-ended number of texts, from all fields of culture. The ostensible abandonment of cultural authoritarianism in this discipline has ironically led many to feel, whether they accept the developments or not, that they now need to demonstrate knowledge in an impossible variety of areas. Indeed, anyone who has been to an academic conference recently will have seen those committed to a radical pluralism and a subversion of hierarchies competing with one another to display their erudition.

This sort of thing has lead to the accusation that a new orthodoxy has developed in academic circles, one that, despite its claims, is intolerant of other approaches. We believe this to be wrong-headed, and evidence of a continued refusal to deal with the dramatic developments in the new humanities, which are an inevitable part of the growth of the field, and an important renewal of its mandate as a crucial human activity. It is always possible to claim that knowledge with which you have not familiarised yourself excludes you. Yet it can only be seen as authoritarian and oppressive from the outside, by those unwilling to investigate its internal tensions and antagonisms.

We hope that in this book we have given some indication of the diversity of standpoints that recent developments in the new humanities are making possible. First, it is important to reiterate the point that recent thinking invites disagreement, and is sceptical of consensus and resolution, both in a theoretical and a political sense. This is one of the hardest points to make to undergraduate students, who have often been trained to think that there is only one correct way to perform a task in the humanities, and that consequently all opinions offered by their teachers need to be reconciled with one another. Second, the idea that a certain project—even a philosophical one—may be open-ended, and even bitterly resistant to resolution (seen as dangerous and restrictive), is also a hard concept for many people coming out of high school to take in. And third, students who are told that some modern ideas are anti-humanist are often flabbergasted, and stunned into silence. We have both had this experience in seminars. What is demonstrated by these three issues is the depth of the assumptions—about unity, teleology, and humanity—that are cultivated in students, often—if not usually—without being directly and self-consciously addressed by teachers. It is these assumptions that many of the theoretical ideas we have introduced here refuse to take for granted. The resultant discomfort for teachers, and especially for academics whose careers are built on these assumptions, and who like to think of themselves as having earned a certain prestige, is what lies behind the often shrill derision aimed at recent developments.

For what is really at stake is a broadening out of cultural analysis from an erudite humanising activity into a critical intervention in the decision-making processes of culture and politics, across the broad

s is not to argue that everything said here is uncontentious.
d it is the role of cultural theorists to invite controversy, some-
we argue is not done enough in the academy. The point here is
at science is simply a free-floating cultural activity, bearing no
on to the human interaction with various, and variously
d, environments. Cultural theory merely wants to propose that
mplexities and politics of culture cannot be removed from any
n activity, and have always to be taken into account. Similarly,
cultural theorists deal with medicine, madness or crime they
simply argue that such phenomena are fantasies generated out
ort of collective cultural imagination at best, and the political
of a cruel ruling class at worst. Cultural theory merely wants
ist that questions of the meaning and status of these things in
ular cultures, described in particular ways and at particular
always have to be taken into account. Scientific truth is not
y, therefore, but nor does it exist independent of the human
ts and cultural processes that produced it—that needed it—at
in time and place and in a certain form.
e humanities academics dealt with the history of certain tex-
ractices that they believed embodied a cultural or moral worth
nproved the lives of the students they taught, and consequently
epth of sensibility and sensitivity in society generally. More
than not, unfortunately, they chose not to share these assump-
with their students, who were expected to understand the cul-
excellence to which they were being introduced, and the
al discipline into which they were being inducted. The status of
knowledges has now been thoroughly challenged, and it is dif-
o promote ideas like beauty, cultural worth, and excellence in
nple way. This is not to say that certain things are not done
by certain people. Often when rejecting recent developments
cademics draw attention to the self-evidence of this statement:
eople simply write stories better than others, and these differ-
eed to be evaluated. Yet, this was not what was claimed in the
onal humanities. What was promoted was never simply the
of certain work, but the *significance* of that quality: it was
t in that quality the whole of culture, even of the human being
ver defined), was at stake, and that in certain practices, the

field from theoretical disharmony to influencing
ernment. We are aware that many radical schol
seen themselves as performing such a task, and v
academics, no matter how up to date they are
ments, have a rationalisation for the social wor
In this sense, the developments we have canvasse
new. This sits with their general postmodern sc
elty. Yet shifts of emphasis have taken place, an
to allow a generalised and automatic scepticism
resent no significant change from what has be
Take, for example, recent controversies about
part of many cultural studies theorists that scier
tural rather than an 'objective' practice, in an
argument proposes simply that all knowledge,
of its empirical method, is at least mediated,
human conventions of communication. It cann
of language, for example, which can never be p
ities and ambiguities, let alone its status as prim
of this, the work of science is always historicall
of objects, its selection of issues, the targeting
all determined for it by economic and political
it (something made painfully clear by the budge
Australian universities in 1996 by the Howard
just to draw attention to the cultural context of
its simplest level, without dealing with scienc
often invisible culturally defined practices to
hand, the theoretical questions of meaning, c
and, on the other, the political questions of gene
policy. The fierce reaction to these claims, an
ridicule directed at them in the name of a com
itself to be situated and interrogated, shows the
of workers in these fields to take theoretica
Indeed, too often the latter have been swept asi
tory statements that present science in the te
Enlightenment—as part of the absolute expa
knowledge against the obfuscations and ambig
a self-image is hard to give up.

Th
Inde
thing
not
relat
defin
the c
hum
whei
rarel
of a
needs
to in
parti
times
fanta
subje
a cer
On
tual
that i
the d
often
tions
tural
cultu
these
ficult
any s
better
some
some
ences
tradit
quali
felt th
(how

best human values were incarnated. In the discussions that still seem to have to go on in the academy and elsewhere, it is rare to hear a clear defence of these older values. Instead, the newer developments are held up for ridicule in the name of a common-sense humanism that is little more than unarticulated and uninterrogated prejudice. Over and over again we hear versions of the claim that Shakespeare is better than Schwarzenegger. Yet what needs to be interrogated is the meaning of such a relativism: why does it arise in the first place? What is at stake in this judgment? Who needs to make it, and what do they gain by it? And so on. These questions are what is now at issue in the new humanities. What is to be garnered from such analysis is greater understanding of the unstable and provisional bases on which the meanings that define our lives are made. It is above all the *seriousness* of this enterprise that explains why critics, once content to talk about the value of organic form, now want to talk about gender, sexuality, and power.

Glossary

Abjection Originating in the anthropological works of Mary Douglas, this term gained wider usage with Julia Kristeva's study *Powers of Horror* (1982). Put simply, the definition of the self is threatened by those things that can cross, and thus defy, the imagined perimeters of the body. The most straightforward examples are bodily fluids (blood—especially menstrual blood—urine, semen, tears, faeces, etc.), although the term is used to describe anything ambiguous or plural. As a consequence, whatever is associated with these abject things, or anything ambivalent, threatens the unity of the subject. The experience of the abject is therefore commonly one of horror associated with the body.

Aphanisis A key term in Lacanian psychoanalysis. Aphanisis, along with alienation, represents in Lacanian theory the fear of loss of subjectivity for the subject.

Avantgarde The most famous and controversial aspect of the modernist movement was its commitment to experimentation in the arts and life. The avantgarde derives its name from the military term for those troops that go ahead of the main body of the army into enemy territory. Avantgarde artists 'lead the way' into new and untested forms. Although postmodernism has inherited much from the dominant avantgarde movements of modernism (such as surrealism and dadaism), it is contemptuous of their élitism, and believes that their subversive ambitions were lost as they became increasingly successful and academic.

Binary opposition A critical strategy developed in structuralism and derived largely from the social anthropology of Lévi-Strauss. Binary oppositions (light/dark, good/evil, masculine/feminine, writing/speech, etc.) were used to explore structures of texts, social institutions, and relations, and so on. Poststructuralism was particularly critical of the idea that there can be such things as binarisms, and that they could have any critical value. Feminism, for example, argued that the binary opposition of masculine/feminine restricts the possibilities of identity and social positioning.

Body Ideas about the body have existed for hundreds of years, but more recently we have witnessed a sustained set of theories that have placed issues of corporeality at their critical centre. In this way the body has come to be seen as part of a sociopolitical landscape by being theorised variously as a site of resistance (e.g., Foucault, feminism, postcolonialism), a producer of meanings (e.g., the semiotics of the body), or a declaration of subjectivity (e.g., psychoanalytic studies). The body has also been approached in terms of its integration with the non-corporeal (e.g., postmodernism, theories of the cyborg).

Canon In historical terms the canon is the set of texts selected for reasons of cultural value, national history, or generic significance as those most worthy of being transmitted from generation to generation, and which thus become the most studied. With the development of cultural studies and semiotics (which invite us to examine more carefully the idea of the text and its social contexts) the term has become much more politicised.

Concretisation A term from phenomenology used to describe an important part of the act of reading. When we read we automatically 'fill in' the details of what the text offers, usually by supplementing it with material already significant to us. When a text announces that a character is walking down a street, for example, we complete the scene according to our own priorities. As with other issues in theories of the act of reading, 'concretisation' is significant not only for its interpretive potential, but also because it indicates the active and creative aspects of reading.

Cultural studies A new academic discipline dealing with a broad range of different types of texts for what they can tell us about the ways in which meanings, identities, and values are produced and reproduced in the world. Cultural studies is particularly interested in the political meaning of culture, dealing with issues such as gender, sexuality, ethnicity, class, technology, nationality, and so on. In contrast to the 'older' humanities, such as English studies, it is these theoretical and political issues that matter to cultural studies, rather than the value of the particular texts studied.

Culture A collective term for all human values, practices, customs and artefacts, the word culture often appears in contradistinction to 'nature', which is seen as outside of and preceding human influence. Often encountered in the phrases 'high' or 'low' (mass or popular) culture, and 'subculture'. The first refers to those artefacts most seen to exhibit fundamental or authentic human values in the most exquisite form. The second refers to those artefacts produced for a large, usually commercial, market. The third refers to the behaviour, habits or mores of a specific social minority, defined ethnically, socially or historically.

Cyborg The term 'cyborg' combines the two words cybernetic and organism. It describes a being that shares animal and technological attributes. Recently, especially since the work of Donna Haraway, the term has been used to describe the contemporary situation of human beings.

Deconstruction The evolution of this term surprised even its creator, Jacques Derrida. Initially proposed in a list of terms to describe and define processes of critical thought in philosophy, deconstruction was quickly taken up as a representative term for a larger challenge to many of the ideas and methods of establishment philosophy. Put simply, deconstruction is an analytical strategy in which the unquestioned philosophical assumptions on which a text is based—often inherited and uncritically accepted binary oppositions—are exposed and presented as artificial. Consequently, the text's meaning is seen to break down. In this sense the essence of the term can be traced back to Derrida's 1966 conference paper 'Structure, Sign, and Play in the Discourse of the Human Sciences', although its critical legacy reaches as far as Heidegger and Husserl.

Dialogism An influential theory of language, particularly as defined in the work of Mikhail Bakhtin, that sees texts as the dynamic and volatile exchange between a number of competing voices, not all with equal social power. This idea is one of the sources of the theory of intertextuality.

Différance A neologism devised by Derrida to indicate some of the problematics of meaning. *Différance* takes into account the processes of deferral and difference that are necessary parts of the operations of meaning and interpretation. It is important to realise that terms such as *différance* are significant not simply as critical ideas, but as political acts. Derrida's strategy with such a neologism was to continue his attack on structuralism and its need/desire to fix meaning.

Discourse A way of connecting certain texts with one another as the enactment of fundamental political and social value systems. In this way, individual texts are seen as part of, and always referring to, a larger collection and co-ordination of texts reproducing similar, or related, points of view. For example, a negative portrayal of women does not primarily express an individual's attitudes, but draws on, reasserts, and justifies the great body of texts that have done the same throughout society and history ('sexist discourse'). Similarly, another example of discourse is the group of texts that define the assumptions, truths, and practices in a certain intellectual or adminsitrative area, such as 'medical discourse'.

Ecriture féminine A term developed by Hélène Cixous to suggest a powerful and alternative way of 'writing'. If masculine writing is dominated by unity, meaning, and theory, feminine writing is said to be plural, expansive, and unaccountable to theory. As a result, the term is used speculatively to describe an ideal writing project, rather than a genre. Founded on the idea of difference, *écriture féminine* is not so much an issue of gender for Cixous, but of writing/thinking outside of the dominant phallogocentric paradigm.

Empiricism The belief that the truth is best achieved by the systematic and objective observation of the real world, and that all theory and generalisation should be secondary to this.

Eurocentric Term used to describe works or theories that fail to acknowledge that the priorities that have dominated Western discourse (such as individualism, formalism, and humanism) are not shared by all ethnic and national groups.

Gaze Theories of the gaze in poststructuralism are much less about perception than about the subject's relationship to others and the self. Sigmund Freud's works on scopophilia have been influential both in the development of the ideas and in the directions they have taken. By aligning the gaze with sexual identity and crisis, Freud provided a critical platform for theories of subjectivity.

Gender One of the most important ideas in feminism is the distinction between the reproductive reality of the body (its 'sex'—understood as male or female) and its cultural identity ('gender'—understood usually as masculine and feminine). Femininity and masculinity are not seen as naturally occurring, therefore, but as products of history, politics, and culture.

Genre The subgroup into which a text is classified according to the style in which it is written and the audience for which it is written. Genres may be understood in simple formal terms, such as fiction, poetry, and drama; or according to more complex and precise classifications, such as science, detective, or romance fiction.

Grand Narratives An important term in the theory of postmodernism, especially as outlined by Jean-François Lyotard. Lyotard argues that modernity is defined by its faith in several overarching principles—for example, the progress of spirit, and the march to freedom. These are ways of constructing human history, and of justifying certain cultural, political, or social projects. Postmodernism is defined by its failure to believe that history is progressing in this way.

Hermeneutics The theory of interpretation. Hermeneutics argues that the fundamental aim of reading texts is to work out the meaning that has been encoded within them. In this way, hermeneutics, which originated in the reading of Scripture, contrasts with poststructuralist modes of reading that see texts not as the expression of a single meaning, but as complex and unresolved fields of conflicting and contradictory meanings.

Historicism A wide range of methods and theories that see the truth of a text or event in terms of its relationship to the historical context in which it has appeared, rather than its own internal qualities.

Humanism The basic value system of the traditional humanities, humanism has its origins in the Renaissance commitment to the study of human beings and their artefacts. Cultural work is evaluated by humanism according to the contribution it makes to the development, clarification, or cultivation of liberal moral values, including individualism, pluralism, and social justice. Recently, humanism has been attacked for its usual claim that there are universal human values that transcend history, ethnicity, gender, and class. This is seen to disregard the importance of difference in defining the culture of human communities.

Humanities The academic disciplines most closely associated with the study of human arts and cultures, such as literature, history, fine arts, philosophy, and languages.

Idealism The belief that the most fundamental level of truth is to be found in systems of thought, rather than in political structures or historical circumstances. In fact, the general validity of thought is seen by idealism to transcend the flux of history and society, and the most worthwhile cultural work is to advance the project of abstract generalisation.

Intertextuality The understanding of texts as determined primarily by their relations to other texts, rather than to their author or historical context. Derived from Mikhail Bakhtin, and developed by Julia Kristeva and Roland Barthes, intertextuality sees texts as part of a vast, intersecting field of meanings, representations and part meanings, on which all social values and ideas blend and clash, and on which human subjects must position themselves in order to partake of their culture.

Jouissance A term left untranslated because of a lack of equivalents in the English language. In one sense it translates simply as pleasure or bliss, but both these terms lack the sexual and excessive qualities that the original French contains. It is particularly important in psychoanalytic theory, with its associations of transgression and the unconscious. A number of feminist theorists (notably Hélène Cixous) gave the term a powerful political dimension.

Lacunae A term from phenomenology describing the gaps or absences in a text. It is particularly important in refiguring the reader as an active and creative agent in the formation of the text.

Literature In its broadest sense, this term refers to anything that has been written, but it is now usually taken to mean those texts (in the genres of fiction, poetry, and drama) that are considered to be of the highest quality, and that most promote the serious discussion of moral values. In practice, this usually means texts that advance or discuss humanist values in a realist or modernist form, especially the novel of social relations.

Modernism The historical and cultural movement that dominated the first half of the twentieth century in the West. In broad terms, it refers to the rejection of tradition in the name of either a fundamental commitment to the new, or to the rationalisation of society, economics, and culture. In the arts, it refers to work that saw itself as partaking of this project, emphasising the experimental and art's claim that it could replace other, older ways of making values.

Naturalism A literary movement, with its origins in realism, which emphasised the painstaking empirical observation of human life as the purpose of literature. Naturalists argued that realism tried to present an overview of social relations as played out by social stereotypes, rather than by detailing the specific material realities of contemporary life. The term 'naturalistic' is often used to refer to texts (particularly in drama and film) that concentrate on the direct representation of social relationships, rather than abstract reflection or subjective experience.

New Criticism A United States literary critical movement of the middle of the twentieth century. The most famous tenets of the New Critics are their concentration on the close reading of the literary text, separate from any context ('the words on the page'); their belief that the text should not be dominated by outside material to do with the author, even what he or she might have said about the work ('the intentional fallacy'); and their belief that texts could not be reduced to a single meaning, and should be allowed to maintain the irony and paradox that are their most significant features ('the heresy of paraphrase'). The New Criticism, combined with the Leavisite movement and its concentration on morality, has been a defining influence on the traditional teaching of English in high schools and universities.

Objet petit a A term from Lacanian theory that denotes the objects of desire in the 'other'. Quite literally, it is the 'objects of the little other'—manifestations of the other in objects of desire.

Other A complex term, perhaps impossible to define because it shifts depending on the critical context in which it is located. In its simplest usage, the other is defined in opposition to the same or the self. The fundamental assumption here is that identities are not derived autonomously, but by interaction with some double or opposite (some 'other') that can be excluded or contradicted in order for identity to be produced. Masculine identity, for example, is derived from the exclusion and rejection of the feminine other. In psychoanalysis the term is tied to the unconscious (derived, in Jacques Lacan's works at least, from Jean-Paul Sartre's idea of alterity and consciousness); in feminist theory it is often employed in terms of the alienated position of women in a phallocentric society; in postcolonialism it is used to demonstrate the cultural and historical differences between colonial and postcolonial, and the cultures of alienation derived from such historical moments.

Phallocentric A term used especially by French psychoanalytic feminism to describe the relationship between culture and masculine power. Masculinity is seen to exert not just a material control over the society, but to have dominated language and culture with masculine values, identified with the symbol of masculine power, the phallus (understood as distinct from the biological penis, even though an image of it). The values associated with masculinity here include unity, authority, hierarchy, meaning, presence, force, and teleology. The related term **phallocratic** describes this formation of masculinity as a political order, and **phallogocentric** emphasises (following deconstruction) the connection between this masculine hegemony and the idea that language has fixed meaning.

Pluralism The promotion or tolerance of a wide range of differing or contradictory points of view. Pluralism is one of the key values of liberalism.

Postcolonialism A theoretical and critical movement that sees national cultures as defined by the internal tensions and stresses produced by the history of colonial domination, usually by one of the European empires of the nineteenth and early twentieth centuries.

Postmodernism Variously an attitude to the modern, or a period of history after the modern. While accepting modernism's contempt for tradition and liberal humanism, postmodernism sees the modernist project as dead, dangerous, or outmoded. It defines modernism either as the period of commitment to radical novelty or the rationalisation of society, economics, and culture. It rejects these modern impulses because they have proved to be restrictive, authoritarian, or murderous.

Poststructuralism As with so many 'post' terms, poststructuralism suggests both a link with a historical movement (structuralism) and a break from it. Poststructuralism comes out of structuralism with its common interests in how meaning is generated and sustained within various cultural processes. However, the break with structuralism is what is so essential to poststructuralism. In short, figures such as Jacques Derrida, Jacques Lacan, Julia Kristeva, Michel Foucault, and the postmodernists (e.g., Jean-François Lyotard and Jean Baudrillard) have enabled us to rethink concepts such as 'meaning', 'truth', 'subjectivity', and 'culture' by examining the very premises on which they are based. The reason why this is seen as poststructuralism is that there is a rejection of the structuralist idea that final models of social processes and humanity itself can be produced (usually in terms of stable binary oppositions).

Queer theory A recent development in gay and lesbian studies, which first sees its constituency as the broad field of oppressed sexualities, and second sees sexuality not only as an issue of the social rights and freedoms of a minority group, but as a key to the politics of culture, particularly as it relates to gender, power, and the body.

Reader The reader has become an empowered site, no longer the passive receptor of the text. In turn, issues such as power and control have become foregrounded in various approaches to the act of reading and the status of the text.

Readerly/writerly texts These are terms introduced by Roland Barthes to suggest not so much a classification of textual systems, but the active/passive roles of the reader. The readerly text is one that is merely consumed by the reader; the writerly one is a text actively constructed by the reader.

Realism The dominant literary movement of the nineteenth century, which sees the purpose of texts to be the representation of the real lives of real people, particularly as they are lived in the present. Realism's understanding of 'real' life emphasises people's belonging in social groups, defined as occupying a certain place in history, and determined by public factors, such as money, property, and politics. Realism also asserts that language and texts can represent the world without undue distortion.

Romance The literary form against which realism defined itself. Romance is seen as unrepresentative of real life and as artificial, producing colourful events and heroes at the expense of a serious consideration of human life. The contrast between realism and romance still influences debates about the so-called seriousness of purpose of high culture, and the frivolousness of popular culture.

Semiotics A broad, interdisciplinary, and international movement, which has its origins in linguistics and structuralism. Like poststructuralism, semiotics rejects much of the limited nature of structuralism in order to develop a complex set of theories about meaning and culture. Key figures include Umberto Eco and Roland Barthes, who have demonstrated how semiotic analysis can be applied to a wide range of disciplines, including film, literature, cultural systems (such as fashion, food, architecture, cars), and painting.

Sexuality Ever since Sigmund Freud produced his theories on sexuality the term has become invested with an expanding set of connotations. Freud's work (whether we accept it or not) has been tremendously influential because it positions sexuality as a cultural construction as well as a process heavily invested in the unconscious. Similarly, feminist theory has aligned sexuality with power and control; and Foucault has argued that it is a social institution used to construct and contort subjectivity.

Sign In structuralism the sign is made up of the signifier and signified (see structuralism). However, in poststructuralist theories, such as Lacanian psychoanalysis, deconstruction, and semiotics, this structure has been scrutinised and reworked in different ways. It still retains its essential feature of a cultural production of meaning, but the internal 'logics' are under question. So, for example, Jacques Lacan uses the structure of the signifier 'over' the signified to represent a relationship of the unconscious to discourse; Umberto Eco challenges the idea that meaning can be fixed (that there can be a stable relationship between the signifier and its signified) by proposing unlimited semiosis—the continual capacity for meaning to be generated from a sign; feminists have argued for an alternative to the binarism of signifier/signified, positing instead difference; and Jacques Derrida's term *différance* is a challenge to this relationship.

Signified See **Structuralism** and **Sign**.

Signifier See **Structuralism** and **Sign**.

Structuralism A vastly influential movement in linguistics, anthropology, and cultural studies that sees all human behaviours on the model of or as determined by a specific model of the sign. The structuralist sign is divided into two components: signifier (the material form of language) and signified (the concept to which the signifier is connected). In analyses of culture, structuralism generalises this binary opposition until it is seen as fundamental to all social processes and meanings.

Subjectivity The meaning of the word 'I'. Recent theory claims that the individual human subject is not naturally occurring, but is a construct of history and culture, particularly in terms of language, textuality, gender, and sexuality. Therefore, discussions of subjectivity stress its relationship to politics, history, and culture, and the way it varies between different cultures, ethnic groups, and historical periods.

Text A broad term for all human activities, products, and representations, when seen as readable. All 'texts' can be deciphered as the sign of some deeper social, cultural or political reality, usually according to the semiotic or structuralist model of the sign. In this way, all human activities are seen as cultural rather than natural, and overflowing with associations and suggestions, providing insight into the way in which meanings and values are produced and reproduced in a given society.

Unconscious For psychoanalysis, the unconscious is the part of the mind that contains the highly charged material that cannot be dealt with in day-to-day (or conscious) living. This material must be repressed in order for the individual to become a subject, and partake of either the social life or the symbolic order. It is material from the unconscious that tries to resurface in dreams, slips of the tongue, and art.

Bibliography

Abelove, Henry, Michele Aina Barale and David M. Halperin (eds), *The Lesbian and Gay Studies Reader*, Routledge, New York, 1993.

Acker, Kathy, *Great Expectations,* in *Blood and Guts in High School Plus Two*, Pan, London, 1984.

Appignanesi, Lisa (ed.), *Desire*, Institute of Contemporary Art, London, 1984.

Arnold, Matthew, *Culture and Anarchy*, Cambridge University Press, Cambridge, 1961 (1869).

Ashcroft, W.D., et al., *The Empire Writes Back*, Routledge, London, 1989.

—— (eds), *The Post-Colonial Studies Reader*, Routledge, London, 1995.

Bakhtin, Mikhail, *Rabelais and His World*, trans. H. Iswolsky, M.I.T. Press, Cambridge, Mass., 1968.

——, *The Problem of Dostoyevsky's Poetics*, trans. R.W. Rostel, Ardis, Ann Arbor, 1973.

——, *The Dialogic Imagination*, ed. Michael Holquist, University of Texas Press, Austin, 1981.

Balzac, Honoré de, *Eugénie Grandet*, Penguin, Harmondsworth, 1955.

Barthes, Roland, *Mythologies,* trans. Annette Lavers, Paladin, London, 1973.

——, *S/Z*, trans. Richard Miller, Hill & Wang, New York, 1974.

——, *The Pleasure of the Text*, trans. Richard Miller, Hill & Wang, New York, 1975.

——, *Image—Music—Text*, ed. Stephen Heath, Fontana, Glasgow, 1977.

——, *Camera Lucida* trans. R. Howard, London, Flamingo, 1984.

——, *A Lover's Discourse: Fragments*, trans. Richard Howard, Penguin, Harmondsworth, 1990.

Baudrillard, Jean, *Simulacra and Simulations*, Galilee, Paris, 1981.

——, *In the Shadow of the Silent Majorities*, Semiotext(e), New York, 1983.

——, *Seduction* trans. Brian Singer, Macmillan, London, 1990.

——, *The Gulf War Did Not Take Place*, trans. Paul Patton, Power Press, Sydney, 1995.

——, *The Ecstasy of Communication*, trans. B. & C. Schutze, ed. S. Lotringer, Autonomedia, New York, 1996.

Baudry, Jean-Louis, 'The Apparatus: Metapsychological Approaches to the Impression of Reality in the Cinema', *Camera Obscura*, no. 1, Fall 1996.

Becker, George (ed.), *Documents of Modern Literary Realism*, Princeton University Press, Princeton, 1963.

Belsey, Catherine, *Critical Practice*, Methuen, London, 1980.

Bennett, Tony, *Outside Literature*, Routledge, London, 1990.
——, Culture, *A Reformer's Science*, Allen & Unwin, St Leonard's, 1998.
Berger, John, *Ways of Seeing*, Penguin, Harmondsworth, 1972
Bersani, Leo, 'Is the Rectum a Grave?', *October*, no. 43, 1987, pp. 197–222.
——, *Homos*, Harvard University Press, Cambridge, Massachusetts, 1995.
Bloch, Ernst, et al., *Aesthetics and Politics*, NLB, London, 1977.
Bloom, Harold, *The Western Canon: The Books and Schools of Ages*, Harcourt Brace, New York, 1994.
Boundas, Constantin V., and Dorothea Olkowski (eds), *Gilles Deleuze and the Theater of Philosophy*, Routledge, New York, 1994.
Brontë, Emily, *Wuthering Heights*, Penguin, Harmondsworth, 1989.
Bryson, Norman *Word and Image: French Painting of the Ancien Régime*, Cambridge University Press, Cambridge, 1981.
——, *Vision and Painting: The Logic of the Gaze*, Macmillan, London, 1985.
Butler, Judith, *Gender Trouble: Feminism and the Subversion of Identity*, Routledge, New York, 1990.
——, *Bodies That Matter*, Routledge, New York, 1993.
——, *The Psychic Life of Power*, Routledge, New York, 1997.
Case, Sue-Ellen, 'Tracking the Vampire', *differences: A Journal of Feminist Cultural Studies*, 3, no. 2, 1991, pp. 1–20.
Chandler, Raymond, *The Big Sleep*, Penguin, Harmondsworth, 1991.
Cixous, Hélène, 'The Laugh of the Medusa', trans. K. Cohen and P. Cohen, *Signs*, 1, 1976, pp. 845–93.
——, 'Castration or Decapitation', trans. A. Kuhn, *Signs*, 7, 1981, pp. 36–55.
——, *Angst*, trans. J. Levy, John Calder, London, 1985.
——, and Catherine Clément, *The Newly Born Woman*, trans. B. Wing, University of Minnesota Press, Minneapolis, 1986.
Connor, Steven, *Postmodernist Critique: An Introduction to Theories of the Contemporary*, Blackwell, Oxford, 1997.
Conrad, Joseph, *Heart of Darkness*, Penguin, Harmondsworth, 1989.
Copec, Joan, *Shades of Noir*, Verso, London, 1995.
Culler, Jonathan, *Flaubert: The Uses of Uncertainty*, Cornell University Press, Ithaca, 1974.
Dean, Mitchell, *Critical and Effective Histories*, Routledge, London, 1994.
de Lauretis, Teresa, *Technologies of Gender: Essays on Theory, Film and Fiction*, Indiana University Press, Bloomington, 1987.
——, *The Practice of Love*, Indiana University Press, Bloomington, 1994.
Deleuze, Gilles, and Felix Guattari, *Capitalism and Schizophrenia, Volume 1: Anti-Oedipus*, trans. Robert Hurley et al., Athlone Press, London, 1977.
——, *Capitalism and Schizophrenia, Volume 2: A Thousand Plateaus*, trans. Brian Massumi, University of Minnesota Press, Minneapolis, 1987.

——, *Foucault*, trans. Sean Hand, University of Minnesota Press, Minneapolis, 1988.

Derrida, Jacques, *Of Grammatology*, trans. Gayatri Chakravorty Spivak, Johns Hopkins University Press, Baltimore, 1976.

——, *Writing and Difference*, trans. Alan Bass, Routledge, London, 1978.

——, *Dissemination*, trans. Barbara Johnson, Athlone Press, London, 1981a.

——, *Positions*, trans. A. Bass, Athlone Press, London, 1981b.

——, *Glas*, trans. J.P. Leavey Jr. and R. Rand, University of Nebraska Press, Lincoln, Nebraska, 1986a

——, *Margins of Philosophy*, trans. A. Bass, Harvester Press, Sussex, 1986b.

——, *The Postcard: From Socrates to Freud and Beyond*, trans. A. Bass, University of Chicago Press, 1987a.

——, *Truth in Painting*, trans. G. Bennington & I. McLeod, University of Chicago Press, Chicago, 1987b.

——, *The Ear of the Other*, University of Nebraska Press, Lincoln and London, 1988.

——, *Memoirs of the Blind*, trans. Pascale-Anne Brault and Michael Naas, University of Chicago Press, Chicago, 1993.

——, 'Sending: On Representation', in Patrick Fuery (ed.), *Representation, Discourse and Desire: Contemporary Australian Culture and Critical Theory*, Longman, Melbourne, 1994.

——, and Marie-Françoise Plissart, 'Droit de regards', trans. D. Wills, *Art and Text*, no. 32, 1997.

Docherty, Thomas (ed.), *Postmodernism*, Harvester Wheatsheaf, Hemel Hempstead, 1993.

Dollimore, Jonathan, *Sexual Dissidence*, Clarendon Press, Oxford, 1991.

Doty, Alexander, *Making Things Perfectly Queer: Interpreting Mass Culture*, University of Minnesota Press, Minneapolis, 1993.

During, Simon, *Foucault and Literature*, Routledge, London, 1992.

——*The Cultural Studies Reader*, Second Edition, Routledge, London, 1999.

Eagleton, Terry, *Literary Theory: An Introduction*, Blackwell, Oxford, 1983.

Eco, Umberto, *A Theory of Semiotics*, Indiana University Press, Bloomington, 1976.

——, *The Role of the Reader*, Indiana University Press, Bloomington, 1979.

——, *Semiotics and the Philosophy of Language*, Macmillan, London, 1984.

Ellison, Ralph, *Invisible Man*, Gollancz, London, 1953.

Flaubert, Gustave, *Sentimental Education*, Penguin, Harmondsworth, 1977.

Foucault, Michel, *Madness and Civilization: A History of Insanity in the Age of Reason*, trans. Richard Howard, London, Tavistock, 1967.

——, *The Order of Things*, Tavistock, London, 1970.

——, *The Birth of the Clinic*, trans. A.M. Sheridan Smith, Pantheon Books, New York, 1973.

——, *The Archaeology of Knowledge*, trans. A.M. Sheridan-Smith, Tavistock, London, 1974.

——, *Discipline and Punish: The Birth of the Prison*, trans. Alan Sheridan, Allen Lane, London, 1977.

——, *The History of Sexuality, Volume 1: An Introduction*, trans. Robert Hurley, Vintage Books, New York, 1980a.

——, *Power/Knowledge*, Colin Gordon (ed.), Pantheon Books, New York, 1980b.

——, *This is Not A Pipe*, trans. James Harkness Berkeley, University of California Press, California, 1982.

——, *The Foucault Reader*, Paul Rabinow, (ed.) Penguin, Harmondsworth, 1984.

——, *The History of Sexuality, Volume 2: The Use of Pleasure*, trans. Robert Hurley, Vintage Books, New York, 1985.

——, *The History of Sexuality, Volume 3: The Care of the Self*, trans. Robert Hurley, Pantheon Books, New York, 1986.

Freud, Sigmund, *The Interpretation of Dreams*, trans. James Strachey, Penguin, Harmondsworth, 1986.

——, *On Metapsychology: The Theory of Psychoanalysis*, trans. James Strachey, Penguin, Harmondsworth, 1987a.

——, *On Psychopathology*, trans. James Strachey, Penguin, Harmondsworth, 1987b.

——, *The Psychopathology of Everyday Life*, trans. James Strachey, Penguin, Harmondsworth, 1988.

——, *Art and Literature*, trans. J. Strachey, Penguin, Middlesex, United Kingdom, 1990

Frow, John, *Cultural Studies and Cultural Value*, Oxford University Press, Oxford, 1995.

Fuery, Patrick, *Theories of Desire*, Melbourne University Press, Melbourne, 1995a.

——, *The Theory of Absence*, Greenwood Press, Westport, Connecticut, 1995b.

——, *New Directions in Film Theory*, Macmillan, London, 2000.

Girard, Rene, *Deceit, Desire and the Novel: Self and Other in Literary Structure*, trans. Yvonne Freccero, Johns Hopkins University Press, Baltimore, Maryland, 1972.

Gombrich, E.H., *Art and Illusion: A Study in the Psychology of Pictorial Representation*, Pantheon Books, New York, 1960.

Goodchild, Phillip, *Deleuze and Guattari: An Introduction to the Politics of Desire*, Sage, London, 1996.

Grossberg, Lawrence et al. (eds), *Cultural Studies*, Routledge, New York, 1992.

Grosz, Elizabeth, *Space, Time and Perversion*, Allen & Unwin, St Leonard's, 1994a.

——, *Volatile Bodies: Towards a Corporeal Feminism*, Allen & Unwin, St Leonard's, 1994b.

Gutting, Gary (ed.), *The Cambridge Companion to Foucault*, Cambridge University Press, Cambridge, 1994.

Haraway, Donna, *Simians, Cyborgs, Women: The Reinvention of Nature*, Free, London, 1991.

Healy, J.J., *Literature and the Aborigine in Australia 1770–1975*, University of Queensland Press, St Lucia, 1989.

Heidegger, Martin, *Being and Time*, trans. John Macquarrie, Basil Blackwell, Oxford, 1962.

Hobson, Marion, *Jacques Derrida: Opening Lines*, Routledge, London, 1998.

Hodge, Bob, and Vijay Mishra, *Dark Side of the Dream: Australian Literature and the Post-Colonial Mind*, Allen & Unwin, Sydney, 1991.

Hoffmann, E.T.A., *The Best Tales of Hoffmann*, Dover, New York, 1967

Husserl, Edmund, *Cartesian Meditations*, trans. D. Cairns, Martinus Nijhoff, The Hague, 1960.

——, *Ideas: General Introduction to Pure Phenomenology*, trans. W.R. Boyce Gibson, Allen & Unwin, London, 1969.

——, *The Paris Lectures*, trans. P. Koestenbaum, Martinus Nijhoff, The Hague, 1975.

——, *Ideas Pertaining to a Pure Phenomenology and to a Phenomenological Philosophy*, 3 vols, trans. F. Kersten, Martinus Nijhoff, The Hague, 1980.

Ingarden, Roman, *Cognition of the Literary Work of Art*, Northwestern University Press, Evanston, Illinois, 1973a.

——, *The Literary Work of Art*, Northwestern University Press, Evanston, Illinois, 1973b.

Irigaray, Luce, *Speculum of the Other Woman*, trans. Gillian Gill, Cornell University Press, New York, 1985a.

——, *This Sex Which Is Not One*, trans. C. Porter and G. Gill, Cornell University Press, New York, 1985b.

——, *Marine Lover of Friedrich Nietzsche*, trans. G.C. Gill, Columbia University Press, New York, 1991.

——, *Elemental Passions*, trans. J. Collie and J. Still, Routledge, New York, 1992.

——, *Sexes and Genealogies*, trans. Gillian Gill, Columbia University Press, New York, 1993.

Iser, Wolfgang, *The Act of Reading*, Indiana University Press, Indianapolis, 1978.

Jagose, Annamarie, *Queer Theory*, Melbourne University Press, Melbourne, 1996.
Jameson, Fredric, *The Political Unconscious: Narrative as a Socially Symbolic Act*, Methuen, London, 1981.
——, *Postmodernism, or The Cultural Logic of Late Capitalism*, Verso, London, 1991.
Jay, Martin, *Downcast Eyes*, University of California Press, Berkeley, California, 1994.
Jenks, Christopher (ed.), *Visual Culture*, Routledge, London, 1995.
Jordan, Glenn and Chris Weedon, *Cultural Politics: Class, Gender, Race and the Postmodern World*, Blackwell, Oxford, 1995.
Jose, Jim, *Biopolitics of the Subject*, Northern Territory University Press, Darwin, 1998.
Joyce, James, *Ulysses*, Penguin, Harmondsworth, 1986.
Kant, Immanuel, *Critique of Judgment*, trans. Werner S. Pluhar, Hackett Publishing Company, Indianapolis, 1987 (first published 1790).
Kaplan, E. Ann, *Psychoanalysis and Cinema*, Routledge, New York, 1989.
Kristeva, Julia, *Powers of Horror: An Essay on Abjection*, trans. Leon S. Roudiez, Columbia University Press, New York, 1982.
——, *Desire in Language*, trans. T. Gora et al., Basil Blackwell, Oxford, 1984a.
——, *Revolution in Poetic Language*, trans. M. Waller, Columbia University Press, New York, 1984b.
——, *Tales of Love*, trans. Leon S. Roudiez, Columbia University Press, New York, 1987.
Kuhn, Annette, *Women's Pictures: Feminism and Cinema*, Routledge, London, 1982.
Lacan, Jacques, *Encore*, Seuil, Paris, 1975.
——, *The Four Fundamental Concepts of Psychoanalysis*, trans. Alan Sheridan, Hogarth, London, 1977.
——, *Ecrits: A Selection*, trans. Alan Sheridan, Tavistock, London, 1985.
——, *Freud's Papers on Technique*, trans. S. Tomaselli, ed. J-A. Miller, Cambridge University Press, Cambridge, 1988.
——, *L'envers de la Psychanalyse*, Seuil, Paris, 1991.
——, *The Ethics of Psychoanalysis*, trans. D. Porter, Routledge, London, 1992.
——, *The Psychoses*, trans. R. Grigg, Routledge, London, 1993.
Leavis, F.R., *The Great Tradition*, Peregrine, Harmondsworth, 1962.
——, *Revaluation: Tradition and Development in English Poetry*, Peregrine, Harmondsworth, 1964.
Leavis, Q.D., *Fiction and the Reading Public*, Chatto & Windus, London, 1932.

Lechte, John, *Fifty Key Contemporary Thinkers: From Structuralism to Postmodernity*, Routledge, London, 1994.

Le Doeuff, Michelle, *The Philosophical Imaginary*, trans. Colin Gordon, Athlone Press, London, 1989.

Lucy, Niall, *Debating Derrida*, Melbourne University Press, Melbourne, 1995.

Lukacs, Gyorgy, *Studies in European Realism*, Grosset & Dunlap, New York, 1964.

Lyotard, Jean-François, *The Postmodern Condition: A Report on Knowledge*, trans. Geoffrey Bennington and Brian Massumi, Manchester University Press, Manchester, 1984.

——, *The Inhuman*, trans. G. Bennington and R. Bowlby, Polity Press, Cambridge, 1991.

——, *The Postmodern Explained to Children*, Power Publications, Sydney, 1992.

——, *Libidinal Economy*, trans. Iain Hamilton Grant, Indiana University Press, Bloomington, 1993.

Mansfield, Nick, *Masochism: The Art of Power*, Praeger Press, Westport, Connecticut, 1997.

McNay, Lois, *Foucault and Feminism*, Polity Press, Cambridge, 1992.

Metz, Christian, *Film Language*, trans. M. Taylor, Oxford University Press, New York, 1974.

——, *The Imaginary Signifier*, trans. C. Britton et al., Indiana University Press, Bloomington, 1982.

Millet, Kate, *Sexual Politics*, Doubleday, Garden City, New York, 1970.

Milner, Andrew, *Literature, Culture and Society*, Allen & Unwin, Sydney, 1996.

Mirzoeff, Nicholas (ed.), *The Visual Culture Reader*, Routledge, New York and London, 1998.

Modleski, Tania, *The Women Who Knew Too Much: Hitchcock and Feminist Theory*, Methuen, London, 1988.

Moi, Toril, *Sexual/Textual Politics: Feminist Literary Theory*, Methuen, London and New York, 1985.

Morton, Donald, *The Material Queer: A Lesbigay Cultural Studies Reader*, Westview Press, Boulder, Colorado, 1996.

Mulvey, Laura, 'Visual Pleasure and Narrative Cinema', *Screen*, 16, no. 3, 1975.

Nicholson, L. and S. Seidman, *Social Postmodernism: Beyond Identity Politics*, Cambridge University Press, Cambridge, 1995.

Nietzsche, Friedrich, *Ecce Homo: How One Becomes What One Is*, trans. R.J. Hollingdale, Penguin Books, London, 1992 (1888).

Prado, C.G., *Starting With Foucault*, Westview Press, Boulder, Colorado, 1994.

Ramazanoglu, Caroline, *Up Against Foucault: Explorations of Some Tensions Between Foucault and Feminism*, Routledge, London, 1993.

Rosen, Philip (ed.), *Narrative, Apparatus, Ideology*, Columbia University Press, New York, 1986.

Ruthrof, Horst, *The Reader's Construction of Narrative*, Routledge, Boston, 1981.

——, *Pandora and Occam: On the Limits of Language and Literature*, Indiana University Press, Bloomington, 1992.

——, *Semantics and the Body: Meaning from Frege to the Postmodern*, University of Toronto Press, Toronto, 1997.

Salinger, J.D., *The Catcher in the Rye*, Penguin, Harmondsworth, 1958.

Sardar, Ziauddin, *Postmodernism and the Other: The New Imperialism of Western Culture*, Pluto Press, London, 1997.

Sarup, Madan, *An Introductory Guide to Post-structuralism and Postmodernism*, Harvester Wheatsheaf, Hemel Hempstead, 1993.

Sedgwick, Eve Kosofsky, *Between Men: English Literature and Male Homosocial Desire*, Columbia University Press, New York, 1985.

——, *Epistemology of the Closet*, University of California Press, Berkeley, 1990.

Selden, Raman, *A Reader's Guide to Contemporary Literary Theory*, Harvester Press, Brighton, 1985.

Shoemaker, Adam, *Black Words, White Page: Aboriginal Literature 1929–1988*, University of Queensland Press, St Lucia, 1989.

Sim, Stuart, *The Routledge Critical Dictionary of Postmodern Thought*, Routledge, London, 1999.

Smith, Cherry, 'What is This Thing Called Queer?', in Donald Morton (ed.), *The Material Queer: The Lesbigay Cultural Studies Reader*, Westview Press, Boulder, Colorado, 1996, pp. 277–85.

Warner, Michael, 'Introduction—Fear of a Queer Planet', in Donald Morton (ed.), *The Material Queer: The Lesbigay Cultural Studies Reader*, Westview Press, Boulder, Colorado, 1996, pp. 286–91.

Williams, Raymond, *Keyword*, Fontana, Glasgow, 1976.

Winterson, Jeanette, *Oranges Are Not the Only Fruit*, Pandora Press, London, 1985.

Wolfreys, Julian, *Applying to Derrida*, St Martin's Press, New York, 1996.

Woolf, Virginia, *To the Lighthouse*, Grafton Books, London, 1977.

Index